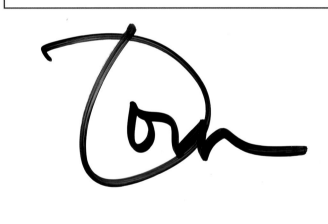

The SHOWMAN of the Pacific

50 Years of Radio and Rock Stars

The SHOWMAN of the Pacific

50 Years of Radio and Rock Stars

BY TOM MOFFATT

WITH JERRY HOPKINS

WATERMARK
PUBLISHING

© 2005 Watermark Publishing

Text © 2005 Tom Moffatt

ISBN 0-9753740-7-9

Library of Congress Control Number:
2005937013

Design/Production:
Leo Gonzalez, Gonzalez Design

Design/Production Assistant:
Joy Oshiro, Oshiro Design

Watermark Publishing
1088 Bishop Street, Suite 310
Honolulu, HI 96813
Telephone: Toll-free 1-866-900-BOOK
Web site: www.bookshawaii.net
e-mail: sales@bookshawaii.net

Printed in Korea

For Sweetie

Credits

A very special mahalo to Hawaii's first rock-and-roll photographer, John Lau of City Art Works, and to Eddie Freeman, Harold Higashi, Robert Knight, Andy Leong, Richard Upper and Terry Luke. Supplemental photos from the Tom Moffatt Collection. Additional studio photography by Harrington Photography.

6 Karen Goldman FYI	110 Richard Upper (left)
7 Tina Lau	112-13 Richard Upper
19 DeSoto Brown (left)	114-15 Richard Upper
19 Hawaii State Archives (right)	116-17 Richard Upper
20 HONOLULU Magazine (top)	118-19 Richard Upper
29 Hawaii State Archives	120 Richard Upper (right)
32 *Hawaii Business* Magazine (top)	126 Robert Knight
32 Hilton Hawaiian Village (bottom)	131 Mountain Apple Co.
33 Hilton Hawaiian Village	133 Tina Lau
36 John Lau	136 Brett Uprichard
42 Larry Ichinose	140 John Lau
44 Pipi Wakayama	155 Foto Lisa/Lisa Oshiro
52 Hilton Hawaiian Village	174 Tina Lau
54-55 John Lau	181 Foto Lisa/Lisa Oshiro
70 John Titchen (lower left)	182 Tina Lau
87 John Lau (right)	183 Tina Lau
94 Robert Knight	18 Tina Lau (left)
103 Richard Upper	190 Foto Lisa/Lisa Oshiro
106 Richard Upper	217 John Lau
108 Robert Knight	219 Tina Lau
109 Richard Upper (left and right)	221 Gil Gilbert

Contents

A Day in the Life...

It was Thursday, and the air was wet and sunny as I left my home in Nuuanu Valley for a day of back-to-back meetings. It looked to be a busier day than most, but it began, at 7 o'clock, as slowly as I could wish, with breakfast on the beach fronting the Kahala Mandarin Oriental Hotel with one of my favorite people, Jimmy Buffett.

I'd known Jimmy for more than 25 years, going back to 1979 when he opened for the Eagles at Aloha Stadium. I'd presented him as a headliner six times or so since, in both the Waikiki Shell and the Blaisdell Arena, and two days before our breakfast he'd played the Shell again to a sell-out crowd. We'd gone to Tahiti together and done some shows there. He helped with a Hurricane Iniki benefit concert. Besides Key West and the Caribbean, I think Jimmy loves Hawaii more than any other place on earth.

It's been nearly 50 years since I promoted my first show, and I've met, presented and gotten to know hundreds of the biggest names in entertainment. With the possible exception of Don Ho and Willie Nelson, I can't think of anyone who's more laid back and unaffected by his fame than Jimmy Buffett. When we met for breakfast, practically the only ones in the restaurant on the beach, he was at the end of another big tour. He had a hit CD on the charts, and his new novel, *A Salty Piece of Land*, was at the top of the *New York Times* bestseller list. And his Margaritaville bar and restaurant chain was the hottest thing in hip nightclubs since the early days of the Hard Rock Cafe.

We talked a little business, I admit. He'd wanted to do a benefit for the Red Cross in Diamond Head Crater, but after checking it out, his technical people told him it was unlikely. Then he said he was thinking about opening a Margaritaville restaurant in Honolulu. I said I thought it was a natural for Waikiki. I was bowled over, though, when he asked if I'd like to get involved.

I was very aware of how successful the chain was, especially after observing the operation at the newly opened Margaritaville in Las Vegas, when I'd visited Jimmy during his performance at the MGM Grand Hotel a few months earlier. I told Jimmy to count me in.

Then he brought out a copy of his novel. I'd already read it and knew he had based one of its minor characters more or less on me. It was in a chapter about Tahiti, and he called me Tom Prophet. "Colonel," he now wrote across the page where my fictional character makes his entrance—he always calls me "Colonel"—"be careful who you take to the Pacific. You could wind up in a book. It goes without saying, thanks for years of friendship."

He signed his name and then signed an earlier book of his for one of my closest friends, Glen Larson. Glen's probably best known for creating and producing television shows: *McCloud, Magnum P.I., Quincy, The Hardy Boys, The Fall Guy, Knight Rider, Buck Rogers in the 25th Century* and *Battlestar Gallactica*. He was also one of the founding members of the Four Preps (above, with Glen on the right), and he wrote their biggest hit, "26 Miles across the Sea." Jimmy said that song was one of his greatest inspirations when he was starting out, and he signed the page in his book where he quoted some of

the lyrics, then gave me the book to pass along to Glen.

Do I sound like a shameless name-dropper? Maybe I do, but when I was at the University of Hawaii in the early 1950s, all I wanted to be was a radio announcer. Look what happened! Believe me, there's no one more amazed than I am. Much of the time I feel like Forrest Gump, the man who epitomizes the phrase about being in the right place at the right time. And having been in so many right places at the right times, now what I want to do here is share with you a little of the fun I've had over the years with these guys.

After leaving Jimmy at the Kahala, I swung by Glen Larson's Hawaii home to deliver his book—Glen was very pleasantly surprised. It was also "Aloha" time, as Glen and his party were due to leave in a couple of hours to return to Los Angeles. Then I drove to Maryknoll School. I have strong connections there. My son Troy is a graduate, and Yvonne Morris, one of the young dancers on a television show I hosted in the 1960s, is now on the Maryknoll staff. She'd asked me if I'd help the school organize and promote a fund-raising concert starring one of their famous students, Jasmine Trias, one of the finalists in the TV show *American Idol* and a performer in the subsequent *American Idols Live* shows I'd promoted at the Blaisdell Arena. It started out with my agreeing to be the emcee, and then I got involved in the technical aspects of doing the show, as well as helping with a silent auction and a live auction. This would be Jasmine's first big concert in Honolulu since *American Idols Live*, and I was pleased to help the school raise money for a good cause: a new gymnasium and auditorium.

Then I had to go to another meeting at the Blaisdell Center with the city's new director of auditoriums, Sidney Quintal, and John Fuhrman, the director of operations. Sid had recently won a big victory for me. I'd been trying for years to get the regulations changed regarding the sale of alcoholic beverages at the city's concert venues. The rule was that you could only order one drink at a time, so if you wanted to buy a whisky for yourself and another for your wife, your wife would have to stand in line, too, or you'd have to stand in line twice—while someone who wanted six or eight shots of whisky in a single cup could order it and be served, no problem. I'd been trying to push a change through the Liquor Commission without success, and when I told Sid I thought it was a stupid rule—it didn't make any sense, it pissed people off and the City lost money from their share of the food and beverage concessions—he took it to the City Council. The Council went along, and the Jimmy Buffett concert two days before had been

the first test. Food and beverage sales that night broke all previous records. I don't get any of that money, by the way; it's split between the concessionaire and the City.

So Sid and I were in a pretty good mood when we met to discuss future improvements to the City-owned venues and ways to cooperate on the actual production of the shows. I was hoping to bring in Kenny Loggins and Jimmy Messina, who were talking about a tour that would be their reunion after 25 years. I thought they could fill the Arena, but I wasn't sure. At the end of the meeting, with the City's cooperation promised, I called Hollywood and put in an offer.

My day was picking up speed. A lunch meeting followed that one, in the Topa Financial Center downtown, where I met with the Road Runner people from Oceanic Time Warner Cable. This was about the promotion of my annual "Soul Jam" show, this year with the Stylistics, Peaches & Herb, the Delfonics, Heatwave and the Persuaders. Road Runner, a high-speed Internet service provided by Oceanic, wanted to offer something to their subscribers. We agreed that if they promoted the concert on all their channels at no cost to me, I'd give their subscribers a $10 discount on tickets and a full week to reserve seats ahead of the tickets' going on general sale. Oceanic also planned to use this as an incentive to attract new subscribers, so it was a pretty heavy meeting. By the end of lunch the deal was done, with plans to do further co-promotions in the future.

Still another meeting came next, this one a short one in my office with my security and technical staff. Norah Jones (below) was to appear at the Blaisdell Arena on Saturday, and all her equipment was coming in the next day, Friday. I wanted to be sure all the bases were covered.

We did have one small problem. The City wanted us to hire two police sergeants and eight officers, the usual contingent for a rock-and-roll show. Well, Norah Jones isn't rock and roll—she's mellow, and her audiences are different from those attracted by rock bands. When we suggested that we might need fewer personnel, we were told we had to take all 10 or none would come. We decided to hire other security.

While in the office, I returned some calls. I'd been working on a break-dancing show that was going to Singapore, and I got a good price from the producer in New York who wanted the Honolulu exposure. He said I had to call a guy in Germany who actually owned the show to get a final okay, though. I said, "It's late now in Germany." He came back with a line I'll never forget: "When it comes to money, there are no time zones." I

called, and the guy said it wasn't possible, because the stop in the Islands would cost an extra $12,000. But he was up to take the call.

A surprise call came in from my old friend, Bob Rogers, one of Australia's all-time great deejays. Bob accompanied the Beatles when they flew from England to Australia for their first "Down Under" concerts. We had started exchanging potential-hit 45's through our mutual friend, Art Thurston, beginning in 1958. I remember sending Bob a brand-new 45 by a group that was unknown in Australia. He made "Lonely Bull" a number-one hit Down Under, and a few months later Herb Alpert & the Tijuana Brass toured Australia and broke all kinds of attendance records. Anyway, Bob asked if I'd go on the air on his top-rated Sydney radio show and talk about Israel "Bruddah Iz" Kamakawiwoole. I'd presented Iz in concert, and I had some interesting stories to relate. So a few minutes later I'm on the radio in Australia, talking about Iz and a song of his that Bob was getting big reaction on, "Somewhere over the Rainbow/What a Wonderful World." Then the subject of Elvis in Hawaii came up, and what was scheduled to be a five-minute or so interview ended up going for about 20!

Another call was from Doug Sharfsberg at

World Wrestling Entertainment (formerly the World Wrestling Federation), to confirm the date when I'd start selling tickets for my umpteenth sports event in the Blaisdell Arena (the same day the "Soul Jam" tickets would go on sale).

Finally, I made a call about bringing the Dave Matthews Band to Hawaii. Another promoter and good friend, Bill Silva, was interested in the band, so I called him to suggest that we do it together. We'd been partners previously, presenting other shows. He said he knew the group's manager and thought he could strike a good deal. I told him to go for it.

My last meeting of the day was the biggest of all, literally. I met with three businessmen who'd approached me over the years wanting to become silent investors. As a rule, I don't look for outside backers in day-to-day events, but for the project we were going to discuss at the meeting, I needed help. It was just too big. You could say the size was titanic.

In 2005, was there anyone, anywhere movies were shown, who didn't know about the *Titanic*, the "unsinkable" cruise ship? It struck an iceberg in the North Atlantic and went down in 1912, taking 1,513 lives—and it wasn't seen again for 75 years. Not long after the wreck was discovered by Robert Ballard—who believed it should be left untouched—a team of entrepreneurs led seven research and recovery expeditions between 1987 and 2004, bringing up some 5,500 artifacts ranging in size from a 17-ton part of the hull to a child's glass marble measuring a half-inch in diameter. Four shows called "Titanic: The Artifact Exhibition" were touring the world in 2005, and I wanted to bring one of them to Hawaii.

I'd flown to Baltimore to see the show there, and I was impressed. Big-time! The entrance was in front of the actual door that first-class passengers used when they entered the ship. There was a full-scale replica of the ballroom staircase that was featured in the movie. For mood and atmosphere there was a wall of solid ice. Real ice! Delicate porcelain dinner settings, jewelry and perfectly preserved leather boots were among the hundreds of items appearing on amazing display, nearly a century later. I wanted Hawaii to see this.

The biggest problem was the cost. The show we decided to bid for had just opened in Columbus, Ohio, and I knew it wouldn't be cheap to move 10 containers of stuff from there—by truck or rail to the West Coast and then to the Islands by ship. Fortunately, we had a place in which to stage the show—the harbor-front building constructed by the State government for an inter-island ferry. The building was standing empty, waiting for final approval of the ferry system, but the State wanted $40,000 a month for rent, a figure set by the federal government since it had paid for the building's construction. The owners of the show also wanted a guarantee of $100,000 up front against a percentage of the gate for a minimum of five months. With shipping, staging and promotion, I'd need as much as $400,000 before I could say I'd do it.

I'd once been offered Elvis Presley at his peak, and I didn't have the cash. I didn't want to miss out on something that big again. At the 3:30 meeting, my investors and I agreed that one way or another we'd make it happen. We'd try to negotiate the rent down and offer the show owners a guarantee of three months, with an option for two more, one month at a time. Come hell or high water, or icebergs in Honolulu Harbor, we were determined: the *Titanic* was coming to Hawaii. It wasn't an opportunity I wanted to pass up.

Promoting's handed me many opportunities I never would have had otherwise. On the same trip where I'd checked out the *Titanic* display, I'd also gone to the Football Hall of Fame in Canton, Ohio, as Steve Young's guest, to see him get inducted. This was a heady experience for me. I retain a love of football from my old high school playing days, and it's a big deal to be inducted—only a very small percentage of the thousands who ever play are so honored—or to be there at the induction of a friend. It was through promotion that I met Steve Young (opposite with his wife, Barb), though the trail's a little twisted: Barb Young has an aunt, Judy, who's Dick Jensen's ex-wife and the mother of my goddaughter, Summer. And back in my early days of promoting, I got Dick (I changed his name to Lance Curtis for a while) his first exposure as a musician. This life is a roller coaster; you just hang on for the ride and enjoy where it takes you, whether it's to the Football Hall of Fame—or just home.

With visions of icebergs and footballs dancing in my head, I drove back to Nuuanu, where the damp still dripped from the leaves and the afternoon light leaked between the branches of the big trees. I thought about my day. Wow! Breakfast with Jimmy Buffett. Making an offer to Loggins & Messina and introducing Jasmine Trias (above) in her hometown solo debut. Planning shows for Norah Jones and a half-dozen of the best soul acts, Dave Matthews and a stage full of sweaty, noisy wrestlers, followed by the *Titanic*.

And it wasn't even cocktail time. 🎤

CHAPTER I

Coming of Age in Michigan

I never enjoyed my birthdays quite the same way most of my friends did. No kid does when he's born in late December. All I remember hearing is, "Merry Christmas and Happy Birthday!" One present instead of two.

Birthday greed aside, I really had nothing to complain about. I had what few people who write their life stories seem to have experienced: a happy childhood. I don't remember my parents ever really arguing. There were no broken bones, no big diseases. About the worst thing that ever happened to me was getting burned by my mom's iron when I was eight. About the same time, I got lost in the Sears department store. And the dad of one of my best friends—a cop—killed himself when we were in the fifth grade. Otherwise, though, my childhood was squeaky clean and trauma free.

My father was a Canadian, from a big family in Winnipeg. Born in 1895, he served in World War One in France. He was a brilliant man who got caught in the Depression, working odd jobs in Canada after the war, then moving to Detroit where he met Mom, an American who'd also been raised in Canada. My brother Norman was born in 1927, I followed along in 1930—on December 30—and my sister was born three years after that. By then, my father was working as an electrician at the General Motors plant.

After a time, he had to quit. I never understood

My father, James Cecil Moffatt (right), served in France during World War One. Opposite: At South Lyon High, the "Big Four" was inseparable (left to right: Dick Lloyd, Bill McCormick, me and George Bridson).

exactly what happened because I was young, but there was a dispute between the union and management, and Dad sided with the bosses. It wasn't something Mom and Dad talked about, but it was serious enough that we had to leave town for part of a summer. My parents decided to make a vacation of it. They had a Pontiac coupe, and my dad rigged a steel rod that held the trunk lid up. My brother and sister and I rode in the trunk—for 200 miles. We had a ball. People along the highway and in the cars behind us smiled and waved. It was one of the best summers of my life. But when we went back to Detroit, my

Brother Norman, sister Anne and me.

father had to find a new job.

I remember the times just after the Depression. Dad gave me a dime to buy some lemons at the neighborhood store, and I lost the dime. He made me go back and look for it. He said, "Go back and find that dime." I finally found it. I remember that. That's how tight money was.

The biggest thrill I got as a kid was when I was in the sixth grade and Jo Jo White, the center fielder for the Detroit Tigers, moved in next door. It was beyond the realm of comprehension that something like that would happen. I was a very big Tigers fan, and I didn't believe it until I saw his baseball uniform hanging on the line next door to my house! The Detroit Tigers—was I excited! Unfortunately, he got traded, so he was only there for one season.

But it wasn't all middle-of-the-road and middle-class cliché. When I was 13, I left home. During the summers of my sixth and seventh grades I had stayed with my mother's cousins, who had a mink ranch about 60 miles from Detroit, and for the eighth grade I went to school there, transferring from a pretty good school system in Detroit to a one-room school with kindergarten and the

first eight grades in it, and only one teacher. That's when I became a mediocre student. I was good at spelling and fine at math, but the rest was pretty much a write-off.

Each week the teacher gave me 10 cents to come in early on Monday and start a fire in the furnace so the school would be warm enough when the others came in at 8 o'clock. Weekdays she'd just bank the fire and it would stay lighted overnight, but over the weekend the coals would die. I'd ring the school bell sometimes, too, to bring the kids in from the playground to start classes. There were three of us in the eighth grade—that was our "graduating class" at the end of the year.

I worked long hours after school and weekends at the mink ranch, feeding the animals ground horsemeat and grain. What wasn't eaten went to the pigs. I was raising a couple of hogs, and the 315-pounder, Herman, won first prize at the Jackson County Fair. I was a 4-H Club member, and I went to the State Fair in Lansing with Herman, showing him on the same field where Michigan State played its football games. He didn't win. The meat companies all supported the 4-H clubs by bidding on the pigs, paying a premium price. Whatever they offered for

My mother's name was Eunice, but everyone called her June.

The family gathers for Thanksgiving dinner at home in 1949.

him was mine to keep. Hot stuff when you're going into your teens.

I moved back in with my parents to begin high school in 1944 and started working as a dishwasher in a restaurant called Curly's after school and on weekends. Curly Hock and his brother, Ed, had worked for the Ford Motor Company, and on the weekends the two brothers' families had a popcorn business together. Their formula was to fill the container halfway with hot popcorn, then pour in a quarter of a cup of heated butter, then fill it to the top with more popcorn and put another quarter-cup of butter on top. This was twice as much butter as other people gave you, and it soaked all the way to the bottom. People would drive miles to get the stuff, and the owners parlayed this money into Curly's Restaurant. It wasn't a big place. They sold hamburgers. There weren't any tables and chairs, just a counter with a row of stools.

I wasn't happy back in Detroit. It was just a big city that I really didn't care for. I liked the green of the farm. The country was clean and the city was dirty. So at the end of my freshman year I went to work at the Hocks' farm for the summer. The Second World War was winding down and rationing was still in effect, but on the farm the chickens and livestock provided everything we wanted. There were pork chops and steaks. Sometimes I'd eat six eggs for breakfast, or drink half a gallon of milk.

Posing with Stank, my pet skunk.

siding beside the elevator from time to time, and I'd have to offload the bags of grain that would later be sold to other farmers in the area. Once in a while I'd help offload a carload of really heavy bags of cement. That helped me stay in shape.

Ed and Marion had a son a couple of years younger than I was, Eddie, and I became sort of a big brother to him. Curly and Ruth didn't have any children of their own, so Ruth became sort of my second mother. I loved my own mother too, of course, and she was very supportive because she knew I wanted to live out in the country, where I had two families. And that's where I learned my work ethic.

The farm was about 180 acres, and every morning I'd milk the cows, feed the pigs, feed the cattle, feed the chickens and gather the eggs, and go to school. I had my own steer named Stevie, which I raised from a calf. I knew that eventually we would eat him. When you grow up on a farm, that's just the way of life. And you always worked hard.

Running all over the farm were about 25 cats and a dog. I also had a pet skunk I'd found when he was a baby. We took him to the vet's to be de-smelled, but he still could squirt a little bit, so I called him Stank and kept him in an unroofed pen behind the house. Near that was the building where we'd peel potatoes every weekend for the next week's French fries in the restaurant. We'd listen to the radio to help make time pass, and I remember peeling potatoes with Eddie when Michigan State beat Southern Cal in the Rose Bowl, 49-0.

There was a huge barn, with a silo that wasn't used, and we stored the baled hay upstairs to feed the cattle during the winter. A few times every winter we'd get snowed in and I wouldn't have to go to school. Before I got a car my junior year, a Model A Ford that I bought for $35, we walked to town, three and a half miles, or we'd hitch a ride.

Dad was working in a factory that supplied parts for military vehicles by then, and I asked my parents if I could stay in the country, live with the Hocks, and go to school there. I think I was my mom's favorite—I had her features—so it was difficult for her, but they both said okay. I changed from MacKenzie High School in Detroit to South Lyon High, where there were about 38 people in my class.

Ed and Curly and their wives lived in the same big farmhouse together. Ed's wife Marion ran the restaurant in Detroit, coming home on the weekends, while Ed ran the farm and Curly ran the grain elevator in New Hudson, a few miles away. A railroad car would be left on a

The Hocks also ran a custom hay baling business. If you grew hay, when it was ready to harvest, you'd hire the Hocks to come bale it after it was cut. I rode on the wagon behind the baler and stacked the hay. Usually we'd let the hay dry in the sun before baling it so some of the water content could evaporate. That made the bales a little lighter, but they sometimes still weighed 100 pounds or so apiece. I thought of my buddies back in Detroit hanging out at the soda shop while I was spreading manure and throwing bales of hay around…I thought I had the better life!

Because of all this work, when I went out for football and basketball I was in really good shape—a little over six feet tall and weighing 175 pounds. I played varsity in both football and basketball at South Lyon. In football, I played tackle, both offensive and defensive, which meant I sometimes played the whole game. I wasn't what's called a "natural athlete," though. I tried out for baseball and didn't make it. But we were in a tough league, and I was pretty good. We never won any championships, but our last game one year was against a team that hadn't let any other team get within their 20-yard line all season—we didn't score, but we got within their five-yard line in the first

I played tackle on the football team. Joe Muir (left) played an end, and Frank Bishop (center) was a guard.

few minutes of the game. To us, that felt like a victory.

We also had to try harder in basketball. Because we practiced on a court with a low ceiling, we never learned how to throw the ball any way other than pretty much straight at the net. Somehow it worked for us, but there were never any of those high, arcing swishes that our opponents got.

South Lyon wasn't very big. It was about 35 miles from Detroit, halfway between Ann Arbor and Pontiac. The town had only 3,500 people. A few blocks away from the center of town there was nothing but big farms. Everybody knew everybody else. There were two cops, the chief of police and his assistant. The chief busted us one night

LYON TOWNSHIP HIGH SCHOOL
Football - Basketball
BANQUET
I. O. O. F. HALL, SOUTH LYON
Tuesday, Apr. 19 - 7:00 p. m.
$1.75 per Plate
Sponsored by Board of Commerce

Coach Donley gives the basketball team a halftime pep talk. You can tell by the long faces that we were way behind.

I was elected student body president in my senior year at South Lyon High.

My senior year I was student body president, and my girlfriend was a popular cheerleader. There were four of us guys who hung out together. We were called "The Big Four." We were all jocks; we played football and basketball together. One day, a bunch of us drove into Detroit and went to a tattoo parlor in one of those traveling carnivals and had identical American eagles put on our arms. Today tattoos are no big thing, but in the 1940s, except on military returning from the war, you never, ever saw them. We were proud. Years later it'd be an embarrassment.

Another thing I remembered years later was how we snuck in to see University of Michigan games in Ann Arbor. My buddies and I would drive there, and a friend who was already inside the stadium would collect as many ticket stubs as we needed from other friends already seated, then pass them to us; we'd walk in showing those stubs. Twenty years later, as a promoter of shows, I figured others would get the same idea—so whenever anyone leaves the venue with a ticket, I punch it or mark it in some way.

I say that where I grew up was rural, but there was a twist: in the immediate post-war years, when the factories stopped making military vehicles and returned to manufacturing civilian ones, there were a lot of new cars on the roads or being driven on special tracks. Three or four miles from the Hocks' farm, Henry Ford's brother had a farm. I remember baling hay there. And Henry Ford had his cars making a circuit up what was called Eight Mile Road to Pontiac Trail, into South Lyon, then returning down Ten Mile Road, 24 hours a day. (Fifty years later, Eminem would star in a movie about, and rap on the soundtrack for, that very same Eight Mile Road.) Not so far away was the Sorenson farm, owned by the man who made Willys Jeeps, so that had been the testing ground for Jeeps. And a few miles south of us was where Henry J. Kaiser built his cars, the Kaiser-Frasers. This was in 1945, 1946. He had built airplanes during the war and converted the factory to make cars. So we were very car conscious. One of my

when we bought some beer and went out driving, and then he called all our families.

Another time I barely escaped trouble of another sort. Driving to Detroit, I stopped to visit a girlfriend on the way. In those days, in small towns, when you picked up the telephone to make a call a real live person came on to make it for you. You gave her the number and she connected you—and you hoped she wouldn't listen in. Well, in my girlfriend's town, the operator was her *sister*. After visiting my girlfriend, at her sister's house, I was about halfway to Detroit when I discovered I didn't have my condoms in my pocket. I'd left them under my girlfriend's bed. And I knew I couldn't call because her sister would know. So I had to drive all the way back.

buddies in high school became a driver for GM's proving grounds a few miles away.

Radio was different in those days, and I was hooked on it from when I was a little kid. I guess we all were. "I Love a Mystery" played three times a week, and that was all anybody talked about the next day at school. This was long before TV, and I loved getting sick so I could stay home and listen to the soap operas: "One Man's Family," "Backstage Wife," "Pepper Young's Family," "Ma Perkins." "The Lone Ranger" was broadcast from Detroit, and some of the actors lived in the same building where my Aunt Hazel lived. I also liked "Gangbusters" and "Suspense."

The first national deejay music program I remember was a show called "Paul Whiteman Presents." He was a bandleader with a 35-piece orchestra. His regular vocalist was Dinah Shore, and every week he'd have guest stars like George Burns and Gracie Allen, Red Skelton, Bing Crosby or Jimmy Durante. I liked music. Sinatra was big. He was the first idol with the girls at Curly's. I was washing dishes there when Sinatra came to Detroit to perform, and that's all the girls talked about at work. The restaurant didn't have a big jukebox, but there was one of those sound systems with small Select-O-Matic-style jukeboxes on the counter with little pages listing the songs. You turned the pages until you found the song you wanted, then put your money in and punched in the song's numbers. There was one for every customer. At home we had a round-topped radio. It was a time when the family ate together and listened to the radio together.

Radio was a theater of the mind for me. You could "see" Fibber McGee's closet when Molly opened it and everything came crashing out. It wasn't as funny when they did it years later on television. And when the Lone Ranger galloped across that little black-and-white screen… I remembered it as being much bigger and better on radio, when I created the same picture in my mind.

Sometimes I went to live broadcasts. In my junior

I got an early taste of show business when I acted in a school production of *Wedding Spells*.

"Wedding Spells"
Three Act Comedy
Presented By
Senior Class of South Lyon High School
SATURDAY, JANUARY 29
Place: Quick Hall — Curtain Time 8:00 p.m.
Admission: 42c, plus 8c Fed. Tax—Total 50c

year I went to see "The Camel Caravan," with Vaughn Monroe. He had three or four hits, and his theme song was "Racing with the Moon." He came to Detroit, and Bert Parks was his announcer. My Aunt Isabelle in Detroit got us really good up-front seats to the broadcast, and I remember both these guys, Vaughn Monroe and Bert Parks, looking at my girlfriend Ruth. She was really cute. Another time, we went to the Fox Theater in Detroit where I saw my first live variety show. Between movies a live show would come on. That was when I saw the Mills Brothers and Frankie Carle's Orchestra in a twin bill. I was really impressed with the Mills Brothers, four guys getting such a great sound backed only by a guitarist, Cliff White. Nine years later I would be introducing Sam Cooke at Honolulu's Civic Auditorium, with the band conducted by the very same Cliff White. At the Olympia in Detroit, where I saw the Detroit Red Wings play, I also saw Sonja Heine, the Norwegian ice skating star who'd made a number of movies and was touring with her own ice show.

I finished high school and moved back with my folks in Detroit. I'd broken up with my girlfriend and thought I should try to go to college. In my senior year, George Allen—who later went on to coach the Los Angeles Rams and the Washington Redskins—had just graduated from the University of Michigan and had gotten a job as coach at Morningside College in Sioux City, Iowa. He knew the caliber of football in South Lyon, and he asked my old coach, Lee Donley, if he had anybody he'd suggest. Coach Donley recommended me as well as our outstanding end, Joe Muir. Morningside wanted to go big-time in football, and George Allen invited us to see them play at Bowling Green, Ohio. We actually sat on the bench with the team, and I was impressed. But when he offered me a full scholarship, I asked him what would happen if I got injured. Would my scholarship remain in effect? I didn't get a straight answer from him, so I can't say I was ever

During my junior year, my cute girlfriend Ruth (right) even caught the eye of Bert Parks.

coached by the great George Allen.

That's when I took a job washing parts at the Dodge plant in Hamtramck, Michigan, figuring maybe I could save enough money to pay my own way. I worked the 4-to-midnight shift, and I was making good money. But I wasn't happy at all. I was back in the city and it was summer and it was hot. I had to catch the bus down Grand Boulevard every day past what would become, several years later, the original home of Motown Records.

After I'd worked for two or three months, the factory went on strike, and I was unemployed. I returned to South Lyon and went to work for the Michigan Seamless Tube Company, cutting steel tubes. I worked double shifts, 16 hours straight when someone got sick, so I could get the overtime. Lots of times I worked from 4 o'clock in the afternoon until 8 o'clock the next morning. And as my savings began to grow, I started wondering about schools again.

Except for a senior trip to Niagara Falls, I'd never been farther away than Ohio, and now I wanted to travel, to get as far away as possible. I remember going to the corner drug store where I saw a magazine that listed hundreds of U.S. colleges. I bought it, and on the final page two universities were listed, one in Puerto Rico, the other in Hawaii. The University of Hawaii was the farthest away, so I wrote them a letter, thinking I might study law.

At the time, I knew nothing about Hawaii. I'd heard "Hawaii Calls" on the radio, and I remembered hearing the surf and listening to Webley Edwards announce the temperature of the air and the water. That was the way the show opened every week, and in the winter in Detroit, it sounded pretty good. Aunt Hazel had stopped there once on her way back from Guam, and she talked about a place where you turned on a spigot and pineapple juice came out. I knew that Hawaii was where World War Two started; we all sat around the radio together on December 7th. But that was all I knew. Except for my aunt, nobody

The "Big Four" at graduation. Right: "Moonlight and Roses" was our prom theme in 1949.

Moonlight AND Roses

in Michigan that I knew had ever been there. Except for "Hawaii Calls" and a few movies I'd seen that were filmed there, the Islands were a mysterious place where there were hula dancers and, we thought, people lived in grass huts. It wasn't advertised like it is today.

In the immediate postwar years, Hawaii was only beginning to attract tourists. Most of the people who went there traveled by boat and were super rich. But the tuition at the university was just $100 a semester. I'd saved $1,200, and when I got my letter of acceptance, not long before the start of classes in September, 1950, I packed my bags, booked a flight on Northwest Airlines, said goodbye to my parents and the Hocks and my friends, and was gone. I left on a Thursday night and arrived on a Saturday morning. It was a long flight, and I felt as if I were millions of miles from home. 🎙

CHAPTER 2

University Days and Army Life

It was a prop plane that brought me to the Islands, and it was the first plane I'd ever been on. So I welcomed the camaraderie between passengers that existed then—something I don't see any more. Nowadays the flight from the mainland is like spending five hours in a school auditorium with strangers, every minute of the trip programmed with meals and drink and video. In 1950, by the time we finally landed in what was then a U.S. territory, we'd had no such distractions and time enough to become friends. When the wheels touched down, we applauded and whistled and yelled. Our adventure in paradise had begun.

It was morning, so I had nearly a full day ahead of me. Nervousness and excitement in equal parts accompanied me to a taxi queue. What I later learned were called "trade winds" softened the heat and humidity. I remember being knocked out by all the flowers and the green mountains. The dark faces of the Hawaiians seemed more exotic than I'd imagined. And everyone seemed to be dressed for the beach. Hawaii even smelled good!

In the 1950 many still arrived in the Territory of Hawaii by ship. At far left center in this photo of Honolulu is the Alexander Young Hotel, where I first stayed for $4 a night. When I came back for good in 1955, I sailed from Los Angeles aboard the *Lurline* (lower left). Opposite: Me and my Army buddies, Schofield Barracks, 1953.

I went first to the university campus, where I learned that because of my late arrival—it was September 16—the only dormitory was fully booked. I was told to return on Monday to get a list of rooms for rent in private homes in the neighborhood and, in the meantime, I was informed that hotels on Waikiki Beach cost $6 a night and that the Alexander Young Hotel downtown had rooms with baths for $4. I found my way downtown.

For what little remained of my first day in Hawaii,

Now, as I stood at her door looking for a room in 1950, after her fourth husband and everyone in his family had died, here she was, this grand old lady, living in this big beautiful house with a view of all Honolulu below, struggling on a trust fund that was established in the 1920s that didn't quite give her enough to live on. So she rented out rooms to pay for groceries.

"Mrs. Hawes, my name is Tom Moffatt and I'm really pleased to meet you," I said.

At the time, I knew nothing about her and had no idea how lucky I was that her name and address were the first on the university housing list. She took me to look at a room about four times the size of a dorm room. She told me that Jack London was a friend of her husband's and that he used to play poker in the room next to mine.

She also told me that she had helped start the Hawaiian Humane Society, and she gave me a picture of her placing a lei on the trans-Pacific cable when it came ashore at Sans Souci Beach in 1901. Before that, she explained, it took several days when something happened in the U.S. before a ship arrived with the news. I later heard from someone else that she had been the mistress of a famous writer she was very secretive about, that she had spent much of her

Francesca Hawes, my landlady, had draped a lei on the trans-Pacific cable when it first came ashore in Waikiki in 1901.

and all the next day, I explored, traveling by bus to Waikiki to walk along the beach road where the palm trees and the rolling surf—both totally new sights for me—delivered everything promised in those Dorothy Lamour movies and radio's "Hawaii Calls."

On Monday I went to the university housing office and was given the address of a house in Manoa Valley owned by an elderly socialite named Francesca Hawes, a woman in her 80s whom I later learned had been married and widowed three times before the turn of the century. (You do the math. She was still in her 30s when her third husband died!) She then met Alexander Hawes, whose father was a Civil War hero, one of John Brown's men. Her husband was several years younger than she was, and his family lived in Sans Souci, a big home that gave the beach its name. Her father-in-law was a very powerful man, one of the founders of the Bohemian Club in San Francisco, and here was his only son married to this three-times-married older woman. I don't think her parents ever accepted her, but they built the couple a big home and put it in a trust so it could never be sold.

Thanks to my previous disk jockey experience, I was able to remain in Hawaii at the height of the Korean War.

time sailing on ships to London and New York.

She couldn't see very well, but she'd get on a bus by herself and go downtown. One day a few weeks later—this was after she had seen me in a bathing suit and told me I had legs like her husband's—I boarded the bus a few blocks after she had and took the adjacent seat. I said hello and she said hello back and started talking to me about this wonderful young man who had taken one of her rooms. And when she talked about her boarder's legs, I realized she was talking about me…and that in her near-blindness she hadn't known it was I sitting next to her. She might have been in her 80s, but she was one of the most charming and elegant women I ever met.

So that was my introduction to Hawaii. It was all so romantic, you could die for it. You can't make up stories that good.

At the time, the University of Hawaii had an enrollment of about 2,000. When I arrived, they'd just built a big new administration building, Hawaii Hall, at the corner of University Avenue and Dole Street, and there was an old gymnasium where they played basketball. Some of our PE classes were conducted in a quarry where the Stan Sheriff Center is today; the football team practiced there, too, all of us getting down into it and back out of it on wood stairs that were built against one of the steep sides.

Most of the students were then, as now, of Asian or Pacific heritage. For a guy who hadn't even seen a Chinese face except on a quarterback who played for another high school in Michigan, this represented a big change. There weren't so many Caucasians, *haoles*, as there are today, either, and the majority were Hawaii residents. Most of the others were guys on the GI Bill who had served in Hawaii during the war and came back because they loved the Islands.

I was one of the very few non-resident, non-veteran haoles in my class. I mixed in pretty well, but I got my first taste of prejudice when there was this girl I really liked.

I scored my first lodgings in Hawaii partly because the landlady thought I had legs like her husband's!

Her name was Jeannie Lum; she was Chinese, and her family owned a nightclub on Ala Moana Boulevard called Leroy's. We wanted to go out, but her family said no because I was white. The same thing happened a couple of years later, when I started dating a Chinese girl who was a senior, two years ahead of me. We became very close. She had a Chinese boyfriend and she strayed from him to be with me, so when she graduated her family shipped her off to grad school in New York. I think they wanted to get her away from me.

Mostly, there was no problem. One of the first guys

At Tripler's Armed Forces radio station I interviewed celebrities like Hawaii's all-time boxing great Carl "Bobo" Olson, the middle-weight champion of the world, and country favorite Tennessee Ernie Ford.

who befriended me was Japanese, Harry Takane; he used to call me Tom Mafia. I'd meet him again, many years later. One of my PE teachers was also Japanese. Soichi Sakamoto was one of the most acclaimed swimming coaches in the world, the Olympics coach for Hawaii. I remember reading about him when I was still in Detroit. They had the Olympics trials there in 1948, and I remember the Hawaii swimmers dominated.

So here Soichi was at the UH, an Olympics coach, teaching local kids how to swim. I was astonished how many couldn't. Living on an island, I figured, would get everyone swimming before they could walk, but no. The weird thing was that Soichi couldn't swim himself. An amazing story.

I never did get into sports, by the way. My freshman year, I tried out for football. I practiced a few days, and I was in pretty good shape and I held my own, but I knew it wasn't for me. The weather dehydrated me, and I felt like an outsider. All the others had grown up together and played together in local high schools. I didn't have my buddies around me, so on the third or fourth day I went to the coach, Tommy Kaulukukui, and turned my uniform in.

My speech teacher, Mr. Spencer—I never knew or probably ever heard his first name—told me I had a good voice and should go into radio. They had a radio guild on campus with a makeshift studio where you could try out. They produced these little radio shows that were given to local radio stations as a public service, and some of the commercial radio announcers in town would come out and announce for the shows. One was named John Needham, and that was the first time I'd ever been close to a professional announcer and watched him work the microphone. Here's a guy who picked up a piece of paper and it just rolled off; it was natural for him. I wanted to be like that. That really impressed me. I liked the glamour of it. I thought there'd be glamour in radio.

By the way, Mr. Spencer may have liked my voice, but he gave me a "C" in the class.

At the time, there were only five stations in Honolulu, one for each of the four mainland-based networks and one independent. KHON, the independent, was Aku's station. He didn't own it—in fact, he never owned a station in Hawaii—but wherever he worked, that station was always known as Aku's. Because in the history of Hawaii radio,

there never was anyone who was bigger, brasher or made more money. At least that's what we were told.

Aku had several names in his life. He was born in Brooklyn in 1917 as Herschel Laib Hohenstein, and when he arrived in the Islands he was Hal Lewis, a name he legally adopted. He was a professional violinist, touring with vaudeville acts as a kid, and it was the fiddle that brought him to the Islands with a small, shipboard orchestra in 1946. A succession of radio jobs followed, and by the time he was at KHON, he'd become known for his on-the-air stunts.

One day he gave all the time signals an hour earlier than they were, causing a woman listener to call in, mad, because he'd made her husband late for work. She called him names, said he was *pupule*, Hawaiian for "crazy." Somebody else called him "fishhead," and soon after that he started calling himself J. Akuhead Pupule, *aku* being the Hawaiian word for skipjack tuna. From that time on, I doubt anyone on the street could've told you his real name.

One of the real highs I got while at UH was being taken by a friend to see the great Aku at work in the studio. He greeted us graciously and, in the brief conversation that followed, he said he needed the sound of a toilet flushing, because he couldn't find that on any of the sound-effects

In 1952 I sent out this homemade Christmas card featuring a picture of me behind a KGU microphone.

records he used while expressing his opinions about the morning's news. My friend and I returned to the UH campus and strung a microphone cord from the studio to a nearby toilet in Hawaii Hall and next day delivered the tape to KHON. Soon after that, when we listened to Aku in the morning, we heard our toilet flush.

There was another reason I listened to KHON. On Sunday afternoons, KHON played our little recorded dramatic shows. My sophomore year, I became the public relations guy for the Associated Students of the University of Hawaii (ASUH), and one weekend I accompanied members of the student government to Hilo where there was a branch of the university. The student body president was Shunichi Kimura (who later became mayor of Hilo and a well-respected judge). One of our hosts at UH-Hilo was Ronald Bright, who went on to become a teacher and producer of shows at Castle High School. (Later, the school named the auditorium in his honor.) Another was James Komeya, who would reappear later in my life, on Guam. Two more were Dick Hashimoto, who became

As the PR guy for the Associated Students of the University of Hawaii, I flew to Hilo on the Big Island with members of the student government.

an executive at Sheraton Hotels, and Barney Menor, who became prominent in Hawaii politics. On that trip, on a Sunday afternoon, we visited Kulani Prison, which was located at a high elevation. Because of that, KHON's signal came through all the way from Honolulu—and for the first time, I heard myself on the radio.

At the end of my freshman year, I wanted to get a job as a junior announcer and applied for a job at KGU and got turned down. So I went to the Dole Pineapple cannery, and the local kids pretty much had a monopoly on that. I was fairly adept at handling farm machinery, so I applied as an equipment operator, but if you had a relative who already worked for Dole, you went to the front of the line.

So next I went to the military, and they were hiring. I ended up with a job at Tripler Army Hospital as a janitor. That's how I spent my first summer in Hawaii, mopping stairs from the first floor up to the ninth. It was the tallest building in Hawaii at the time, and that meant there were a lot of steps. I knew them all.

I got more involved with school activities my sophomore year and also more involved in partying. I remember when they opened a warehouse where they'd kept all the Japanese goods confiscated during the war. We bought this 10-year-old beer for a dollar a case that was not quite as good as the local brew and lugged eight cases of it back to my room. After the Japanese beer ran out, we stocked my closet with our local favorite, Royal. We also liked to get a watermelon, cut a hole in the top and hollow out most of the fruit. We'd pour in a bottle of rum, put the top back in and carry the thing up to the roof to ferment for a few days. Then we'd all sit around with straws and get blotto.

One time we went aboard the *Lurline* with a watermelon to see off some friends who were going to the mainland. All of a sudden the ship started off—and we panicked! Where do we hide? Are we stowaways? Were we

KIKI was one of only five radio stations in Honolulu in the early 1950s.

relieved to find that if we slipped the tugboat captain a few bucks he'd return us to shore!

I was also the PR guy for the Pineapple Bowl, and I'd take the contestants for Miss Pineapple around to public events. (One of the contestants was the Olympic swimmer Evelyn Kawamoto, who later married Hawaii swimming great Ford Konno. It was a real kick when, years later, Evie called me to get tickets for her grandchildren for a Michael Jackson concert.) Another beauty contest, the Ka Palapala Pageant, had a queen of each nationality competing: Chinese, Japanese, Korean, Filipina, Caucasian and "cosmopolitan." I'd get information out to the media. Once, I was dressed up in a kimono, pulling this cute girl in a rickshaw on campus, and someone took a picture just as my pants were falling down beneath my kimono. The guy who captioned the picture was John Griffin, a staff writer for *Ka Leo*, the campus newspaper, and he'd go on to become one of the top editors of the *Honolulu Advertiser*; in the caption

he called me Tom "Rickshaw" Moffatt.

I think if I had stayed at the university, I might have gone for a degree in public relations. But at the end of the school year in June 1952, a year after they rejected me, KGU offered me a full-time position as a junior announcer. I was fascinated with professional radio and didn't return to classes that fall.

KGU was one of the oldest stations in the United States, first going on the air in 1922. KGU was also one of the earliest affiliates of NBC, the first U.S. network, and it was one of the two Honolulu stations (with KGMB) that the Japanese planes homed in on the morning of December 7, 1941. When I joined the staff, the station occupied the top floor of the *Honolulu Advertiser* building, its walls covered with traditional Hawaiian *tapa* and *lauhala* mats and hung with big photographs of NBC stars like Edgar Bergen and Jack Benny and Bob Hope. Another NBC star, Dave Garroway, had actually worked at KGU before going on to New York. Could we have talked into the same microphone? I remember being quite impressed.

I met Ella Fitzgerald after a few months on the job. She was doing "Jazz at the Philharmonic" at McKinley High School. Vincent Priore, a former road manager for Louis Armstrong, was taking her around, and when he brought her to KGU he introduced me to her. He was now working at KGU, too, and he became one of my mentors, despite the fact that he smoked *pakalolo* (marijuana) occasionally, which at the time I found both shocking and *avant garde*. I had tickets to go to Ella's concert that night, and when I went home to change my clothes, I was on a real high. But the mail that was waiting for me completely changed my mood—it included my draft notice. I'd thought the draft board in Michigan might not have noticed, but I guess the university blew the whistle on me. So I went to the concert with mixed emotions. It was a hell of a concert, with Barney Kessel on guitar, Ray Brown on bass, Oscar Peterson on piano, Lester Young on sax, Buddy

Rich on drums and several other jazz greats of the time.

My draft notice arrived November 20, and I reported to Schofield Barracks on December 9. This was at the height of the Korean War. During the 16 weeks of basic training, it was understood that the whole company was going to Korea, so it was pretty heavy. We spent a couple of weeks up in the wilds of Kahuku in a foxhole. And it wasn't simulated weapons fire.

The final week, the drill sergeant we all thought was so tough took me aside. He told me, "You don't want to go to this war." He said the military was looking for a disc jockey for a closed-circuit radio system at Tripler, and he loaned me his car to drive up there for an interview. He may have saved my life.

They had a studio right there inside the hospital, and we were on the air from 6 in the morning until 10 at night, playing to a captive audience: the patients. We got these big transcriptions, 16-inch ones, with the programs on them. Bob Hope, Jack Benny, Bob & Ray, all the network shows. Every once in a while we'd do a disc jockey show, play Frank Sinatra, Patti Page, June Christy, the Mills Brothers, Nat "King" Cole and people like that.

During that time, a lot of the wounded came back from Korea to Tripler, and a lot of entertainers who came to Hawaii to perform would come to Tripler to see the GIs. Because I was the only professional radio announcer on staff, I'd interview them on the "Bedside Network" so all the patients could listen. Some even performed at the post theater, and all of them at least walked through

During my sophomore year, my closet doubled as a storeroom for our favorite beverage, locally brewed Royal Beer.

the wards to say hello. My favorite was Louis Armstrong, who disappeared minutes before I was to introduce him at the theater. I found him in the hospital parking lot, warming up, blowing his trumpet in the tropical sunlight, trademark handkerchief in his hand. I rushed the great Satchmo back into the building.

So it was pretty easy duty. I worked six days a week, and at the same time I worked part-time at KGU and KIKI. I didn't like living in Army housing, so eventually I drifted out of the barracks and moved into town.

A friend was an announcer at KAHU in Waipahu, and he was living with these two old gals in Waikiki on the beach between the Royal Hawaiian and Halekulani Hotels. They lived in the front of the house and he had a room in the back. He didn't pay any rent, because they just wanted him on the premises. He left Hawaii and introduced me to the ladies, so I moved in and continued to serve my country.

At KIKI, I was doing a disc jockey thing. At KGU, I was the staff announcer, and I'd run the board for some of the sports shows, including the re-creation of major league baseball with Joe "Rack 'em Up" Rose doing the play-by-play. He was given the basic facts, and he'd re-create the game as if he were really there. He'd talk about a little disturbance in the stands, just make things up, and people thought it was real. I'd do the sound effects and read the commercials. We had four turntables. One was for a normal crowd, another for an excited one, another for a booing crowd and another for the sound of a vendor selling 7-Up, which was one of his sponsors.

During the Korean War, some of our military were thought to be cooperating with the communists while in prison. They were called "turncoats." When the first planeload of released prisoners was shipped back to the States, they stopped in Hawaii for medical examinations. A Congressional committee examining the allegations wanted the men interviewed, and I was picked to ask the questions on camera. I was told at the time I couldn't even talk about it to my friends—which I didn't. I was scared to death. After an afternoon of interviews, the film was put on a plane that night for Washington, for the committee to view.

So it was very interesting duty, and when I was discharged on December 8, 1954, except for basic training, I didn't even feel as if I'd been in the Army. More important, I'd moved my career ahead.

When I got out of the army, it'd been four years since I'd left the mainland, and I was supposed to go directly to my folks' home in Michigan. But my friend Jim Wahl—whose uncle had been Webley Edwards' announcer on "Hawaii Calls" and occupied another room

When I wore this get-up in an early publicity stunt for a beauty pageant, the campus newspaper identified me as Tom "Rickshaw" Moffatt.

in Mrs. Hawes' house—had been hired by a radio station in El Paso, Texas. So I went there first, and together we crossed the border into Juarez, Mexico. While we were there, we went to a bullfight. My mother was an animal lover, and she was not pleased.

I finally made it back to Detroit, but I didn't stay long, and when a friend of the family who was a car dealer asked if I'd like to drive a Cadillac to a buyer in Los Angeles, I was gone again. I picked up an Army buddy and headed west, visiting Dodge City and Las Vegas. Dean Martin and Jerry Lewis appeared at the Sands and came out to the table where I was playing blackjack, taking turns as the dealer. I think they came to my table because Louis Prima was sitting next to me. And for the record, Jerry Lewis paid me even when I lost, and Dean Martin played it straight. Then after delivering the car, I got onto the *Lurline* and came home to Hawaii.

This time I planned to stay. 🎙

CHAPTER 3

Early Hawaii Radio

Pre-statehood Hawaii was very different from what it is today. The population was small, less than half a million in 1950. Tourism was still in its infancy, and the economy was driven mainly by sugar, pine and the big military bases. Because it was a territory, its citizens couldn't vote in presidential elections. They couldn't even elect their own governor, who was appointed by the President of the United States.

There was no television; instead there were drive-in movies. There were no jet planes landing at Honolulu's airport. Commerce remained largely in the hands of the companies known as the Big Five: American Factors, Castle & Cooke, Alexander & Baldwin, Theo. H. Davies & Co., and C. Brewer & Co., long-time sugar planters with deep missionary roots.

Radio was different in the 1950s, too. The national network affiliates—KGU for NBC, KGMB for CBS, KULA for ABC, KPOA for Mutual—all ran the same shows that were broadcast on the mainland, but a week or more later, after the recorded programs reached the Islands (on 16-inch discs like those we played at Tripler).

KIKI was the only independent station, and so it had many of the local personalities. Jimmy Walker was the morning guy. Gene Taylor, a transplanted Englishman, had an afternoon easy-listening show. Jack Tasaka had a Japanese language program. Tommy Tomimbang, father of Emme Tomimbang (later to become a major Island TV

In the 1950, Hawaii's economy was still driven mainly by the sugar and pineapple industries and the big military bases. Opposite: As a young radio announcer, I found myself making more and more public appearances.

personality) hosted a Filipino language show. That was typical. A lot of the local programming followed racial lines. And a station's programming might bounce all over the map, so that some big-name network show would be followed by something in another language!

When I returned to Honolulu, I went right back to KGU. I went on the air with a 10 p.m. to 1 a.m. show called "Moffatt Past Midnight." In the summer of 1955 I did Honolulu's first radio "sock hop," with a remote broadcast from Rainbow Rollerland on Keeaumoku Street, located

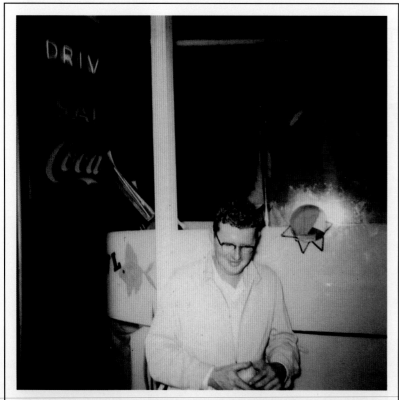

The original Uncle Tom's Cabin at the Ilima Drive-In on King Street.

halfway between downtown and Waikiki. Sometimes, when it was slow at the rink, I'd put on a longer record and join some of the Rollerland staff to watch a movie on the screen of the Kapiolani Drive-In Theater nearby, where the Daiei store is now. The operation was that loose.

The music was a mish-mash, what later came to be called Middle of the Road—people like Tony Bennett, Les Baxter, Nat "King" Cole, Don Cherry, the Four Freshmen, Sinatra—the popular artists of the time. On Sunday mornings I had to host a piano show; I remember playing a lot of Andre Previn music.

It was at KGU that I met Ron Jacobs. Ron began his radio career while he was still in school in 1952, after he transferred from Punahou School after seven years and before he dropped out of Roosevelt High after two to take a job as a disc jockey at KHON. He came aboard at KGU at the ripe old age of 17.

I remember my first impression: "Who is this pompous ass?" Later we became on-the-air adversaries and have remained off-the-air close friends for half a century! I have always, always, stood in awe of his quick and perverse mind.

It was also at this time that I got to see how the politics of both radio and Hawaii came together to play dirty tricks. Eddie Sherman was a stand-up comic and amateur boxer from the Borscht Belt in New York who had settled in the Islands and become a friend. The fast-talking Sherman wanted to do a breakfast program from the Moana Hotel, following Aku's top-rated morning show. I became the announcer who'd say, "Now, ladies and gentlemen, from the beach at the Moana Hotel, 'Breakfast in Waikiki' and your host, Eddie Sherman."

The show was a hit, with Eddie interviewing visiting celebrities. Well, when Webley Edwards heard about it, he went to the hotel and the radio station and said, "If anyone should be doing a show from the Moana, it should be me." After all, he said, hadn't he'd done "Hawaii Calls" from the Moana for years? He also had gone into politics and was in the State Legislature, so Eddie was told "Aloha" and Web took over the show. I thought it was crappy, but there I was announcing in Waikiki and introducing Webley Edwards, who had introduced me to Hawaii with "Hawaii Calls" when I was a kid.

There was another show from the Moana Hotel, broadcast on Sunday evenings with a guy we nicknamed Major Hoople, and this was when I saw the bizarre Jacobs sense of humor for the first time. It was a kind of classical show and Jacobs was running the engineering board. One night, after a KGU baseball broadcast, when the concert show was under way, Jacobs put on a sound effects record of a dog barking. The barking began every time Major Hoople opened his mouth. Major Hoople couldn't hear it, and anyone listening to the radio would've thought there was a dog loose on the beach. The sportscaster, Joe Rose,

My interview deal with NBC let me get up-close and personal with celebrities like jazz singer June Christy.

fell down on the studio floor laughing.

Ron had a serious side, too. When former Mayor John Wilson died we stayed up all night to produce a news special for Aku to play during the morning news. Mayor Wilson was a former civil engineer for whom the Wilson Tunnel would be named, and Ron tracked down another engineering student who'd gone to college with the Mayor: former President Herbert Hoover. RJ tape-recorded the ex-President's memories of Mayor Wilson on a long-distance call. That was Ron's first documentary,

but hardly his last.

Around this time KIKI wanted me to do a morning show, and for most of the year I worked at both stations. This was when the recording industry made the transition from 78 rpm records to the smaller, more durable 45s. At the time, some of us deejays weren't sure that these funny little records would last. After a while, KGU wasn't too

My big boss at KHVH was the legendary industrialist Henry J. Kaiser, who was hard at work planning Hawaii Kai—the Islands' first planned residential community.

To the Gala Opening of the
Hawaiian Village
Wednesday
Four to Six
September 14, 1955
for
Cocktail Party
for members of the Press

Henry J. Kaiser and Fritz B. Burns cordially invite you

R. S. V. P.—TELEPHONE 9-0941
PLEASE PRESENT INVITATION AT DOOR

happy that I was competing with them, so they fired me and I went to KIKI full-time.

The Ilima Drive-In on King Street, next to the Wisteria Restaurant, asked me to do a "remote," using a sort of "fish bowl" broadcasting booth that I christened Uncle Tom's Cabin, a name that would stick with me for the rest of my life. I got a better offer from the White Top Drive-In on Ala Moana Boulevard, where Ward Warehouse is now, and moved my "cabin" there. At the time, I was doing a show in the KIKI studios that ended at 10, then I drove like a bat out of hell to the remote location, covered by a long recorded intro that my announcing buddy Jim Wahl

had produced at KGU for me using dozens of bits and pieces of songs.

The KIKI equipment was pretty primitive. I had a turntable that didn't stop, so there was no such thing as cueing up the record. The turntable just kept running. So I would drop the record onto the spindle and talk and slowly bring the sound up and hope for the best. Occasionally I'd get a request for a track from a long-playing record, with as many as eight songs on a side of the disc with no discernible break between them. It was a real challenge to cue up any track other than the first.

My show really took off, though. This was early 1956 and a musical revolution was brewing, one that soon would grab me by the ears and change my life. But at the time I still loved jazz, and when singers like June Christy, Carmen McRae, Mel Torme and others came to town to perform, I interviewed them and fed the interviews to "Monitor," a nationwide program broadcast by NBC on the weekends. I didn't get paid much. I did it mostly for the prestige.

One night, I went to the Clouds nightclub in Waikiki to see June Christy, and after her set she said, "Let's take a walk." As we went down the stairs from the club, someone said, "Boy, are you lucky!" I couldn't have agreed more. We spent the week together. At the end of the week, Jacobs knew I was flying to San Francisco to visit a girlfriend who was in school there. He came to the airport to see me off, and you cannot imagine what his face looked like when I arrived with June Christy on my arm. He also was a big fan, and I hadn't told him I was seeing her.

There was another show I did at KGU that not many people knew about. Station management thought there was an audience for a country music program, and I was drafted along with the other announcers to create one. So we did this show called "The Rootin Tooters." I used a country voice that sounded like a screechy old man and called myself Jermiah Grundy. Dick Halverson, who had

KHVH was one of Kaiser's pet projects, located at his newly opened Hawaiian Village Hotel. Erected in a single day, the hotel's geodesic dome was built by Kaiser in 1957 to promote the world premiere of *Around the World in Eighty Days*.

the best pipes and phrasing in Hawaii, was Silo Sy. Jim Wahl was Cowpatch Kelly and Ken Alford, who on weekends led Hawaii's top Dixieland band, the Dixiecats, was Cornfed Ken.

We had fun with it. We'd come up with make-believe song titles, like "When the Sump Backs Up, I'll Come Back to You." The show didn't last long, and no one ever knew that I was Old Man Grundy. When a friend asked to meet him, I merely smiled and said he was a very private person.

So there I was, a jazz disc jockey faking it with a country show, and I was getting all this fan mail about rock and roll. Everybody around me in the business was "talking stink" about this new music, and more and more this was what I was getting requests to play. I remember going to dinner at a musician friend's house with June

Christy. Elvis was on the cover of *Life* magazine that week, and everybody was laughing about the guy with the funny name.

Eventually I did what I'd always done and have tried to do ever since: I listened to my listeners. I think that's what made me successful. I wouldn't put my own taste in. I'd put a record out there, but if it didn't get reaction I'd drop it. It was because of requests that "Rock Around the Clock" by Bill Haley & the Comets was the first rock-and-roll record played on the radio in Hawaii. And I was the one who dropped it on the turntable, in 1955. I'm proud of that.

Years later, after *Life* had (perhaps reluctantly) changed its own tune, Frank Zappa wrote a story recalling when he first heard Haley's song in the movie *Blackboard*

Jungle. "He was playing the Teen-Age National Anthem and it was so LOUD I was jumping up and down. *Blackboard Jungle*, not even considering the story line (which had the old people winning in the end), represented a strange sort of 'endorsement' of the teen-age cause: They have made a movie about us; therefore, we exist…"

Haley wasn't alone in 1955. Chuck Berry, Little Richard, the Platters, Fats Domino and Ray Charles were leading the same attack. I remember *Billboard* magazine called 1955 "The Year Rhythm and Blues Took Over the Pop Field."

Pretty soon, I phased out of jazz altogether. I continued to play a lot of ballads, though: the Tune Weavers' "It's Almost Tomorrow," stuff like that. Gale Storm. Pat Boone. The McGuire Sisters. These were the white artists

Our Roller Derby promotions at the Civic Auditorium (opposite) featured crowd-pleasing grudge matches between Ron Jacobs and me—like this one (above) with Hal "Aku" Lewis as our official starter.

who "covered" all the black artists. Even some of Elvis' early songs were covers, including "Hound Dog," first recorded by Willie Mae "Big Mama" Thornton in 1953.

It was an earlier song that broke Elvis. This was "Heartbreak Hotel," released by RCA in January 1956. It became a hit after Elvis performed it on *The Dorsey Brothers* TV show, and the song rocketed to number one nationally. Without question, Elvis generated more mail and more requests in Hawaii than any other artist of the time. Of *all* time! I played Elvis' records on my program more than any other artist's and often gave his address on the radio. Hawaii sent Elvis more mail per capita than anywhere else. I would receive letters from Elvis fan club members all over the world requesting that I play his songs.

The year Elvis became the biggest thing in rock and roll I made another move, joining the staff of KHVH. This was a new independent station slated to go on top of the Hawaiian Village Hotel. Both the station and the

hotel were the pet projects of Henry J. Kaiser, the same man whose postwar car, the Kaiser-Frazer, had been tested near the Michigan farm where I grew up. By now, Mr. Kaiser—I always called him "Mister" and will always do so—had become a multimillionaire. Like so many others from the mainland, he was enchanted by the Islands; but unlike most, he set out to change the place he loved—and he succeeded. Statehood was being talked about and Mr. Kaiser wanted to be ready for the popular explosion he was sure would follow.

The Hawaiian Village was the first hotel to challenge Matson Navigation Co., which owned several beachfront hotels in Waikiki. It actually opened in 1954 when Mr. Kaiser bought the old Niumalu Hotel and renamed it. Everything was pink. The hotel was pink; the sheets and pillowcases were pink. It was all low-rise then, but by 1956 a nine-story high-rise was under construction, and the whole top floor was going to be occupied by this new, state-of-the-art radio station.

KHVH was not a rock-and-roll station. No such station existed at the time. In fact, the general manager—the man I idolized back when I was at the university, Hal "Aku" Lewis—hated rock and roll. Hated it with a passion. Years later, in the early 1980s just before he died, Aku would say proudly that he'd never played a single rock-and-roll record, not even one by the Beatles. Aku didn't want to hire me, but Mr. Kaiser gave him no choice.

Mr. Kaiser may have been in his 80s, but he hadn't gotten where he was by being blind and deaf to what the people wanted. He was a man who knew marketing forward and backward, and for his new station he wanted to get a young disc jockey for the kids at night. So he personally canvassed some of the schools and talked to the principals to see whom the kids were listening to. It was me, so he told Aku to hire me. The station was still under construction. The studios at the top of the hotel were ready, but the elevator went only part way, so we had to walk up an outside staircase, like a fire escape. I moved right in.

Mr. Kaiser felt we should have a country and western program, and Ron volunteered my services. So every morning I followed Aku at 9 as Uncle Tom playing today's hits, and then from 11 until noon I turned into Jermiah Grundy. There was a walkway by the studios where the public could watch and listen to the disc jockeys. I insisted that a curtain be put up between 11 and 12 so that I couldn't be seen making a fool of myself. One morning about 11:15 Mr. Kaiser brought his board of directors, who were visiting from Kaiser Headquarters in Oakland, to tour the studios. I was introduced to them, but then I was afraid to open the microphone and come on with

HONOLULU BUSINESS COLLEGE CLUB
Presents:
The Lolly Pop Hop
Music by
Jim Taylor's Rock-A-Billies
MC Tom Moffatt
Ala Wai Clubhouse · · 8-12 p.m.
May 2, 1958 · ·
Informal
Adm. 75¢
FAVORS
ENTERTAINMENT
BOP CONTEST

In May of 1956, "Graduation Day" by the Four Freshman hit number one on "Uncle Tom's Cabin." The song was so popular that I was asked to present them with an honorary degree in a special ceremony held at the University of Hawaii.

the funny voice. I segued about four records before they left—it seemed like an eternity.

My Uncle Tom show was popular; I brought my audience along from KIKI; but in one way I was not a success. Rock and roll wasn't making much money for the station. Not just in Hawaii, but all across the mainland, the guardians of public morality said rock and roll was an evil influence on young people. When Elvis appeared on *The Ed Sullivan Show*, he was shown only from the waist up, to hide his gyrating legs and hips. In Honolulu, as elsewhere, it was hard to get businesses to advertise on shows that featured this new music. In desperation, the KHVH sales staff told advertising agencies that if they bought a commercial on Aku's show, they'd get free spots on Jacobs' show and mine. Ron was playing rock and roll by now, although he claimed to dislike it, too.

We started inventing promotions to draw more attention to the station and to prove to the ad agencies that we had something worth investing in. Jacobs was moon-lighting as an announcer at the Roller Derby at the Civic Auditorium, and when he started putting me down on the air to create a little rivalry, we made a deal with Ralph Yempuku, who was managing the Civic, and the Roller Derby producer, Ed Silver, that Ron and I would race.

The weakest audience night was Wednesday, when the most they ever got was 1,200 people, and we were to get a percentage of the proceeds for everything over 1,200. Jacobs was a good villain and that was the role he took, building the competition to a frenzy on the air on his show, while I took the high road and belittled his efforts at attacking me. Come the night of the race, there were 3,600 people in the audience—a sell-out!—to see who would win: Jacobs wearing the black hat, or Moffatt wearing white.

We had to practice. After all, I didn't want to make a fool of myself. So I got fitted for skates and started practicing on the track. I really got into it. I was doing pretty well, and Jacobs didn't practice that much. He knew he couldn't skate, so he decided to lock the wheels on his skates and run around the track. Aku was the official starter, the gun

Ron Jacobs and I race go-karts in another Roller Derby grudge match.

went off and Jacobs didn't have a chance. Wheels always win over feet, and I won.

But that wasn't the end of it. At the finish line, we had it planned so that one of Jacobs' sidekicks would smash my face with a pie and I would duck and Jacobs would take the hit. Which he did. But then he grabbed the microphone and started to attack me verbally. The audience wouldn't let him speak, covering his rant with jeers. Thus a great fake rivalry was born.

I was doing 9 to noon and 9 to midnight and pro-duction stuff in between. Saturday I'd stay at the station all day. One Saturday I came in, and Mr. Kaiser had his hardhat on, supervising something in the lobby. When I came down that night, the entire lobby had been trans-formed; he'd remodeled the whole thing. At the time, he was planning to build what became Hawaii Kai, so I shouldn't have been surprised.

Another time, he built the Dome for the premiere of *Around the World in Eighty Days*, a blockbuster new film starring a cast of the biggest international stars. When I arrived in the morning, Mr. Kaiser had his hardhat on again and they were starting construction. When I got out that night, the dome was erected.

That gave us an idea, and Jacobs and I went to Aku, proposing to race around the world in 80 hours on Pan Am. Jacobs would go in one direction and I'd go in the other. The idea was we'd end up back in Hawaii the day of the premiere. Aku loved it. Pan Am loved it. Mr. Kai-ser shot it down. He thought it would distract from the movie's producer, Mike Todd, and his wife, Elizabeth Taylor, who were coming to the premiere. It was one of the biggest disappointments of my young radio career.

Little did I know that the best was yet to come. 🎤

CHAPTER 4

The Fantastic Four: Ralph, Earl, Sam and Elvis

Ralph Yempuku was a war hero, and so was Earl Finch, although Earl never went to war.

It's been well over half a century since Pearl Harbor was bombed, and many young people today don't remember, and maybe never knew, a lot about how the United States reacted to that—by declaring war not only on Japan, but also on men, women and children of Japanese ancestry residing in the U.S. Law-abiding American citizens and taxpayers had their schools and businesses shut down, their property confiscated; many thousands were locked up in internment camps where many remained for years because of the mistaken belief that they might be spies.

These second- and third-generation Japanese, whose parents and grandparents came to Hawaii as laborers to work in the fields, and who over the decades worked themselves into positions of success and respect, responded in a way that will stand as a monument against racism for all time. Those who were not incarcerated lined up to enlist in the armed forces. Most were grouped together in the 100th Battalion and the 442nd Regimental Combat Team and sent to Europe, where they became the most highly decorated units in the war.

Before all that happened, these men took their basic training at Fort Shelby in Hattiesburg, Mississippi, a place not then known for its racial enlightenment. Here, too, these men were treated like the enemy. One Hattiesburg

Legendary in the Islands for his support of Hawaii's Japanese-American soldiers during World War Two, my partner Earl Finch (third from left) helped me welcome Teddy Randazzo at John Rodgers Airport. Hawaii's own Robin Luke is between them. Opposite: I interviewed a lei-bedecked Elvis after his 1957 Hawaii debut at Honolulu Stadium. Behind us is a poster for *Jailhouse Rock*.

resident, Earl Finch, was an exception to the rule. Earl was rejected for military service for medical reasons, and when his younger brother was inducted, he hoped his sibling would be greeted warmly wherever he was sent. With that in mind, Earl decided to extend hospitality to the servicemen who came pouring into Hattiesburg. It didn't matter to him that their color and culture weren't the same as his. They were far away from home.

I was thrilled when Ralph Yempuku called in 1957 and asked me to help him and Earl Finch stage live rock-and-roll shows in the Islands. That's Ralph on the right with *Honolulu Star Bulletin* sports editor Joe Anzivino (left) and wrestling promoter Al Karasick.

One day, while walking along Hattiesburg's main street, he saw a couple of the Nisei standing in front of a drugstore. "They looked awfully lonesome," he later told friends. "So I asked them to dinner. They came, and we enjoyed their company—my mother and I. Ordinarily, that would have been the end of it. But the next day the boys came back with a big bouquet of American Beauties for my mother. I'll never forget their thoughtfulness."

One dinner led to the next, and then he organized barbecues for dozens at a time. He had a big cattle ranch and a successful clothing store, and he could afford to do that. Pretty soon, Earl was as much revered by the Japanese Americans as he was reviled by the local community. The *New York World-Telegram* called him a "one-man U.S.O.," and the *Saturday Evening Post* said he was "that rare human being, a man without a single angle. Spontaneously, and with all the fullness of his heart, he became a friend of an

unjustly persecuted and cruelly misunderstood minority, whose minds and whose values were American, but whose skin was the skin of the enemy."

At the same time, Earl's neighbors boycotted his store, his friends wouldn't have anything to do with him, and his fiancée broke off their engagement. He was accused of being a spy for Japan, and rumors said he befriended the boys from Hawaii in exchange for their making him beneficiary of their life insurance polices. It must've been painful, but in all the years I knew Earl, what I report here I heard from others, not him.

Ralph Yempuku was born in Hawaii, and his parents and siblings had moved back to Japan before the war started, leaving Ralph behind. He'd graduated from McKinley High School and was studying at the University of Hawaii and in the Reserve Officers' Training Corps when Pearl Harbor was attacked. Thus, he, too, went to Hattiesburg for basic training. There, like so many before him, he met Earl Finch.

Unlike most of the Japanese Americans, Ralph was sent to the Pacific, where as a lieutenant he was assigned to the OSS intelligence corps, the precursor of the CIA. He served with Merrill's Marauders, parachuting behind enemy lines to destroy supply routes and communications in Burma and to liberate prisoners of war. He didn't talk much about any of this to me or anyone else. Like Earl, he was a hero, but not one to blow his own horn.

When the war ended, he was serving in Hong Kong as an aide to the U.S. Army brass. At the surrender meetings there, he found himself sitting across the table from his brother, who was an aide to a Japanese officer. Because of the circumstances, they parted without exchanging a word.

During the war, Earl Finch became a hero in Hawaii as many of the young soldiers wrote home about him. They said he loaned them money and never pushed for its return. Earl himself wrote letters, and when he learned that one of "his boys" had died on the battlefield, he sent

My good friend "Sad Sam" Ichinose (right) was Hawaii's premier boxing promoter. Here we celebrate at the Ginbasha, later the Forbidden City, with Bobby Darin and the infamous Honolulu nightclub dancer known as "Evil Jezebel" (third from left).

flowers to the boy's folks. And when any of the Japanese-American veterans who'd been wounded passed through Hattiesburg on the way home and stopped to say hello, he treated them to trips to New York, Chicago and Washington, D.C.

In this way, Earl became a legend in the Islands he'd never seen, so in 1946 he was invited to Honolulu by the men of the 442nd. The motorcade that greeted him stretched from where King Street crosses Dillingham all the way to Iolani Palace, where the territorial legislature then met and where he was, on this occasion, praised as a true son of Hawaii. When he returned to the mainland his buddies, with their friends and families, gave him a check for $10,000. Typically, Earl left the money in Hawaii to entertain hospitalized vets.

Earl returned a year later, joining Ralph and the 442nd Veterans Club to stage a "Go for Broke Carnival" at Honolulu Stadium. The show starred Martha Raye,

and the proceeds were used to build a memorial clubhouse on McCully Street near the Ala Wai Canal. It was following this visit that he decided to move to the Islands permanently. He started an export/import company, wholesaling candy and other items, and in 1951 joined Ralph in staging another benefit carnival. After that, he decided to go into what Ralph called "this so-called promotion business."

So I felt unbelievably honored when they called me in 1957 to see if I'd like to go into a partnership with them. Ralph by now was managing the Civic Auditorium, and Earl had some money to invest, and together they thought it was time to start staging live rock-and-roll shows in Hawaii. Rock and rollers, they were not. They were promoters, and like any good promoters, they knew a good thing when they saw it coming over the hill. They proposed that I coordinate the talent, and they'd put up the venue and cash. If the show lost money, I'd get nothing, and if it made money, Ralph would give me a share of the profits.

At the time, the Civic was known more for its sports than its musical events. This big hall on South King Street that Ron Jacobs said looked like an "aluminum Egg McMuffin" had been a venue for the likes of Andre Kostelanetz, Lily Pons, Liberace and Spike Jones and his City Slickers (four acts that showed the place's cultural democracy), but more often it was home to basketball, wrestling (including sumo), professional tennis, the circus and the Roller Derby. Boxing was in its heyday there, too, and the man who was top dog in that field in time became one of my closest friends.

This was "Sad Sam" Ichinose, a nickname he got because of his basset hound expression. He was also a five-star character, one of those people that others love to tell stories about. For example, he was on the Board of Supervisors, the City Council of its time, and when during a re-election campaign his political advisor told him that he ought to say something about juvenile delinquency, he recorded a commercial and ran it before anybody caught it: "This is Sad Sam and I'm running for the Board of Supervisors and I want my constituents to know that I'm 100-percent behind juvenile delinquency." Nobody cared. He got elected anyway.

Sam made his first big money during the war. He got the last liquor license just before December 7, for Sad Sam's at Hotel and River Streets. With the war on, this was like being given the key to Fort Knox. The sailors and GIs lined up when the bar opened in the morning. His wife kept watch, and if a serviceman wasn't drinking, they kicked him out to make room for someone else.

When I knew Sam, he had another bar on Hotel Street, where we all gathered after the fights. He and Ralph were close, but opposites. Ralph was a family man, and he would go home and worry about the next promotion. Sam was a family man, too, but he would go out and party with his friends. Sam always said, "Win, lose, or draw, let's go out and get stinkin' drunk." That was his philosophy. And his motto was: "Every night is New Year's Eve."

He managed Dado Marino, who was the first world champion boxer to come out of Hawaii, a flyweight. When Sam took Dado to England for a bout, he and the trainers went out drinking, and when they got back to the hotel it was locked up. So Sam started climbing up a trellis and when he got to the second floor, it collapsed. Woke everybody up and the manager kicked the whole group out, fighters and all.

Another night they were at Sad Sam's bar, and Ralph was going off to the mainland for a week. Our mutual friend Bill Miller, who later became the manager of boxing

Sad Sam managed flyweight Dado Marino (right), Hawaii's first world champion, shown here in a match at Honolulu Stadium.

great Alexis Arguello, asked Sam if he'd miss his partner. Sam said, "Are you kidding? I don't miss him when he's here!" Another line became a regular part of his party-time vocabulary: "Fuck, fight, or shine the light!" None of us had any idea what it meant, but it had something to do with Sam's adventures in a Japan geisha house.

A character? Yes. But also a great promoter. He was a master at getting the press involved. He entertained them. Once in Japan, when he took Dado over there, they were having drinks at a place where there was a band, and Sam paid the band to come along when they went to the next bar. Then they came along to the bar after that, and on through the night the band played on for Sam and his entourage until the wee hours of the morning. The press loved him, and they got behind his fighters.

Everybody in Hawaii thought we'd finally get rid of the Territory label and become the 49th state. It'd been talked about since before the Second World War, and after it, could there be any question about the Islands' loyalty? By 1950, four out of five residents of Hawaii were citizens, and by the mid-'50s I don't known how many Congressional committees had discussed Island statehood in public hearings. Every time, we got our hopes up, and every time the proposal wasn't passed. Why? Same reason Hawaiians with Japanese ancestry were discriminated against during the war…and most of the "no" votes for admission came from the American South. So Alaska passed us by.

When Ralph and Earl called me, that final vote had not been cast, and they asked if I'd put together a show for what was being called the 49th State Fair. The headliners were Billy Ward & his Dominoes, a group that already had launched two of the most powerful solo artists in R&B, Clyde McPhatter and Jackie Wilson. On his own, backed by a re-formed Dominoes, Billy did a remake of "Stardust" in 1957. It was a pretty big hit, and on the strength of that, I suggested we bring him in, along with two other mainland acts, Don & Dewey and H.B.

We got Elvis fan mail from all over the country; here I've been made a member of a Presley fan club in Mississippi.

Barnum & the Circats. They did three shows a day in a tent, and I doubt anybody in Honolulu noticed that the headliners for the show were black. Nobody in Hawaii did. The "race card" just didn't get played here. Only on the mainland was skin color a big thing.

In a funny way, that message rang out again when I met Billy Ward and drove him in from the airport. I'd been calling my show "Uncle Tom's Cabin" for a couple of years by then, and practically the first thing Billy said was, "What's this Uncle Tom shit?" To call an African American an "Uncle Tom" was an insult, meaning the black kowtowed to the white. I doubt very many in Hawaii had even heard the phrase used in that way. And I didn't have an answer for Billy.

At the time I was emceeing a lot of shows, at least one a week at a school or a dance. I didn't get paid. I did it for the exposure. It was good for me and it was good for the radio station. Between 1955 and 1957, I must've appeared at every school on Oahu and many on the outer islands. One day I was emceeing a talent show at Farrington High School, and Jacobs called me from KHVH to say Elvis was coming to the Honolulu Stadium for a concert. This was big news. So when I announced it from the school

On November 10, 1957, Elvis ended his cross-country tour with two packed shows at Honolulu Stadium. The most expensive seat in the house was $3.50.

stage, the kids went berserk.

Just before joining KHVH, I did a massive contest on KIKI working with a friend, Dick Howard, who was the advertising director for Consolidated Movie Theaters in Hawaii. With Dick's help I was able to give away the hat Elvis wore in his first movie, *Love Me Tender*. The contest generated 53,000 letters. The hat was given away at a special showing of the movie at the Waikiki Theater, on a Saturday morning in December 1956. That was the first time I experienced people screaming in a movie theater.

Now Elvis was actually coming to the Islands to perform. The concert was added onto the end of a long mainland tour despite the promoter's advice to forget it. The promoter was Lee Gordon, an American who brought the first rock-and-roll shows to Australia, and he said he didn't think Hawaii had enough fans to fill the stadium once, let alone twice. Elvis's manager, Colonel Tom Parker, knew better. He was well aware of the *Love Me Tender* hat contest.

There was another attraction for the Colonel in the Islands. This was something none of us knew at the time, probably not even Elvis. The Colonel's real name was Andreas Cornelis van Kuijk, and he was Dutch. Enlisting in the U.S. Army in 1929, he served at Fort DeRussy and then at Fort Shafter, and it wasn't until after he was discharged that he started calling himself Thomas R. Parker, the name of his Hawaii commanding officer!

What happened next was amazing, too. KHVH was Honolulu's rock-and-roll station, the Elvis station, and a few days before the concert date, we were told that Colonel Parker had taken the entire eighth floor of the Hawaiian Village Hotel for Elvis and his entourage, the floor below our studios! As soon as the word got out, the fans

Uncle Tom

We thank you, Uncle Tom
For bringing us pleasures and joys
And your program is a favorite
Of teen-age girls and boys.
You never denounce our Elvis
Like other dee-jays do
You know how much we love him
So you play lots of his records too.
From nine to one, six days a week
You sacrifice your sleep
So to thank you for your efforts
Here's a poem for you to keep.

— Phyllis Fukumoto —

began to gather. One girl from Kaneohe strung one of the longest leis ever made and gave it to Jacobs and me. Jacobs hung it from the lanai outside Elvis's suite, and it reached all the way to the ground. It was there when Elvis checked in, after a four-and-a-half-day cruise on the S.S. *Matsonia*.

Of course, we had our own welcome planned. It was Ron's idea: what we did was create the world's first Elvis impersonator. The day before the shows, Donn Tyler, a member of the station staff, was dressed and made up to look like Elvis, given an Elvis wig, and put in the back seat of a white convertible next to a make-believe Colonel Parker. The idea was that Jacobs would then give them a tour of the island while I went on the air. It was Saturday morning, and every record I played was one of Elvis'.

First they went to Kalihi, and someone called the station to say they'd seen Elvis driving down King Street. Then they drove over the Pali to Kailua. It got bigger and bigger, and I kept taking the calls from people on the street. The plan was for Ron and his friends to arrive at the stadium during one of the biggest high-school football games of the year, a contest between McKinley and Punahou.

After bluffing their way through the gate, the car halted in front of the stands and, as Ron described it later in *HONOLULU* magazine, "Gene Good [who was broadcasting pre-game activities live on KGU], in the midst of discussing the undefeated Punahou team, froze in mid-sentence—gasped—whispered to someone—paused—then raved hysterically, 'Ladies and gentlemen, believe it or not, Elvis Presley, the King of rock 'n' roll, has pulled into Honolulu Stadium right before our eyes!'"

The stadium went bananas. Both teams stopped their warm-up exercises. The McKinley band stopped playing and chased the car as it now started circling the field. The Punahou band struck up "Hound Dog" while Gene Good announced, "You're hearing it all exclusively here on KGU, 760 on the dial!"

I'd played Elvis records for about six hours when Ron and the others got back to the studio, reporting what had happened. I signed off at 3 and was told someone wanted to talk to us on the phone. An anonymous voice told us that Colonel Parker wanted to see us downstairs. We went down, scared to death. He was wearing a straw hat and a string tie. He looked at us for a minute. He wasn't smiling. Then he said, "You boys got a fair sense of humor. Now, I heard your little stunt. And you know what? It should sell some tickets."

It was at that point Elvis entered the room. "Elvis, say hello to Mr. Moffatt," the Colonel said. I shook hands, and he said, "Pleased to meet you, sir. Sure is a pretty place y'all got here." He was then introduced to Mr. Jacobs, and the Colonel said, "Elvis, these boys got us some good publicity today, gonna sell tickets. Okay if they emcee the shows tomorrow?"

"Sounds good to me," said the man whose records I'd played all day. "Nice meetin' you fellas. See y'all at the show."

I was to emcee at the afternoon concert, Jacobs at the one that night. I was wearing my white jacket, and when I walked out onto the field, there was this huge reaction from the crowd. The Colonel told me to get up on the stage and introduce Elvis.

"Where is he?" I said.

"Don't worry about it," the Colonel said back, "—just introduce him."

The band was already in place. Then Elvis arrived

in a limo with his Memphis Mafia, the gang of good ol' boys he took with him wherever he went. I think about all the technical support the acts use now. All Elvis had was the boxing ring; that was his stage. The sound system was pretty much what they used for boxing. And his lights that night were the boxing lights. But that didn't matter, with the raw excitement projected by Elvis Presley.

One thing I'll never forget was his encore number. He had just done "Hound Dog," started to go off the stage, and of course the crowd went crazy. So he came back and he did this slow, sexy version of "Hound Dog." He jumped off the stage and sang to the audience. And the barriers were nothing like they are today, just a piece of fencing. So you could see Elvis through the fencing, and he was down on his knees singing.

"Yoooouuuuuu ain't nuuuuuuuuthin' buuuut a hoo-ouuuuund dawg…" And the crowd went totally nuts.

Then he was swept away in a limo with his band, another car following close behind containing the Memphis Mafia. Of all the rock-and-roll shows I did, that was the one Rock-and-Roll Moment.

Later there was a press conference at the hotel, and I did a little interview with Elvis. I asked him what he thought of our promotion. He said, "I listened for a little while, but got tired of listening to myself, so I changed the station."

It didn't matter. From that time on, we had the inside track with Elvis. The Colonel always made sure that I was the only one there with a microphone. 🎤

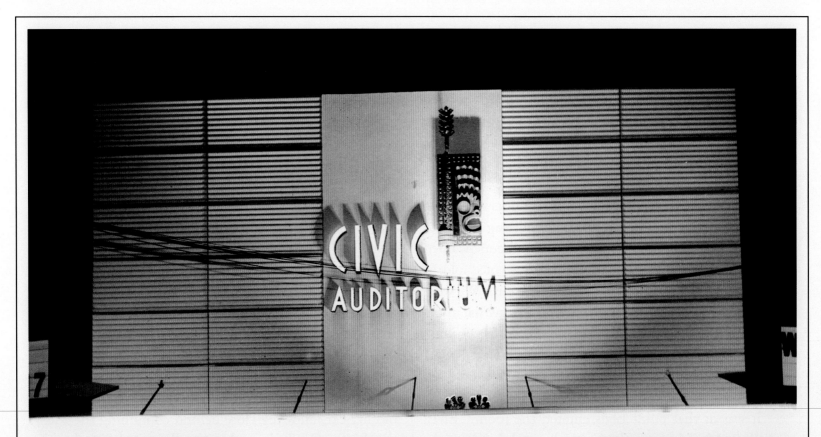

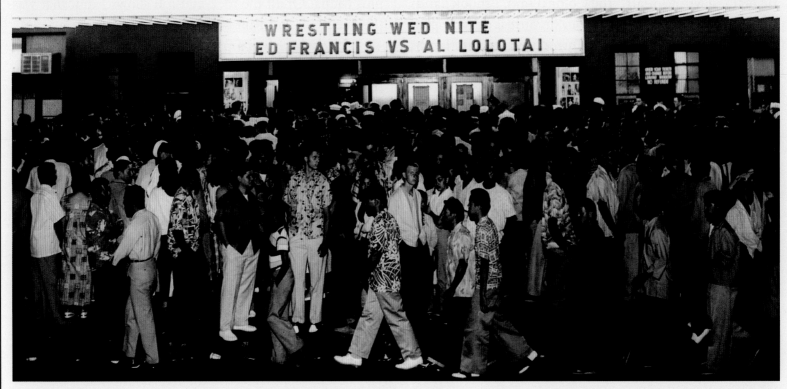

CHAPTER 5

Life after Elvis

After the 49th State Fair, my partnership with Earl Finch and Ralph Yempuku went into high gear. Only a few weeks after Elvis had appeared in the old stadium, we put on the first rock-and-roll show to be held at the Civic Auditorium, with the Five Satins, Don & Dewey and Sonny Knight. We called it the Show of Stars.

This was just after my record came out. Bob Bertram, who'd produced "Susie Darlin'" by a Honolulu high-schooler named Robin Luke—a Top 10 national hit—came to me and said, "All these guys who can't sing that well are making records, and I think I can make you sound okay; you've got a nice voice." We decided to record Alfred Apaka's signature tune, "Beyond the Reef," giving it a rock tempo. There was this black vocal group at Schofield called the Flames—Ron Jacobs had helped them produce a record at the KHVH studios called "Crazy." So the Flames backed me, and it sold pretty well.

I had no plan to sing it publicly until Bertram asked me to do so at a local high school. I had this contest in which students buying tickets for the Show of Stars at the box office would say what school they were from, and the Five Satins would do a show at the school that sold the most tickets. Waipahu High School won, and in the car on the way I rehearsed the song, the Five Satins singing behind me. I cannot tell you how cool I felt. How many other disc jockeys could say the Five Satins had backed

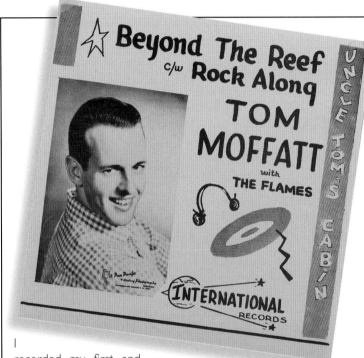

I recorded my first and only record with backup by the Flames, a vocal group from Schofield Barracks. Opposite: The crowd gathers at the Civic before the 15th Show of Stars, featuring the Crests and Clyde McPhatter, in May 1959. Ed Francis, who would soon become Hawaii's top wrestling promoter, was scheduled to battle Al Lolotai later in the week.

them up in concert?

The next weekend we toured the outer islands. At first tickets were going slowly on Maui, so we flew over to promote the concert, went right to Maui High School, (the principal was a friend of Ralph's), and as the kids were walking in the halls between classes, the principal

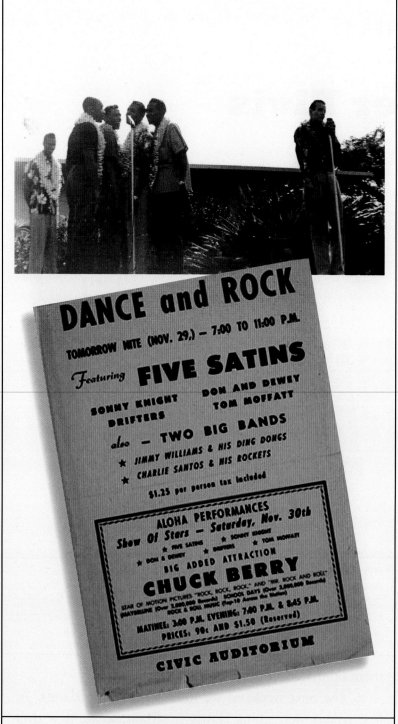

DANCE and ROCK
TOMORROW NITE (NOV. 29.) — 7:00 TO 11:00 P.M.
Featuring FIVE SATINS
SONNY KNIGHT   DON AND DEWEY
DRIFTERS   TOM MOFFATT
also — TWO BIG BANDS
★ JIMMY WILLIAMS & HIS DING DONGS
★ CHARLIE SANTOS & HIS ROCKETS
$1.25 per person tax included

ALOHA PERFORMANCES
Show Of Stars — Saturday, Nov. 30th

BIG ADDED ATTRACTION
CHUCK BERRY

MATINEE: 3:00 P.M. EVENING: 7:00 P.M. & 8:45 P.M.
PRICES: 90c AND $1.50 (Reserved)

CIVIC AUDITORIUM

The Five Satins, famous for their doo-wop version of "In the Still of the Night," headlined the very first Show of Stars. During their visit, they also sang backup vocals for me on "Beyond the Reef" at a high school concert. I cannot tell you how cool I felt!

made an announcement on the public address system, saying, "There's someone here who wants to remind you of an important event happening here on Maui." I took the microphone and said, "Hiiiiiiiiii!" the same way I opened "Uncle Tom's Cabin." Well, the girls' screams throughout the school were unbelievable. And then I plugged the show. Try to get a high school to allow that today. Anyway, the tour was so successful, we decided to do one more show at the Civic and brought in Chuck Berry to add to the lineup.

(There was something else I did at the time that became a kind of signature riff. A group called the Sixteens had a song called "Send Me Flowers," and it opened with some rhythmic gibberish that I occasionally used to sign off my shows: "Mokalakalaka, boom diddy, boom diddy." I even included it in the introduction on "Rock Along," which was on the flip side of "Beyond the Reef." I was told that cheerleaders at one school included it their game routine, and when I went to schools on promotions or to emcee a show, I was knocked out when auditoriums full of kids greeted me with those words: "Mokalakalaka, boom diddy, boom diddy." I still get chills when I remember that. And laugh.)

The Five Satins cost us $2,500 for the whole tour—two weekends, plus two outer islands—and we paid Chuck $3,500 for the one night at the Civic. The morning of the show there was a hurricane warning, and people were told not to leave their homes. It rained a lot and the winds came up a little, but there was no hurricane. Everybody stayed home anyway, though, and we lost money. A lesson I needed to learn. Ralph said, "Don't worry about it. We'll make it up next time."

For the second Show of Stars, in January 1958, the Four Aces were the headliners, and for the third we outdid ourselves. The Australian promoter Lee Gordon was taking a big show to Sydney and offered us a date on the way. The stars included Paul Anka, Jerry Lee Lewis and Buddy

Paul Anka was huge in Hawaii. At the third Show of Stars he even headlined above the great Jerry Lee Lewis (left), Buddy Holly and Jodie Sands (center).

old guy over here who's really been helping me. I'd like to meet him. His name is Uncle Tom." I guess the word "uncle" sounded old. Older than I looked, anyway. Was he surprised when I said, "Hi, I'm Uncle Tom!"

I related real well to the performers. I was a few years older, but I was playing their music. A lot of the jocks on the mainland were older. And I hadn't fully matured—I was a young 26 or whatever I was. I also got a chance to know the performers. They were in town longer than the acts that I bring in now. We'd go to the outer islands together. Sometimes they'd take a few days' vacation after the shows. So I had a chance to hang out.

For the fourth Show of Stars we brought in Frankie Lymon, Eddie Cochran and the Coasters. Frankie had just released the album *Frankie Lymon at the London Palladium*. He was 15 years old, and his stage savvy was like nothing I've seen since. For a kid that age, his confidence and stage presence were incredible.

Holly & the Crickets. At the time, Paul Anka was the hottest star in Hawaii. At the show, "You Are My Destiny" got the biggest reaction. You'd think Jerry Lee and Buddy Holly would be the headliners, but in Hawaii, Paul was.

I was at the Civic when they put the tickets on sale at the box office. This was when King Street had two-way traffic. It was afternoon rush. This city bus pulled over, full of people, stopped, and the bus driver got out and went to the box office and bought tickets for the show. I don't think anyone could get away with that these days.

I really promoted Paul Anka. I announced his fan club address, just as I did for other stars. I did that quite frequently. Paul was 16 or 17 at the time, and when I went to pick him up with his father at the airport and introduced myself as Tom Moffatt, Paul said, "There's this

HONORARY MEMBER
This certifies that
TOM MOFFATT
is a member in good standing of the
PAUL ANKA FAN CLUB
with all due privileges and courtesies extended during tenure of membership.
Anita Ryder
President

I had to do a school promotion at Stevenson Intermediate, and I said to Eddie and Frankie, "Why don't you come along?" They stood in the wings as I introduced the students' band, and after they played a few songs and took a break, I brought out Eddie and Frankie. Eddie picked up the guitar that'd been left on stage and Frankie got behind the drums, and they played the Fats Domino song, "I Want You to Know." It really blew everyone away.

The next day, Frankie's attorney Maxwell Cohen, a nice man, said Frankie's mother was very religious and asked if there was a way to get a picture of Frankie at a Catholic school. I had some friends at St. Francis School in Manoa. I took him up there and classes were going on. When they saw him, the girls went nuts. They were screaming and the classes were disrupted. The principal never forgave me. She thought I was doing a publicity

My First Professional Job
by Neil Sedaka

My first professional engagement was in 1959, with Tom Moffatt. I was 19. This was before jet planes, so my mother, Eleanor, and I took a propeller plane from New York to Hawaii. It took about 24 hours. I was exhausted.

Tom was very gracious to me, but I had never studied singing, so my voice was shaky, as were my nerves. I was on with Jo-Ann Campbell, a hot female singer, and the great guitarist Duane Eddy. They were having a thing together (I think).

I stayed at the Hawaiian Village Hotel. There were no high-rise hotel buildings. I stayed in a little grass shack! Tom gave me confidence despite my voice and repertoire of four songs. I think the audience expected a Japanese American because of my last name. Tom was terrific, a perfect host and mentor.

I am happy to say our friendship has continued for all these years, and I hope it will continue for many more to come.

To Neil, a New Yorker, a thatched-roof bungalow at the Hawaiian Village Hotel was like an authentic "little grass shack."

stunt, and I wasn't. We were there for Frankie's mom.

Next stop was the radio station, where Frankie asked if he could drive my car around the parking lot, as he was just learning to drive. The sales manager had a new Edsel, and Frankie rammed into it. A lot of people got a kick out of it because the Edsel was the subject of a lot of jokes at the time.

Frankie was a nice young man, but you had to keep your eyes open. He had this girl he wanted to take out, and we double dated; Frankie and his girl were in the back seat, and as I was walking my date to her front door at the end of the evening, I saw Frankie and his date scrambling into the front. I got there just in time. They were going to take off in my car! Another time, on the night of the show, Earl Finch entered the Coasters' dressing room. Frankie was in there, and they all were smoking a joint. Earl told Frankie to get the hell out of there and get ready for the show. He then told the Coasters, "What the hell's the matter with you, giving this kid a joint?" One of them said, "Mr. Finch, he brought it to us!"

KHVH had been good for me, but when Mr. Kaiser hired a guy to run the station who didn't like rock and roll, I knew my days were numbered. Aku's hatred of the music I could take. At least he didn't tell me what to play. But when this new guy started dictating a playlist, I quit. At the same time this happened, KPOA was asking its listeners to vote for a new host for a show called "The Big 30 Revue." This was a program that played the top 30 songs every night, changing the list once a week. I got the most votes, and they offered me the job. I said I didn't like being locked into playing music I didn't pick on my own or which wasn't based on listener requests. They said I'd have full freedom to play whatever I wanted in the hour following the "Big 30" show. I accepted the offer and took the "Uncle Tom's Cabin" title along with me.

But before I did, I also said I thought Ron Jacobs should get involved at the station, because he wasn't happy

Dressed in muumuus for an encore, the Four Preps brought down the house at the Civic Auditorium. Second from right is Glen Larson, who went on to become a top TV producer and my good friend.

No 15-year-old performer before or since has had the incredible stage presence of Frankie Lymon.

at KHVH, either. Fin Hollinger, the station manager, said he didn't want Ron, and I said either you take Ron or you don't get me. And he blew up. It took him a long time to forgive me. But he hired Ron, who eventually became the program director. When Fin realized how good a radio guy he was, he ended up sending Ron to the mainland to consult with other stations with the same ownership.

All through 1958 and into 1959, there was hardly a month when Ralph and Earl and I didn't present at least one Show of Stars. Connie Francis, the Diamonds, Frankie Avalon, the Four Preps, the Everly Brothers, Ritchie Valens, the Champs, the Platters, Bobby Darin, Sam Cooke, Dion & the Belmonts—one after another they helped put Hawaii on the international rock-and-roll map.

Alan Freed was having his big shows in New York, and Art Laboe was doing record hops in L.A. But these shows in Hawaii were unique. I don't know another city outside of New York where you had someone doing all this stuff. We got more performers in Hawaii than most cities in the whole country. We weren't a big market, but every-

The Shirelles

Ritchie Valens

Fabian

Jan & Dean

Connie Francis

Sam Cooke

The Everly Brothers

The Platters

Freddie "Boom Boom" Cannon

The Fleetwoods

Dodie Stevens, Bobby Rydell and Chubby Checker

Johnny Mathis

Dion & the Belmonts

Billy Ward

★ SHOW OF STARS ★
PRESENTS THE
PAUL ★ ★ ★ ★ ★

ANKA
SHOW

★ HITS ★

Puppy Love
Diana
You Are My Destiny
Crazy Love
Midnight
Just Young
Teen Commandments
(with Johnny Nash & Geo. Hamilton)
All of A Sudden (My Heart Sings)
I Miss You So
Lonely Boy
Put Your Head on My Shoulder
It's Time to Cry

LP ALBUMS
PAUL ANKA
MY HEART SINGS

Plus
★ AN ALL-STAR SHOW ★

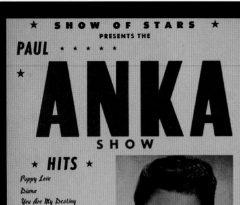

CIVIC AUDITORIUM

| MAR. 18 - FRIDAY
7:00 & 8:45 PM
REGULAR PRICES:
Reserved $2.20 | MAR. 19 - SATURDAY
7:00 & 8:45 PM
2:30 PM MATINEE
Gen. Adm. $1.45 | MAR. 20 - SUNDAY
2:30 PM MATINEE
Teenagers $1.25 | Children Under 12 $.90 |

★★★ SHOW OF STARS ★★★
PRESENTS

PAT BOONE
EXCLUSIVE
DOT RECORDING ARTIST

ONE CONCERT ONLY
WAIKIKI SHELL
FRIDAY NIGHT - AUG 4th 8:15 P M

TICKETS ON SALE: WAIKIKI SHELL BOX OFFICE - THAYER PIANO CO. - DOWNTOWN
CIVIC AUDITORIUM

PRICES: RESERVED $3.50 – $2.50   GEN. ADM. $1.55 TAX INCLD.

7th SHOW of STARS

Teddy
RANDAZZO

Frankie AVALON

HI-FIVES
★ SIX TEENS
★ ROBIN LUKE
★ ALEC RAMOS -- The Drifters
★ TOM MOFFATT, M.C.

CIVIC AUDITORIUM
FRIDAY, SATURDAY & SUNDAY, JUNE 20-21-22

| 2 SHOWS NIGHTLY
7:00 – 8:45 p.m. | SATURDAY & SUNDAY MATINEES
2:30 p.m. |

SPECIAL TEEN-AGE PRICE $.90

GENERAL ADMISSION $1.20
RESERVED SEAT 1.80

Show of Stars
Presents
The SHIRELLES
GENE PITNEY
DICK AND DEE DEE
The CASCADES

with
TOM MOFFATT, M.C.

CIVIC AUDITORIUM
Friday, April 5 - 7:30 P.M.
Saturday, April 6 - 2:30 Matinee
7 & 8:45 P.M.
Sunday, April 7 2:30 Matinee
Prices: $1.45 Gen'l Adm. $2.20 Reserved
Children Under 12 90c.

12th SHOW OF STARS
★ ★ Featuring ★ ★
THE
PLATTERS
GOLD RECORDS
(SALES OVER 1 MILLION COPIES)
★ ONLY YOU ★ MY PRAYER ★ THE GREAT PRETENDER
★ ON MY WORD OF HONOR ★ YOU'LL NEVER KNOW
★ YOU'VE GOT THE MAGIC TOUCH   ★ HE'S MINE
★ I'M SORRY ★ TWILIGHT TIME ★ HEAVEN ON EARTH
★ SMOKE GETS IN YOUR EYES (CURRENTLY THE NO. 1 HIT ACROSS THE COUNTRY)

★ Bobby DARIN
★ Thurston HARRIS
★ Plus AN ALL STAR SHOW ★

CIVIC AUDITORIUM

| THUR. JAN. 1
2:30 Matinee
7:30 Evening | FRI. JAN. 2
7:30 Evening
Only | SAT. JAN. 3
2:30 Matinee
7:00 Evening
8:45 Evening | SUN. JAN. 4
2:30 Matinee
Only |

POPULAR PRICES

RESERVED SEATS . . . . . . $2.20   TEEN-AGERS. $1.25
GEN'L ADMISSION . . . . . $1.45   CHILDREN (under 12) 90

16th SHOW of STARS
★ ★
JIMMY
CLANTON

The CHAMPS ★
Back by Your Request

★ DION
and the
BELMONTS

Also: Ronnie DIAMOND, The DRIFTERS, Al LUCAS,
UNIQUES, Dan DALTON, The JOKERS, BABY DOLL,
CHARLIE SANTOS Orchestra, Tom Moffatt

CIVIC AUDITORIUM

| Friday June 12
7:00 - 8:45 p.m. | Saturday June 13
2:30-7:00-8:45 p.m. | Sunday June 14
2:30 p.m. |

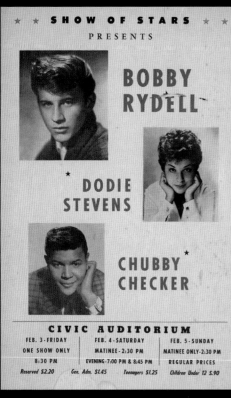

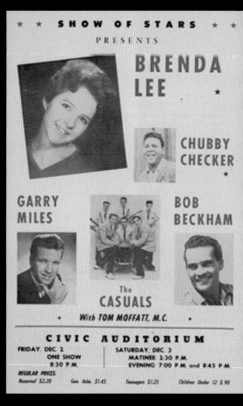

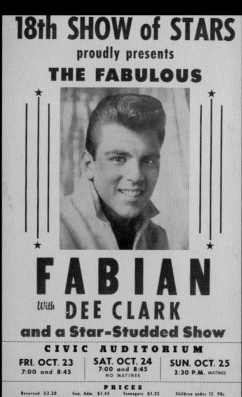

The legendary Bobby Darin performed at the 12th Show of Stars along with the Platters. "Mac the Knife," not yet released, was his last song that evening.

Sometimes we brought in unknowns. Once, he had to go to New York to put together a show with Teddy Randazzo and Frankie Avalon, and I told him to see if he could get the Hi-Fives, five guys who had a real white doo-wop sound. When Earl stopped on the way in L.A., he said nobody had heard of them. He finally found them in New Jersey, and they didn't even have an agent and had never been out of the East. They'd just done local shows. Well, we brought them to Hawaii. The lead singer, David Brigati, later joined Joey Dee & the Starlighters, the group that helped make the twist such a huge success. And a few years after that, David's brother Eddie came to Hawaii as a member of one of Hawaii's all-time favorite groups, the Young Rascals.

We also used local talent. Dick Jensen was renamed Lance Curtis by Earl and me because we thought it sounded more Hollywood. We used Robin Luke several times. Alec Ramos was very popular, and we changed his name to Ronnie Diamond. Earl called Lou Chudd, who recorded Ricky Nelson, at Imperial Records, and said, "I got this kid named Diamond." They recorded "Close to My Heart." The record didn't do what we'd hoped, but this kid from Radford High was booked on Dick Clark's Saturday night show. Everybody did *Bandstand*, but the weekend show was a big deal. It was a very active musical time. A lot of kids got more interested in music because of the Show of Stars and the fact that we put local kids on it.

These mainland acts worked hard for their money, by the way. It wasn't just

one wanted to come here. That made me important to them, because I was the disc jockey in Hawaii. They remembered me more than somebody in Fresno or San Bernardino or Portland because of where I lived. Looking back over the years, I know that helped.

In the Show of Stars partnership, we each had our area of specialty. Ralph was the manager of the Civic and responsible for the business end. Earl was the agency contact, working mainly with the General Artists Corporation in Los Angeles and New York—the agency that had most of the young music acts at that time—and he'd do the actual negotiating for the performers I thought would work best.

We tried changing names to make local talent more marketable: Alec Ramos became Ronnie Diamond, Dick Jensen became Lance Curtis.

Ewa Carnival

2 Big SHOWS NIGHTLY! PRESENTS

"Rockin' For Ewa" *Featuring*

RONNIE DIAMOND
Darling of the Teenagers

AL LUCAS
Hawaii's Fastest Rising Star

DRIFTERS
A Favorite Vocal Group

LANCE CURTIS
A Star Attraction

UNIQUES
The New Sound

TOM MOFFATT
Hawaii's Top Deejay & M.C.

Plus

★ FREE CARS & PRIZES!!
★ EXHIBITS
★ GAMES, RIDES ETC.
FREE PARKING

LIVE FISHING
(IN THE SWIMMING POOL)
BAITS, POLES, HOOKS WILL BE SUPPLIED.

AT THE EWA GYMNASIUM GROUNDS
SEPTEMBER 4, 5 & 6 • 6:30 PM TO 1:00 AM

KPOA THE BIG STATION

KEEP tuned to 630

Presents THE BIG **30**

REVUE'S HITS OF THE WEEK AS DETERMINED BY YOU WHO "VOICE YOUR CHOICE" AND BY THE EXCLUSIVE KPOA AUDIT OF TERRITORY RECORD SALES

OFFICIAL LIST FOR WEEK OF
Monday, November 17, 1958

130th Week of BIG THIRTY REVEUE

1. CLOSE TO MY HEART, Ronnie Diamond, (Imperial)
2. TOM DOOLEY, Kingston Trio, (Capitol)
3. LONELY, Hi-Fives, (Decca)
4. I'LL WAIT FOR YOU, Frankie Avalon, (Chancellor)
5. MY GIRL, Robin Luke, (International)
6. NEED YOU, Donnie Owens, (Guyden)
7. DREAMY EYES, Johnny Tillotson, (Cadence)
8. JUST YOUNG, Paul Anka, (ABC)
9. I GOT STUNG, Pvt. Elvis Presley, (RCA Victor)
10. BIMBOMBEY, Jimmie Rodgers, (Roulette)
11. TEA FOR TWO CHA CHA, Tommy Dorsey, (Decca)
12. CHICKA CHICHA HONEY, Robin Luke, (International)
13. I'LL REMEMBER TONIGHT, Pat Boone, (Dot)
14. TO KNOW HIM IS TO LOVE HIM, Teddy Bears, (Dore)
15. TOPSY (Part II), Cozy Cole, (Love)
16. THE WORRYIN' KIND, Tommy Sands, (Capitol)
17. THE END, Earl Grant, (Decca)
18. GOODNIGHT, Elegants, (Apt)
19. ROCK-IN ROBIN, Bobby Day, (Class)
20. LOVE OF MY LIFE, Everly Brothers, (Cadence)
21. BLUE RIBBON BABY, Tommy Sands, (Capitol)
22. IT'S ONLY MAKE BELIEVE, Conway Twitty, (M-G-M)
23. BEEP BEEP, Playmates, (Roulette)
24. IT'S ALL IN THE GAME, Tommy Edwards, (M-G-M)
25. FALLIN, Connie Francis, (M-G-M)
26. TEEN COMMANDMENTS, George Hamilton IV, Johnnie Nash, Paul Anka, (ABC)
27. DREAM OF ME, Kalin Twins, (Decca)
28. I'M SORRY NOW, Shields, (Tender)
29. SO MUCH, Imperi[...]
30. YOUR LOV[...]

TOM MOFFATT
Hawaii's DJ idol on
BIG 30 REVUE
UNCLE TOM'S CABIN
5-10 P.M. Daily

BETTY SMYSER
Air Hostess of the
SALLY SAMPLE SHOW
8:30 to 11:30 A.M.
Monday thru Saturday

JOHN RUSSELL
Popular Star of
CALLING ALL STARS
11:30 to 1:30 P.M.
Monday thru Saturday

KPOA "BIG PICS"

. . . Ron Jacobs' record research on coming hits in Hawaii and Stateside

1. THE DIARY, Neil Sedaka, (RCA Victor)
2. CORRINE, CORRINA, Bill Haley, (Decca)
3. DONNA, Ritchie Valens, (Del-fi)
4. TRY, BABY, TRY, Vogues, (Dot)
5. I PROMISE YOU, Billy and Lillie, (Swan)

KPOA TOP-15 ALBUMS

. . . based on Hawaii's best-sellers

1. KINGSTON TRIO, Kingston Trio, (Capitol)
2. SANDS STORM, Tommy Sands, (Capitol)
3. JIMMIE RODGERS SINGS FOLK SONGS, Jimmie Rodgers, (Roulette)
4. SURFERS ON THE ROCKS, Surfers, (Hi-Fi)
5. SOUTH PACIFIC, Soundtrack, (RCA Victor)
6. MORE SING ALONG WITH MITCH, Mitch Miller, (Columbia)
7. CONCERT IN RHYTHM, Ray Conniff, (Columbia)
8. MUSIC MAN, Original Cast, (Capitol)
9. PRIMITIVA, Martin Denny, (Liberty)
10. VOICES IN LOVE, Four Freshmen, (Capitol)
11. THE VERY THOUGHT OF YOU, Nat "King" Cole, (Capitol)
12. ONLY THE LONELY, Frank Sinatra, (Capitol)
13. LEI OF JAZZ, Arthur Lyman, (Hi-Fi)
14. KING CREOLE, Pvt. Elvis Presley, (RCA Victor)
15. SONGS OF THE FABULOUS CENTURY, Roger Williams, (Kapp)

ALBUM PICS OF THE WEEK

1. SAM COOKE ENCORE, Sam Cooke, (Keen)
2. DANCE WITH DICK CLARK, Keyman, (ABC Paramount)
3. LOVE AND MARRIAGE, Ray Charles Singers, (M-G-M)

YOU CAN WIN PVT. ELVIS PRESLEY'S FIRST ARMY UNIFORM! KEEP TUNED TO KPOA FOR DETAILS OF THIS EXCITING CONTEST

RON JACOBS
Director of Programs
And Special Events

BOB LANG
Glib and Popular Star of
ALBUMS FOR ADULTS
6:15-6:30 P.M.
WAKE UP HAWAII
5:30-8:30 A.M.

JOHN CONNELL
Your late-nite Star of
LUCKY LAGER
DANCE TIME

Season's Greetings
KPOA UNCLE TOM'S CABIN
Tom Moffatt

When I moved to KPOA to host "The Big 30 Review," I took the "Uncle Tom's Cabin" name with me and even included it on my Christmas card.

The *Tom Moffatt Show* on KHVH (now KITV) followed Dick Clark's *American Bandstand* and *Bandstand's* general format as well, including regular show dancers (right).

they did another sax-oriented song, and I could not speak into the microphone. The audience just overwhelmed me, and I didn't know what to do because I had to introduce Frankie. Finally, the leader of the Champs took the mike and the crowd calmed down, thinking he was going to say something. He then handed it to me and I introduced Frankie. The sax player and the band's drummer, Dash Crofts, later teamed up as Seals & Crofts.

It was during this time that I really noticed how different the Hawaii market was from the ones on the mainland. Partly it was because we were so isolated and the radio competition was not the same as it was in, say, southern California. There, radio frequencies bumped up against each other and often overlapped, crowding the marketplace and making it easy for one market to influence another nearby. San Bernardino could break a record that'd influence Los Angeles, but Honolulu was 2,500 miles out to sea. That, and because we were such a small market, meant we didn't get the attention and pressure from record companies that bigger, mainland radio stations got.

Cut off from all that, Hawaii could, and did, do what it wished. A big star on the mainland could be a minor one in the Islands and vice versa.

A couple of years before, in 1956, Alan Freed had produced a movie called *Rock, Rock, Rock*. It was the first rock-and-roll movie released in Hawaii, and there was a song in it by the Three Chuckles called "Won't You Give

flying to the Islands, singing five songs, then going to the beach. We'd do a rehearsal Friday afternoon. We'd do one show and sometimes two on Friday night, two or three shows Saturday, then Sunday night at Schofield Barracks. On top of that, they did interviews and shows on the outer islands. We did that a lot. If we had a group that was self-contained, they would back the other performers. The Champs backed Frankie Avalon and the Beach Boys backed Dee Dee Sharp.

The Champs show was the only time where I lost control because of the reaction of the crowd to the performers. The Champs did their hit, "Tequila," and the crowd went bananas. Jimmie Seals was a hell of a honking tenor sax player, and he went into "Night Train." The audience just went nuts. I had to bring them back and

Me a Chance?" I started playing it on the radio, and kids went to the movie and started requesting the song. The movie was a smash and ran for months, and the song became number one in Hawaii. Teddy Randazzo, an Italian kid from New York, was the lead singer of the Three Chuckles and he became a big star here, so big that he headlined the seventh Show of Stars two years later over Frankie Avalon. Teddy became one of Hawaii's most popular performers. Yet he never was as big on the mainland.

Another difference was in how the stars were billed. For the 10th Show of Stars we brought in Tommy Sands and Connie Francis, along with the Diamonds. Not many people know it, but Tommy had worked on the road for Colonel Parker as a gofer. When some Hollywood studio wanted Elvis for a network film called *The Singing Idol*, the Colonel said Elvis couldn't do it; give it to Tommy. Well, Tommy got the part and it launched his career. Tommy became so popular here, he headlined over Connie Francis, who was a more established star nationally.

I was doing all right, too, in my own way becoming a local "star" of stage, screen and radio, as the old saying

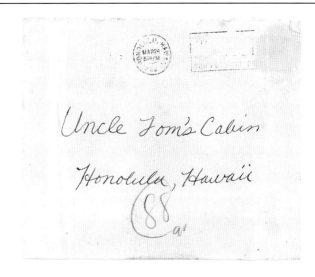

In 1958 you could address an envelope simply to Uncle Tom's Cabin in Honolulu and it would be delivered to our radio station.

goes. I continued to appear on the stage at the Civic Auditorium and in high school auditoriums on all the islands, and I started hosting a television show.

Actually, Mr. Kaiser was the first to put me in front of a TV camera when I was still at KHVH, but that show never happened because sponsors hadn't yet recognized this new market. Then Bob Smith, promotion director of ABC affiliate KHVH, suggested I do a dance show following Dick Clark. With Clark's lead-in audience, the show took off, like, wow. Mostly we played records and a bunch of kids danced, but whenever we could we brought on local and national acts to lip sync to their records. I had regular dancers, and to be seen on that show was a big deal. Dick would do a voice-over announcement at the end of his show: "Now stay tuned for Tom Moffatt and *The Tom Moffatt Show* in Honolulu." Later we moved the show to prime time, and once we got the format down, we taped five shows back-to-back on a Saturday morning. I'd take five changes of clothing and we'd have five different groups of dancers, plus our regulars.

Even Aku liked it. He said he still couldn't understand the music, but it was fun. 🎤

Taking the show on the road: among those boarding an Aloha Airlines DC-10 for an inter-island flight were the Drifters, Ronnie Diamond, Glenn Glenn, Robin Luke and the Tilton Sisters.

CHAPTER 6

POI Boys Just Want to Have Fun

As I write this, I've been a disc jockey and an entertainment promoter for more than 50 years. During that time, I've played records by, interviewed and presented hundreds of acts—from Elvis Presley to Michael Jackson to Frank Sinatra to the Rolling Stones, from Rudolf Nureyev to the American Idols to Bruce Willis (playing harmonica!) to Hulk Hogan to the Shanghai Circus. So what am I remembered for? What do the people of Hawaii want to talk about most when they come up to me?

A radio station that was named for the sticky stuff you get when you boil taro root. From 1959 to 1974 I was one of the "POI Boys." Those 15 years at what must have been the most popular radio station in Hawaii history, K-POI, were wildly unforgettable.

When K-POI went on the air—the call letters were always hyphenated then—the Islands were on a roll. Today, we celebrate statehood on August 21, the anniversary date marking the official Presidential proclamation, but the big blowout in Hawaii came five months earlier, on March 12, 1959, when Congress passed the statehood bill and Lyndon Johnson announced that Hawaii was—finally—one of the United States. The days as a territory were *pau*, over, at last.

Hawaii hadn't seen a celebration like that since the end of World War Two. In Washington, delegate to Congress Jack Burns served fellow politicians a 50-candle

The POI Boys—each one a true radio "personality"—were the first disc jockeys in Hawaii to rock around the clock. Opposite: The K-POI basketball team included (left to right) Bob "the Beard" Lowrie, Dave Donnelly, Mike "Mighty Leader" Hamlin, Kenny Wells, Mel "the Moneyman" Lawrence, me and Steve Nicolet.

statehood cake (flown in by Dole Pineapple), and in Honolulu the people poured into the streets. Those in cars blew their horns. Everybody got the day off, and of course there was a show at the stadium. Twenty thousand came to see an all-star lineup of Hawaiian entertainers, and I was one of the emcees, along with Ron and Ed Sheehan and Lucky Luck.

People had waited for statehood for a long time, and

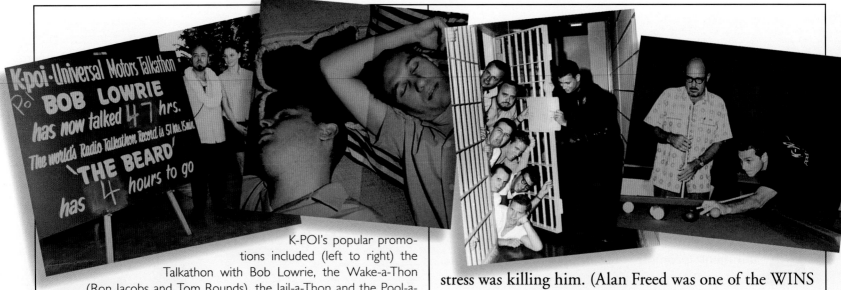

K-POI's popular promotions included (left to right) the Talkathon with Bob Lowrie, the Wake-a-Thon (Ron Jacobs and Tom Rounds), the Jail-a-Thon and the Pool-a-Thon (Mel the Moneyman shooting for the side pocket, with *Honolulu Star Bulletin* columnist Jim Becker).

when it happened I don't think anyone realized how it would open up the floodgate of tourism to Hawaii, how it signified the end of a sleepy town. (Coincidentally, just two months later, the first jet-propelled Boeing 707 arrived.) Before statehood, many people considered Hawaii a foreign land. The only big outside business to come in was Sears; Liberty House and McInerny's were the retail merchants and Lewers & Cooke was the building supply place. There was no Ala Moana Center. Markets were closed on Sundays and holidays. All that would change, and although we didn't realize how different it would be, statehood was embraced. I don't remember any negative feelings about Hawaii's becoming a state. None. Everybody was happy about it. We weren't halfway citizens any more. We were 100-percent American.

At the same time, I left KPOA. Another station, KHON, had gone into bankruptcy and was purchased by KPOA'S general manager, Thomas "Fin" Hollinger, and H.G. "Jock" Fernhead, an Englishman from New York who had run that city's top rock station, WINS, and had been told by his doctor to get out of town because the

stress was killing him. (Alan Freed was one of the WINS personalities.) The price? Just $20,000.

After I'd been hired by Fin and with a month to kill before K-POI went on the air, I went to a club in Japan to listen to a singer named Masaaki Hirao, who had recorded a Paul Anka song. He sent me to his manager in the second basement of the club. I was talking broken English to him, and he finally said, in perfect English, "Hey, man, haven't I met you somewhere before?" This was Tats Nagashima, and we became good friends. He became the biggest promoter in Japan and that country's first major publisher of English-language songs, including the Beatles tunes. Later, we brought Masaaki to Hawaii, and in the years to come, Tats and I worked together frequently.

I returned to Hawaii on Friday, May 15, for the 15th Show of Stars with the Crests and Clyde McPhatter, who performed that night and on the 16th and 17th. K-POI went on the air on Monday, the 18th, and by the end of the summer we were number one in all time slots in Hawaii—the only possible exception being against Aku in the morning.

K-POI had the first consistent format in the history of Hawaii radio. Until then, it had been a mishmash of canned shows from the mainland, local personalities and ethnic programming. The other stations had disc jockeys,

The Donkey Derby
by Tom Rounds

Of all the K-POI promotions, none was wackier and weirder than the K-POI Donkey Derby. This was a race between most of the jocks, mounted on donkeys, and it was arranged, as were most of these extravaganzas, to draw the biggest crowds at the start and finish. We began at the Pearl City Tavern and wound up the next day at the Mynah Bird Drive-In at the corner of Waialae and Hunakai, across from Waialae Shopping Center (now Kahala Mall).

Logistically, we required the traffic control services of the Honolulu Police Department, a rolling donkey diner stocked with feed and water, and our own donkey wrangler, Benny Borges from Koko Head. A few days before the event, Benny rounded up the healthiest animals from a wild herd that roamed the range between Hawaii Kai and Makapuu and trucked them to a cousin's spread in Waipahu a few weeks before the Derby, where they were to be conditioned for the race. "Broken" turned out to be a more apt term, and when I took a look at these untamed beasts, I quickly volunteered to manage the entire event from the driver's seat of the K-POI cruiser.

We started on a Friday before a crowd of 5,000 during afternoon drive time, and the jocks soon began to develop a love-hate relationship with their mounts. These animals did all the things that made donkeys famous, including digging in their heels, bucking, braying and blinking those lovable downcast eyes that betray all sorts of evil intent. They played to the crowd and soon turned the event into man vs. beast—and the beasts were winning the hearts of the fans.

As evening wore on and the crowds thinned, our caravan got down to the business of getting from Point A to Point Z, slogging down Dillingham Boulevard through intermittent showers, getting across to Nimitz Highway and through the sickeningly sweet vapors from the Dole Cannery, munching and pooping onto Ala Moana, cutting across Kapiolani and up to Waialae Avenue. All along the route, the HPD funneled the herd into a traffic lane and let us run the red lights. As the sun rose, and the troop crested the hill by the Queen Theater, the bedraggled POI Boys found that their faithful listeners had reassembled.

The riders by now were at the point of exhaustion. Having

endured the rain, the dark of night and the endless bowls of saimin proffered by the town's major drive-ins, they didn't know their asses from their *okoles*. They just wanted the damned thing to end.

The animals were in great shape, however, thanks to the TLC provided by Benny, and they were still playing to the crowd. So as our Quixotes drew closer to the finish line, who's the tall figure in the lead, the one with his feet dragging on the pavement? Why, it's Uncle Tom! But wait. What's that also dragging on the pavement?

It was then that Hawaii's own presenter of good, clean teen fun realized that (a) he was astride the only male donkey in the pack and (b) the rest of the mounts were mares, one or more of which had clearly gone into heat.

At this point, all control was lost as Uncle Tom's animal, now oblivious to his mission to be first over the line, made for the females with alacrity and considerable vigor. The crowd, aghast, swirled. The kids were quickly led away, and the HPD officers fell down laughing. The Beard, for once, was speechless. And few noticed when a lone donkey named Juan, carrying the irrepressible Michael Gwynne, K-POI's late-night jock, sitting on an inflatable rubber tushie cushion, quietly finished first, the winner by only a nose.

I wanted to win the race; my donkey had other ideas.

This football dream team included Don Rickles, Helen Reddy, Howard Cosell and Muhammad Ali voicing promos for K-POI.

including Michael Gwynne, Jack Kellner, Steve Nicolet, Jim Mitchell, Don Robbs, Dave "the Moose" Donnelly and others I'll talk about later. Each was a "personality" in the truest sense of the word. We might have been loved or hated, but our listeners never felt noncommittal.

A third reason that led to K-POI's domination of the airwaves was our determination to make it fun. Not only did we play the music the kids wanted to hear and put together a gang of crazies to play it, we promoted the station in a way never experienced in radio before.

The first big promotion was handed to us when Colonel Parker offered an interview with Elvis, who was then serving Uncle Sam in Germany. Now, Elvis wasn't doing interviews, as a rule. The Colonel's philosophy was that if Elvis was going off to serve his country, he wasn't going to sing; he wasn't going to do anything connected to show business, including giving interviews. But I think in the back of his mind he wanted to bring Elvis back to Hawaii. And when someone asks if you'd like to interview Elvis—when everyone else in the world is being told no—you don't ask, "Why me?"

We didn't want to promote the interview until we had it down on tape. I interviewed him in the evening, when it was morning in Germany. I remember I had a date immediately afterward, and I was so excited, but I couldn't tell my date that I'd just talked to Elvis. We'd all been sworn to secrecy because we wanted to announce it in a newspaper campaign.

but they'd constantly have to go into a language program, which broke the momentum that we were able to keep going smoothly from one show to the next. And we played rock and roll, as Bill Haley suggested, "around the clock." This was the major reason for our success.

One of the other big reasons was the on-air lineup. Ron Jacobs was the station's program director and the morning man, doing 6 to 9, and I was on next, 9 to noon. Jumpin' George West had the noon to 3 o'clock shift, and he was followed by Tom Rounds, 3 to 6. I came back with "Uncle Tom's Cabin" from 6 to 9, Bob "the Beard" Lowrie was on the air 9 to midnight, and Bob Prescott was the overnight man. Later, there'd be others,

Besides playing records on the air, we also packaged a few albums under the K-POI brand.

The next big promotion was the first of the many stunts that gave the station, and the POI Boys, their reputation as people who would do just about anything. This was the first of our "Thons," the Wake-a-Thon. There was a department store on Dillingham Boulevard called Wigwam, and the idea was for Tom Rounds to set up camp in there and break the world record for going without sleep. We all supported him, but it was Ron who slapped him in the face with a wet towel and screamed at him and kept him going. Once a day TR, as we all called him, would go across the street to Foremost Dairies and get a shower. He was awake for eight days, a record that was in the *Guinness Book of Records* for years. The final Sunday, across the front page of the *Advertiser* was a picture of Tom's eyes. He says that he doesn't recommend the experience!

Some of the "Thons" were competitions between the POI Boys. One time, we did a speedboat race going from Honolulu Harbor and around Sand Island and back, over and over again, to see who could keep going the longest. We had drivers, and TR and I were co-pilots in competing boats. There were a lot of others in this, too, but we were the only disc jockeys. The way the boat bounced up and down over the waves, I thought my kidneys were going to burst. I was in such pain, but I was determined to beat Rounds. We started in the morning and went all day. And when I finally quit, I learned that TR had hung it up an hour earlier.

TR and I squared off again in a charity Bowl-a-Thon. He was at the Waikiki Bowl, next to the Surfrider Hotel, and I was at the Pali Lanes in Kailua. I remembered how important practice was from my Roller Derby contest with Jacobs, so TR and I spent several days bowling before the contest began. We started on a Friday afternoon, and on

We staged the premiere of *A Hard Day's Night* at the Princess Theater, preceded by a Dick Jensen concert. I later greeted Ringo Starr when he arrived at Honolulu International Airport.

the front page of the *Advertiser* on Sunday there was a picture of me holding my thumb up, and my thumb was so swollen it looked like the end of a baseball bat. They had to keep giving me balls with bigger thumbholes. It was around the clock, no sleep, and people came to the bowling alleys to donate money to charity. One time in the middle of the night I was sure I was in the Dillingham Bowl on Dillingham Boulevard and not at the Pali Lanes in Kailua. Once an hour we broke to freshen up, but there were all these people there, so we couldn't fake it. It ended Monday, and I haven't gone near a bowling alley since.

Another was the Hang-a-Thon. Jacobs was going to stay in a car for a week, hanging from a five-story crane. We planned to stage it on a used car lot on Nimitz Highway in Kalihi. Jacobs wasn't too happy about doing it, so we decided I'd "rescue" him at the last minute. It was Sunday and we had a good crowd when Jacobs started freaking out, saying he wouldn't do it. So I got up there and started broadcasting with a mike that we'd strung to the top of the crane. An hour later the state safety inspector showed

Pat Boone's wife told me this was the best interview he'd ever done.

who had refused to put their clients on rock-and-roll radio programs a few years earlier. Nobody had ever done crazy promotions like this before, and now we were on the front page. We weren't just silly; we were news! They couldn't ignore us now. Suddenly, a radio station that was bankrupt a few months before was profitable.

We never had any budget for this, so we had to find sponsors to cover the costs. I remember Wigwam got eight days of round-the-clock promotion for the Wake-a-Thon for a mere $2,000. We had another promotion with Meadow Gold Dairies where they filled a milk can with coins—quarters, dimes and nickels. This is where Mel Lawrence got his nickname "Mel the Moneyman." We announced on the air that Mel was cruising down such-and-such street and the first person to come out of the house and give Mel the Meadow Gold word of the day could reach into the can and pull out a handful of coins. Our general manager had already ordered that most of the coins be nickels, but he still thought this was costing too much, so he made us reduce the size of the hole in the top of the can.

The only competition we had in all of this came from KULA. KULA tried to do promotions, but they couldn't match us. On top of that, we engaged in dirty tricks. TR's wife would call KULA and say she wanted to request a song; they'd put her on the air and she'd say, "I want to hear a song by Elvis and it's K-POI K-POI K-POI…" until they cut her off.

We were working 18 hours a day. I had an office in the station, and I slept there. I would get to my apartment once a week if I was lucky. Sometimes to entertain ourselves we'd make telephone calls. One time, Jacobs called Pearl Harbor and he rolled off names; he didn't know what he was saying; and they connected him to a submarine. Ron said he was the Navy's chief of protocol and said the prince of some country was stopping at the airport, and while the plane was being refueled he wanted

up and ended it. But it still created a lot of talk.

Over the years, there were more than a dozen "Thons." There was a race around Oahu on bicycles. I won that one by a considerable distance, and I still treasure the gold watch awarded me. Dave Donnelly and Jack Kellner, who was very sarcastic, went at each other verbally in an Insult-a-Thon. Michael Gwynne, a professional musician who also was one of our jocks, tried to set a world record in a Drum-a-Thon. The Pool-a-Thon was held in a billiards parlor at the corner of King Street and Kalakaua Avenue, where Mel Lawrence took on all challengers around the clock, including a number of local politicians. We fought mock battles in electric boats on the Ala Wai Canal that fronted the K-POI studios…talked each other to death… and shook more hands than Teddy Roosevelt.

The promotions got the station noticed, by creating a bond not just with our growing number of listeners, but also with the advertising agencies. These were the guys

THE PACIFIC
WAR MEMORIAL
COMMISSION
Proudly Presents
IN PERSON
ELVIS PRESLEY
★ WITH ALL STAR CAST ★
BLOCH ARENA • PEARL HARBOR
Saturday, March 25th, 1961
8:30 P.M.—Doors Open 7:15
All Proceeds For U.S.S. Arizona Memorial Fund
PEARL HARBOR, HAWAII

VIA RCA AH1426 FB1441 DP567
BADNAUHEIM 87 19 1210 PAGE 1/50=
AUG 19 8 35 PM '59

COL TOM PARKER HAWAIIAN VILLAGE HOTEL HONOLULU=

DEAR COL MY SINCERE THANKS TO TOM MOFFAT AND RON JACOBS AND
THE ENTIRE STAFF OF KPOI AND TO ALL THE FANS AND FRIENDS IN
THE HAWAIIAN ISLANDS I AM IN FULL AGREEMENT WITH YOU THAT IF
ALL POSSIBLE WE SHOULD MAKE OUR

DP567 COL TOM PAGE 2/37 =

FIRST PERSONAL APPEARANCE AFTER I RETURN FROM THE ARMY IN
HAWAII PERHAPS YOU CAN WORK THIS IN WITH OUR FIRST TOUR AFTER
WE MAKE OUR FIRST MOVIE NEXT YEAR
      YOUR PAL ELVIS PRESLEY 14
GOETHESTR BADNAUHEIM GERMANY

In 1959, Elvis sent a telegram from Germany offering to do a Hawaii concert right after his discharge from the Army. His arrival for the *Arizona* Memorial benefit drew a huge crowd of screaming fans to John Rodgers Airport.

The *Arizona* Memorial benefit at Pearl Harbor was preceded by a big press conference and photo opportunities for lucky fans.

to inspect their submarine at 1 o'clock in the morning. It was a Saturday night and the commanding officer wasn't available, and the ensign who answered Ron's call figured he'd better get everyone in dress uniforms.

Another time, Ron called Kini Popo, Hawaii's first TV morning personality. He was on at the same time Ron had his morning show, and Ron didn't like competition, so he'd put on a record and call. "Is this Kini Popo?" Ron would ask. "Yes, this is Kini Popo." And Jacobs would deliver a string of obscenities just to see Kini Popo's face.

I'll never forget when Ron said he wanted to see how long he could keep jocks from other stations on the phone, just breathing. He even tried it on me, but when I took a call and said, "Hello, this is Uncle Tom" and the caller didn't say anything, I hung up immediately. But some of the other jocks...one of them started ranting and cursing Ron. And he'd record them and play it back later for our amusement. So I'm cruising along doing a great radio show and these other guys were getting screwed up by Jacobs, who was just breathing.

Probably the best sabotage we ever planned was when a competing station tried a "Thon" of its own and said it was going to put one of its jocks at the bottom of the Biltmore Hotel pool. Rounds, Jacobs and Donn Tyler checked into the hotel under a false name, asking for a room overlooking the pool. It was morning and there was a crowd gathered. The jock jumped into the water in a wetsuit and a few minutes later, Rounds threw packets of dye into the pool, instantly turning it black. The jock must've freaked, because he came right to the top and climbed out, waving his arms and shouting.

When it came to dirty tricks, Nixon had nothing on the POI Boys. The difference, of course, is we were just having fun. And never was it more fun, or more exciting, than when Elvis returned to the Islands.

When I interviewed Elvis when he was in Germany, I asked him if he had a message for his Hawaii fans. "Well,"

he said, "I would like to say that I will never forget the day the ship pulled out, what a good feeling I had. Everybody was throwing leis in the water, you know? And everybody was singing 'Aloha' and all that. It was really a nice feeling, and I certainly hope to come back again someday, I really do."

With Elvis still in the Army, the Colonel visited the Islands on holiday. He came to see us at K-POI and said if we could get 10,000 signatures, he'd make sure Elvis did his first post-Army concert in Hawaii. Ron and I had pictures taken with the Colonel in the studio, and then we took one of those long rolls of teletype paper like the wire services used in our newsroom and set up a table in the brand-new Ala Moana Center. We got many more than 10,000, believe me. And it didn't take very long.

Shortly after that, we got a telegram that said, "COL. TOM PARKER HAWAIIAN VILLAGE HOTEL HONOLULU. DEAR COL. MY SINCERE THANKS TO TOM MOFFATT AND RON JACOBS AND THE ENTIRE STAFF OF KPOI AND TO ALL THE FRIENDS AND FANS IN THE HAWAIIAN ISLANDS. I AM IN FULL AGREE-

Jacobs and I pose with Elvis in his *Blue Hawaii* get-up and K-POI contest winner Maria Velardo.

In 1962 Elvis was back in town to film his second Hawaii movie—*Girls! Girls! Girls!* His fans and I met him at the Hilton Hawaiian Village heliport, where he sported leis up to his ears and the navy blue nautical cap that he would wear in much of the movie.

MENT WITH YOU IF [AT] ALL POSSIBLE WE SHOULD MAKE OUR FIRST PERSONAL APPEARANCE AFTER I RETURN FROM THE ARMY IN HAWAII. PERHAPS YOU CAN WORK THIS IN WITH OUR FIRST TOUR AFTER WE MAKE OUR FIRST MOVIE NEXT YEAR. YOUR PAL, ELVIS PRESLEY."

Well, as it turned out, Elvis did a charity concert in Memphis first, but right after that the Colonel brought him to the Islands, as promised, and said Elvis was going to perform at the 4,000-seat Bloch Arena at Pearl Harbor, another benefit, this one for the *Arizona* Memorial. The Colonel also announced that after the concert, Elvis

would make a movie in the Islands called *Blue Hawaii*. The Colonel invited us to the meeting at the Hawaiian Village Hotel with the Pearl Harbor brass and told us to watch what happened. He said, "You're gonna see a lot of skeptics when they come in, and when we leave, they'll be very positive."

So all these Navy admirals came in with their aides, and this colonel who wasn't really a colonel starts talking. He told them that everybody had to pay to get in, Elvis and his father and the Colonel included; there would be no free passes, so that every penny helped pay for the construction of the memorial. He then told the brass that he had something special for them from Elvis, and he opened a box and brought out some 8-by-10 glossy photographs. And he got away with it. When the Colonel was done, all these officers dripping with gold were practically

Left: Colonel Tom Parker proclaimed himself First High Potentate of his Snowmen's League, a fraternity of special friends. Here he inducts me into this exclusive group. That's Jacobs inside one of those outfits. Above: The Colonel wrote, "I met Tom in 1957 and…we are the same friends today" and presented this to me on his last birthday.

saluting him.

He also paid for several extra tickets himself and gave them to the admirals' drivers, then had them seated in among the high-ranking officers.

After the Bloch Arena concert, the Colonel said we could have a contest where the winner and a guest would go to Hollywood and visit Elvis on the set of *Blue Hawaii*. (Most of the film was made in the Islands, but some of the interior scenes were shot on the Paramount sound stages.) Ron and I accompanied the winning letter writer and her mom, and that was the first time I got a chance to spend any time with Elvis without a microphone or a telephone between us. We talked about ancient Egypt and super-

natural things. He was pretty well read, and I was really impressed.

I do have mixed feelings about one other promotion we did. One of the Honolulu TV stations had a charity auction scheduled to run all weekend. Ron and I were asked to host for a period of time to raise money on it. So we got a pink sheet from the Hawaiian Village Hotel and cut it into one-inch squares and said, "This is the sheet Elvis slept on at when he stayed at the hotel last night." Anybody who made a pledge of at least a dollar while we were on the show got a piece of the sheet. It could've been the sheet…but I wouldn't have bet on it. 🎤

CHAPTER 7

Sweetie and Niniko

Tommy Sands, who was spending a few extra days in Hawaii following his appearance at the 10th Show of Stars, was dating a girl who had a girl-friend she wanted me to meet—and it wasn't until after I picked her up that I learned she was in high school. I wasn't interested in dating a high-school girl, and after dinner we dropped her off at home. I had no way of knowing it then, but she'd later become my wife.

A year passed, and I was emceeing a beauty contest. I made a date for the following weekend with one of the judges, a former beauty queen. She didn't show up. I waited around and waited around and finally gave up. I was in Waikiki, so I went to the International Market-place, where I ran into my young one-time date, Sweetie Cablay, who was then out of school and dancing for Donn Beach at Don the Beachcomber. I hadn't seen her since that night with Tommy, but now that she was older, I was interested.

Sweetie—a nickname given to her when she was very young—was a Radford girl, two years ahead of the school's best-known alumna, Bette Midler. She was a songleader and one of the most popular students, and I don't have to tell you, she was beautiful. Like many Island girls she danced the hula, and she was also an outstanding Tahi-tian dancer, later taking classes from Kent Ghirard. He was the heir to the Ghirardelli chocolate fortune from San Francisco; he became a respected hula teacher and was one

Sweetie Cablay: what a difference between the high-school girl I dated and the Don the Beachcomber dancer (opposite) I saw in Waikiki a year later!

of the few haoles to get the recognition of Hawaiian *kumu hula*, hula masters. He was known for his discipline and perfection of "Hawaiian image." Long hair, no fingernail polish or jewelry. Matching costumes, precision dancing. His Hula Nani Girls performed thousands of times from the late 1940s into the 1960s, dancing down Kalakaua

Sweetie and I were married at the beautiful Fern Grotto on the island of Kauai.

Avenue on "Aloha Wednesdays" and greeting celebrities at the Aloha Tower pier and at the airport for the Hawaii Visitors Bureau. To be a member of his troupe was considered a great honor.

Following a courtship that took me to the mainland on weekends so I could be with her as she toured with Hilo Hattie, Sweetie and I married and had a son, Troy, and in 1962 began looking for a house. One morning when we were to look at a place in Nuuanu, a fascinating article by Bob Krauss appeared in the *Advertiser* telling the story of

a 19th-century mansion there called Niniko. He'd found its history in a book in the Halekulani Hotel library, and when he went to look for the house, he was surprised to see that it still existed.

By an act of the legislature in 1858—the year of the Great Mahele, or Division of Lands—the property on which the house was built was set aside for growing food for men stationed at the fort in downtown Honolulu. It was His Majesty Kamehameha III's decision to relinquish title to much of his domain and give it to chiefs and commoners alike, but he asked his cabinet ministers to secure what then was called Kahapaakai. In 1862 it was presented to him by special act of the legislature, the only instance of

It was love at first sight when we found this beautiful home in Nuuanu Valley, originally built in the late 19th century on land once owned by royalty.

the kind on record.

Two years later a Tahitian princess named Ninito, the niece of Queen Pomare, came to Hawaii to marry His Majesty's adopted son, Prince Liholiho. The king thought the French were using her to get a foothold in Hawaii, so he sent Liholiho and his brother off to England to school. To save face and pacify Tahitian royalty, the king then gave the Tahitian princess this big parcel of land that was now renamed Niniko, changing the "t" to a "k" because there is no "t" in Hawaiian.

Ninito sold the property in 1879 without ever living on it, and it passed through several hands before its purchase in 1892 by Frederick Lowrey, the president of Lewers & Cooke. Lowrey and his wife built a huge home and put in acres of rolling lawn with Japanese bridges over the streams than ran through the land. There were two living rooms, two kitchens and a pantry, seven bedrooms, four bathrooms and two attics. It was one of the most beautiful homes of the time, and it was ranked right up there with the fabled Damon estate as having the most beautiful gardens in Honolulu. A ballroom measuring 30

by 60 feet designed by Hawaii's leading architects, Dickey and Wood, was added in 1927, with a balcony overlooking the ballroom supported by a huge beam with the inscription "It Seeks To Speak That Magic Word Aloha."

(Years later, the Mamas & the Papas stopped at the house on the way to the airport, and when I took them on a tour and we got to the ballroom, all four of them spontaneously started applauding. It's that kind of room.)

Coincidentally, the day Bob Krauss wrote his story, Sweetie and I were to look at a home on Niniko Place. Two doors down from the one we went to see was the one Bob had written about. I looked at it and, wow! We didn't want the one we looked at, and Sweetie told our realtor to let us know if the Niniko house ever went up for sale. About a month later, she called and said the house was going on the market the next Monday for $45,000.

Though the house was old it had extraordinary craftsmanship and charm. It sat on a half-acre of fee-simple land

When I showed the Mamas & the Papas our home's 30-by-60-foot ballroom, all four of them burst into spontaneous applause.

and it had a fireplace; I'd always wanted to live in a house with a fireplace. Even so, we could not have afforded it if it hadn't been for my television show. I had a percentage of the commercials, and I made a lot more money than I could've earned in radio and saved it.

I asked the real estate agent, "Can I put in a bid for $40,000?" She said, "If you want the home badly enough, put in a bid for the selling price and they have to sell it to you. You bid less and someone else comes in with $45,000, they'll get the house." I took the advice, and it was ours.

Two stepdaughters of Charles E. King—the legendary Hawaiian composer—lived there, and it was a house divided. One of the sisters had married a sailor that the other sister didn't approve of, so the house was kind of cut in half. But all the rooms were intact. The sale was going to go through in January 1963, and one of the sisters was nice enough to invite us up at Christmas. Knowing I was a disc jockey, they gave us a wind-up phonograph that played 78s, and when we moved in that was about the only furniture in the house. That is, until Sweetie discovered the auctions held by a dear friend, Moe Lipton. One in particular helped fill most of our bedrooms, when Moe auctioned the contents of the Young home (on Waikiki Beach between the Royal Hawaiian and the house I lived in during part of my stay in the army). Sweetie also discovered the Salvation Army before buyers found out that you could buy an antique there for the price of a piece of junk.

All this time, I continued at K-POI. The promotions continued, too, and still frequently featured members of the station staff. We even made a running character out of the station bookkeeper. His real name was Lin Hon Au, but many second-generation Chinese parents gave their kids American names, often using a U.S. president's last name as the child's first. So Jacobs renamed our accountant "Coolidge Nakamura" (making him Japanese as well). We had him make announcements on the air, and he always screwed it up in a way that was funny, and when he realized what he'd said he'd start giggling. When a dog was lost, it was described in Coolidge's unique fashion as a "lost cocker Spaniard." Followed by a fit of giggles. He also was a spokesman for Waikiki's Beach Market on John Ena Road—this store traded us milk for airtime and beer for any promotion we might give them. Coolidge's commercials were so funny, listeners requested them. Jermiah Grundy also returned to add his unique brand of humor in Beach Market commercials—he'd telephone wrong numbers, like a noodle shop or a poi factory, and start ordering items for delivery like he was talking to George or Eugene Shimizu, the owners of the Beach Market. The recorded results were hilarious.

Coolidge also played a role in a promotion held in Kapiolani Park during one of Hawaii's annual State Fairs. Albert Rego, brother of Leonard Rego of Leonard's Bakery, had created a new kind of Portuguese sausage called a burguesa, and the brothers figured that if K-POI could sell malasadas, it could sell sausages, so they bought a lot of airtime on the station and we agreed to launch a "flying burguesa" at the fair. We acquired a 3,000-cubic-foot barrage balloon left over from the Korean War and some eighth-inch steel cable to keep it anchored to the ground and launched it, saying Coolidge was aboard as pilot. It's a good thing he wasn't. He was sending his messages "back to earth" from inside a plywood Flight Control Center on the fairgrounds, hidden from view, when winds caught the burguesa and slammed it onto the point of an E.K. Fernandez tent pole, deflating it. Our listeners were unaware of this, and the next day Tom Rounds was quoted in the *Advertiser* saying that Coolidge would remain in the sausage's capsule long enough to establish some sort of vague record for K-POI and the state, help the Jaycees by drawing crowds to the fair, and "make a series of tests for several government agencies."

Aside from being a POI Boy, Bob Lowrie

was also known as the "Weird Beard" who hosted horror movies on Saturday nights on KHON-TV. Once when he got sick and was off the air and at St. Francis Hospital for a week or two, I organized an impromptu parade to bring him from the hospital back to the studios in—what else?—a hearse, where he would then go on the air. I don't think we got a permit; we just did it. I thought of it the day before, so we had all our disc jockeys in their cars just in case, but it worked because we had a long line of cars, which caused some traffic problems.

I was always blessed with very loyal fans, who formed fan clubs through the years. One of the early ones was called the Record Squad, and everyone had a number. Record Squader No. 13 was Wayne Harada, who went on to become the entertainment editor at the *Honolulu Advertiser*. Ron had a loyal listener in the morning who attended all our functions, a loyal fan he nicknamed

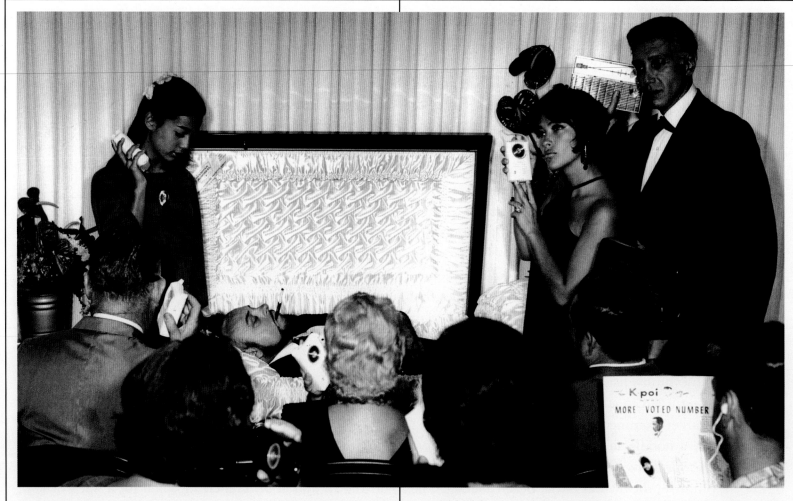

"Mourners" tune in to K-POI on their transistor radios at a mock funeral for Bob Lowrie—the implication being that the only people in town who didn't listen were those who had passed on (note the Beard's ever-present cigarette).

"K-POI Mabel." I remember when Jacobs and I met the guy who owned the Coca-Cola bottling plant and we decided that I'd be the host of "The Coke Hi-Fi Club," which would air in the evenings as part of my show. Over 20,000 people wrote in and joined. We had contests for our listeners and gave away Coca-Cola clocks and transistor radios. Those were pretty good prizes in those days.

That later inspired a stunt. When I became general manager we bought several dozen transistor radios and tuned them to K-POI, then taped them so the tuning would hold, turned the radios on, wrapped them for mailing and sent them to all the ad agencies and big accounts. So the next day, all these guys got packages in the mail with music coming out of them and a POI Boy yelling the station breaks. The post office didn't like it, but it got a lot of talk; it sparked interest in the station.

We were also the first to do bumper stickers, and they were very successful until it was discovered that you couldn't peel the damned things off. Stations are still giving out bumper stickers, but most people just take them for souvenirs and don't put them on their cars.

We had a "Marathon of Hits" every Labor Day weekend, counting down the top 300 songs of all time, as voted by our listeners and the K-POI jocks. It became

More promotions: a Poi Boys schoolbook cover, Miss K-POI contests, me as a convict (the number I'm holding is the station's request number) and the Coke Hi-Fi Club.

a big deal. People actually stayed up and listened from the beginning to the end.

Then we started the Miss K-POI contest. High schools nominated candidates. Sometimes we'd have celebrity guests at the contests and the audiences we attracted were bigger than those for Miss Hawaii. Miss Hawaii would get an audience of a few hundred and we'd get 8,000. I admit the numbers were connected to the talent we had on the show. When we had the Monkees coming in for what was their first live performance anywhere, we gave the Miss K-POI contestants several hundred dollars' worth of "Monkee Money." The bills had pictures of the Monkees on them, and the girl who sold the most won a

TV—and the money could be used to buy tickets to see the Monkees in concert. We did the same thing a year later with "Rascals Revenue."

I remember another guest star, Jack Lord. This was before *Hawaii Five-O*, when he was a rodeo rider in a western TV series called *Stoney Burke*. He appeared at the contest in full cowboy dress, carrying a saddle. When I offered him a ride back to his Waikiki hotel, he let me take him part way and then insisted on getting out to walk

Spinning a disk in the KORL studios, interviewing Joanie Sommers for K-POI.

down Kalakaua Avenue, still carrying his saddle, stopping to say hello to fans and sign autographs.

Another great promotion was our "Blast Off" concert. When another station staged a Battle of the Bands and paid nothing to the winners, we announced our contest and offered $1,500 cash to the winning act, as well as a record deal for the release of a 45 on a national label. Linda Green & the Tempos from Kaimuki High were the winners, and I spent hours recording them in the K-POI studios for a Warner Bros. release. We presented the competition on three stages in the Waikiki Shell before a sell-out crowd of 9,000 K-POI listeners.

We also started a news effort where everyone after their shift on the air had to spend at least an hour making calls to get quotes from people in the news that we'd use the next morning. Our news director was Don Robbs, and this made it sound like he had a big staff. And on the big events, we put everyone to work. When Eisenhower came

to town, the first president to visit the Islands since the war, we had somebody at every important intersection between the airport and downtown Honolulu, reporting in: "This is so-and-so reporting for K-POI and the President is just passing Kalihi Street…" We had every salesman, every disc jockey, the whole staff.

One time, the Beard cut into the John F. Kennedy motorcade. Here comes the President and the Secret Service, and right in the middle of it is the K-POI cruiser, with the call letters all over the side. He got into the parade somehow, and I don't think the Secret Service was too happy—thousands along the parade route ended up waving at the President and our Beard.

We had a slogan that said if you heard news, you heard it first on K-POI. If you called K-POI and reported a news event, you got $1.38, and if it was the best tip of the week, you got $13.80. That was our frequency on the radio dial, 1380. So people would call us sometimes before they called the police. The police got sort of ticked off at us about that. They'd get to the scene of a crime and we'd be there ahead of them.

The biggest thing we jumped on—and it was unfortunate because the family learned about it on K-POI before someone was able to break it to them gently—someone called Ron on a Saturday morning and said there was an unreported death at the YMCA, which was just a few blocks from the station. This was in the handball courts, where a lot of prominent people played. So we went down there, and it was Alfred Apaka, the biggest singing star in Hawaii.

More often we went for laughs. During the time I was at K-POI, there were two shipping strikes, and a lot of the things you took for granted suddenly weren't available. Like toilet paper. You couldn't find it in a store. There was a song called "Roll On," and we told our listeners every time we played it, the first person to call in would get a free roll of toilet paper. Our janitor had access to the PX at Pearl Harbor, and he got us cases of the stuff. Winners would come from all over the island to collect their coveted prize, and we got a big laugh when one day a Cadillac drove up and the chauffeur came in to collect the roll that his Kahala boss had won.

Our competition hired a detective to try to find the Golden Hibiscus we buried.

We also had a Treasure Hunt where you could win $1,380. You had to listen to clues given every day on the radio and then go dig something up. Holiday Mart was the sponsor of the hunt, so we planned to bury a Golden Hibiscus, the Holiday Mart logo. We didn't actually bury it until we were close to broadcasting the final clues, because we didn't want it to be discovered accidentally. Finally, we buried it on a construction site on the Windward side.

Our main competition, KORL, started saying they would find the Golden Hibiscus, and they hired a detective to discover its location. We didn't know it at the time, but the detective worked for the security company that was guarding the site where we buried the Hibiscus. They hired this genius to find it, and it was right where his company was responsible for the security, and they were guarding it when we snuck in and planted it.

The genius never found it. One of our listeners did. 🎤

CHAPTER 8

Changes

When I was a jock at the other stations, before K-POI, I could promote the Show of Stars on my show, but not on any other program. At K-POI, the shows got promoted around the clock. So attendance continued strong.

Most of the concerts, still being held at the Civic, were hassle free. Dion & the Belmonts, Neil Sedaka (making his first-ever professional appearance), Duane Eddy, Jan & Dean, Bobby Rydell, Bobby Vee, Ray Peterson, the Ventures, Chubby Checker (three times!), the Shirelles (our first black girl group), Gene Pitney, Brenda Lee, Freddie Cannon and Paul Anka (again) all went down well. Johnny Crawford was another repeat performer. He was playing Chuck Connors's son in *The Rifleman*, so he came out with a lariat and his high, little voice, but he was a pretty good singer, and the kids loved him.

Sometimes we turned the shows into a promotion for the station. Johnny Crawford became very popular on the radio from his appearances in the live concerts.

I decided to break his new album, and a new jock, Fred Kiemel, was to play the bad guy who'd try to steal the album from Uncle Tom. So it's Saturday morning and I'm playing the record and there's the sound of a needle being dragged across the record, and then Kiemel says, "We're not going to play this piece of junk on K-POI. I'm taking off with it." There's the sound of a door slamming, and Uncle Tom says, "Wow, why did he do that?" Then I ask

The Sunshine Festivals inside Diamond Head Crater (above and opposite) helped us promote K-POI FM Sunshine, one of the first underground rock stations in the country.

the listeners to help me find Kiemel and the album, so I can play it.

For reasons I'll never understand, KORL went on the air and said there was no album out yet, said what we were talking about was a fake—and they were going to get the album first and introduce it to Hawaii on Monday. They were playing right into our hands, because we did have the album and what Kiemel had, physically, in his hands was a package with another record inside, bound up with so much tape it was practically impossible to open. We said the listener who recovered the album would get 10 tickets to the next Johnny Crawford concert and get to meet Johnny and so on. We gave clues about Kiemel's location

When Fabian came to town for a Show of Stars, he made a grand entrance by helicopter on our radio station roof.

and finally announced that he'd be in Ala Moana Park at three o'clock that afternoon. The listeners didn't know, but we put Kiemel in a helicopter *over* Ala Moana Park and he *dropped* the album. Somebody grabbed it and rushed to the station. We then took the real album from where we'd stashed it in the studio and started playing it, while the jocks at KORL sucked wind.

We used a helicopter again when Fabian came to town. We'd made arrangements with his manager, Bob Marcucci, to have a chopper meet them at the airport and take him to the K-POI roof. The helicopter guy checked it out and said the roof was stable enough, so I was on the roof with a microphone, and the building was surrounded by kids who were cutting school to see it happen.

Performers kept telling us we had to get Bo Diddley, and we hyped ourselves into it. Not many in Hawaii knew his music, but we thought La Verne Baker could carry the show. On the bill we also had Larry Williams with "Short Fat Fanny" and "Bony Maroney," and this kid Johnny Tillotson, who'd just hit with "Dreamy Eyes." Johnny credits K-POI with saving his career. We played

"Dreamy Eyes" and it became a number-one hit in Hawaii. He was with Cadence Records, which was owned by Archie Bleyer, Arthur Godfrey's bandleader. Cadence had hit first with the Everly Brothers, and they also had Andy Williams. Johnny was the first young solo singer on the label, and he wasn't happening, so they weren't going to renew his contract. But on the strength of "Dreamy Eyes" in the Islands, they gave him another shot and he came out with "Poetry in Motion," which became a national hit. Anyway, Bo Diddley didn't do it for Hawaii. He may have stopped the show at the Apollo Theater in Harlem, as many performers told us, but it didn't happen here. And for some reason, Larry Williams never showed up.

There was only one other instance like that, when we had the Flamingos booked to appear. They were busted on their way to the Oakland airport when they pulled into a gas station; the attendant became suspicious about the aroma coming out of the car and called the police. Earl Finch was at the Honolulu airport waiting for them when the story came into the K-POI newsroom.

We also booked the Beach Boys for the first time. I was on the air when the record promo guy brought Carl Wilson into the studio. I asked him, "Are you going surfing this afternoon?" I don't know who was more embarrassed

Jerome and the Frog

by Johnny Tillotson

I was on the Show of Stars tour for Tom Moffatt in Hawaii in 1960, sharing the bill with Bo Diddley, La Verne Baker and Eugene Church. The cast and crew had gotten along famously.

At the end of the tour Tom was throwing a party for all the performers at the Hawaiian Village; it was outside, and he had pulled out all the stops. There were all kinds of fabulous Hawaiian foods and *hors d'oeuvres*; all the good stuff. To a kid like me in 1960, it was heaven. I was there with La Verne and all these great performers; it was a beautiful balmy evening in Hawaii; it's just something you would never forget, even if nothing else had happened.

But Bo Diddley's right-hand man was a fellow named Jerome—he was a tall man who had tremendous charisma in person and on stage. He played shakers (percussion instruments) for Bo. Now we're at the party and Jerome calls me over; he's standing behind a giant silver punch bowl filled with a lime-sherbet punch. He says, "Johnny, would you come here a minute," and I say sure and go over. He says, "I'm going to play a little joke on Bo. Look what I've got here." Behind his back, he's holding a *big green frog*. Now, I've got a little phobia about frogs myself, and they have some big ones in Hawaii. But Jerome says to me, "Call Bo over here and I'll ask him if he'd like some punch" (which was also green). I said OK.

"Bo, can you come over a second? It's Johnny." Bo says sure, and heads our way. Now, just as Bo's getting near, Jerome slides the frog into the bowl. Well, the frog starts sinking to the bottom, and Jerome calmly says, "Bo, do you want some punch?" and hands Bo the ladle. So Bo takes the ladle and puts it in to get a nice big scoop of sherbet.

At that point, the frog jumps on the ladle like it's a lifeline, then takes a big leap and lands on Bo's shoulder—and then Bo starts jumping! I thought Bo was going to lose his mind; he was as scared as the frog for a second. Finally, the frog jumped off Bo's shoulder and Jerome started laughing and we all started laughing, and Bo was laughing too. It was one of the funniest things I've ever seen.

So now it's 2003, and Bo and I are both shooting the PBS special *Rock at 50* in Pittsburgh, and we're talking backstage in Bo's dressing room. I said, "Bo, do you remember the night in Hawaii?" and he slapped his leg and said, "Man, I will never forget that! Jerome and the Frog." And we both had big smiles on our faces.

Bo Diddley never forgot the frog in the punchbowl.

The Beach Boys first appeared in Hawaii at the 30th Show of Stars, where they performed on their own and also served as the backup band for Jackie DeShannon and Dee Dee Sharp!

when he told me that he had never been on a board in his life. Ralph and Earl and I were upset because we thought the sex symbol of the group was Carl's brother Brian, and he didn't come. And Mike Love had a saxophone, which I didn't realize was a stage prop that he wasn't really playing. So I kept putting a microphone in front of the sax.

The Treniers opened the show, two of a group of brothers who had started their careers with the big bands in New York. One brother would walk off the stage singing and the other brother would enter singing from the opposite side of the stage. (They were identical twins.) It was hilarious. They and their other brothers were a good act. The Beach Boys followed, and then Jackie DeShannon and Dee Dee Sharp, with the Beach Boys as their backup band, as unbelievable as that sounds today. That was our 30th Show of Stars and one of our last.

By now, Jacobs had earned his chops as a program director, so the company that owned K-POI sent him to K-MEN in San Bernardino and K-MAKE in Fresno, California, stations it had just purchased, to knock some efficiency and excitement into them. In Fresno, he hit his

stride, adopting and adapting many of the K-POI promotions in a battle for ratings with Bill Drake, a young programmer on a competing station. (Rumor has it that for a Thanksgiving promotion, Ron dropped a live turkey from a helicopter, the idea being that the listener who found it would win a big prize. Ron didn't know turkeys couldn't fly, and it plummeted through someone's roof!) Ron says he got bored and, unable to decide whether to go to San Francisco or Los Angeles, returned to Honolulu and went back on the air at K-POI. That was when he and I and TR and Mel "the Moneyman" Lawrence decided to form a new entertainment company that took us into show business big-time and led to the dissolution of my long partnership with Ralph and Earl.

On April 10, 1964, the Honolulu entertainment scene took a big leap forward. No, it wasn't us, but it took the four of us along. That was when the City opened the Honolulu International Center (HIC) on Ward Avenue, a structure that Ron would compare to a flying saucer but which I always thought looked like one of Leonard's Bakery's malasada doughnuts on steroids. The Civic Auditorium would continue its operations for another 10 years, but from this time forward what was later renamed the Neal Blaisdell Center (for the longtime Republican mayor) would be the premier venue for the city's entertainment, and we, as the newly formed Arena Associates, would be in the thick of it from day one.

It wasn't easy to leave Ralph and Earl, although I had their blessings and we remained friends. In the years to come, I'd continue to work with Ralph when we used the Civic for some of our shows. Sadly, Early died just a year after we ended the partnership. He was only 49 when the bad heart that kept him out of World War Two ended his generous life. He got a grand send-off. Services were at Central Union Church, where Governor John Burns delivered the eulogy. After the funeral, Earl's brother, a master sergeant in the Army, came to me and said he had wanted to take his brother home to bury him in Mississippi, but he was afraid he wouldn't have been able to find pallbearers. After all that time, his neighbors had not forgiven him.

It's said that timing is nine-tenths of everything that works, and it certainly worked for us. Two San Francisco disc jockeys who were friends of ours, Tom Donahue and Bob Mitchell, were promoting a monster rock concert the same weekend that the HIC was to open. Our idea was to bring the same acts to Hawaii as soon as the California show was done. Donahue and Mitchell agreed to pay the talent, a travel agent gave me credit for the airfare, and we pledged the jocks in San Francisco 50 percent of whatever profits there might be.

We called it A Million Dollar Party and promoted it on K-POI around the clock. We lost two of our headliners when Lesley Gore got the measles and Chuck Berry was forbidden by his parole officer to "leave the country" because of statutory rape charges he had against him at the time. I got Chuck on the phone and said I was going to protest because Hawaii was now a state. I was going to call Senator Dan Inouye. But Chuck said no, it would only get him in more trouble with his P.O. So I called Teddy Randazzo and Ray Peterson to fill in.

Others on the bill were Bobby Rydell, Jan & Dean, Johnny Crawford, April & Nino, Paul Revere & the Raiders, Paul & Paula, the Dovells, Betty "Shoop Shoop" Everett and Bobby Freeman, plus Hawaii's bands the Telstars and the Casuals. A good friend, Hal Blaine, the top studio drummer in Hollywood, came in to lead the rhythm section, and Joe Castro, a friend going back to my days as a jazz jock, conducted the orchestra. Joe was a hell of a piano player and was for many years the companion of tobacco heiress Doris Duke. I well remember special occasions when I was invited by Joe along with some musician friends for late-night jam sessions at Shangri La, Doris Duke's fabled home at Black Point near Diamond

In 1964 A Million Dollar Party inaugurated the new Honolulu International Center, later renamed the Neal S. Blaisdell Center. Lesley Gore got the measles and Chuck Berry bowed out at the last minute due to a statutory rape charge, but teen heartthrob Johnny Crawford of TV's *The Rifleman* helped fill the bill.

Head. I especially remember one time when the guys played all night and shortly after sunrise we were all served a delicious breakfast cooked by Doris herself.

With Joe conducting the orchestra and with the exciting lineup for the show in Honolulu's first modern concert venue, we knew we were home free. The problem was that the building wasn't really ready on opening day, and we were wiring seats together to form rows at the last minute. The kids had been waiting in line for hours, and when the gates opened, there was a big rush for the toilets. Unfortunately, someone had forgotten to unlock the ladies' restrooms. It all worked out, though. And when the box office was

K-poi presents A MILLION DOLLAR PARTY

APRIL 10 ONLY ... IN PERSON:

BOBBY ★RYDELL
LESLIE ★GORE
★PAUL & PAULA
RAY ★PETERSON
PAUL ★REVERE & THE RAIDERS
and the CASUALS with the JOE CASTRO ORCHESTRA featuring HAL "Drummer Man" BLAINE

CHUCK ★BERRY
★JAN & DEAN
DIANE ★RENAY
THE ★DOVELLS
BETTY "SHOOP SHOOP" ★EVERETT
and TELSTARS

ALL SEATS $2.00
HONOLULU INT'L. CENTER ARENA
FRIDAY, APRIL 10 • 6:30 & 9:15 P.M.

counted, everybody involved was happy.

Shortly thereafter, Ron went to Hong Kong to check out a radio station in neighboring Macao and was arrested upon his return at the Honolulu airport. The charge? Possession of a minuscule amount of what the newspapers called "marihuana." The problem was, it gave the cops reason to search Ron's home, where they found more of the stuff. The story was on the front page of the papers, and our competition, KORL, really made a big deal of it. After serving 30 days and paying a $1,000 fine, Ron's radio career in Hawaii was finished. (Or so we all thought at the time.) Fortunately for him, his old Fresno nemesis, Bill Drake, was reprogramming a new station in Los Angeles, and he hired Ron to be his main man.

All this had no negative effect on Arena Associates. In fact, it made us stronger. Ron quickly turned "Boss Radio KHJ" into the number-one station in "Boss Angeles," and a year later TR landed the program director job at "The Big 610 KFRC" in San Francisco. Arena Associates found itself a major influence on pop music in Hawaii and on the West Coast. Three months later we promoted another Million Dollar Party with a couple of the same acts (Jan & Dean and Ray Peterson), plus the Beach Boys, Jimmy Clanton, the Kingsmen, the Rivingtons, Jody Miller and, "direct from London," Peter & Gordon, the first English group to appear in Hawaii. Plus a group we called the K-POI All Stars that included Hal Blaine and a young studio guitarist yet to make himself known as a vocalist, Glen Campbell. That show was a sell-out, too. At the last moment we added Screamin' Jay Hawkins, who was appearing at Jack Cione's Forbidden City nightclub to sing his hit "I Put a Spell on You." When I introduced him the spotlights went to the entrance of the Arena, and here comes Jay in a coffin with the Rivingtons as pallbearers. It was wild—and so was the audience's reaction.

My "promotion" to K-POI's general manager a couple of years later—in 1967—was a mixed blessing.

At the second Million Dollar Party, Screamin' Jay Hawkins made his entrance in a coffin with the Rivingtons as pallbearers.

Radio was always more than music, time and temperature to me. It was a special kind of communication, both in performance and in one-on-one contact with an audience. I missed talking to the listeners, the hands-on approach to radio that goes with being on the air and answering the phone. (Something that's not done much nowadays, except in talk radio, where it's a battle of neuroses and egos.) That said, being the boss gave me the opportunity to reprogram K-POI's FM station, which was then was playing elevator music and losing money, and turn it into a big success.

At the time, what came to be called "underground radio" was hardly known. This was a programming concept credited to the guy who was our partner in the first Million Dollar Party, Tom Donahue. He and Bobby Mitchell were the top deejays at KYA, which had been the number-one station in San Francisco until TR came to town and took over the market with KFRC. Shortly afterward, Donahue left KYA and soon created the new format for another Bay Area station, KSAN FM. Playing album tracks that never got programmed on AM stations sounds simple enough, but at the time it was considered radical. It wasn't only

After teen heartthrob Ricky Nelson failed to show up for an interview, we quit playing his songs on K-POI, much to the consternation of his fan club, his father and his record label. (Turns out he'd never been told about the interview in the first place.) Such was the uproar that Ricky later made it a point to stop over on his way to Australia for a terrific interview.

hits that got played, but also some of the tracks that were too long to program on what was called "Top-40 radio." Where the AM stations would play the Doors' three-minute version of "Light My Fire," Donahue played the unedited seven-minute version from the band's album. Where no AM station could find room for the Rolling Stones' 20-minute-long "Coming Home," Donahue told his jocks to play whatever they wanted. Radio was suddenly "hip" in a way that the Top 40 stations weren't thought to be. After leaving KYA, Bobby Mitchell went to work for Ron in LA and became Boss Jock Bobby Tripp on KHJ.

That's when Jesse Sartain, a bright guy still in his teens whose parents owned the Brown Derby nightclub downtown, came to me with an idea for the station's programming. He had previously suggested that Arena Associates erect a tent behind the International Marketplace on Kuhio Avenue and call it The Summer Place. This was to be a hangout for teenagers. It didn't really take off the way we'd hoped, but it started us thinking about open-ing a club in Waikiki. Now Jesse was urging me to bring "underground" FM to Honolulu.

He was young, but I told him to go for it. He got a group of guys together, and we started playing album tracks and called it "K-POI FM Sunshine." Bang! All of a sudden, I had the hottest new radio station in town. The station owners went along with me, and after KSAN, we had one of the first underground stations in the country. K-POI FM. Sunshine around the clock.

Now, FM radio was not in vogue then, and you never, ever saw it in a car radio. But they had these big eight-track cartridge decks. So we rigged them to take FM, and the first time I listened to K-POI FM in the car, on comes Country Joe & the Fish with their "Fixin' to Die Rag": "Gimme an F, gimme a U, gimme a C…" I went ballistic. What the hell was this?

Maybe I reacted the way I did because I was now station "management," and I worried more than I had when I was a jock about things like "policy" and the possible loss of our FCC license. More likely, I was still the upright, straight-ahead square that environments like my folks' and the Hocks' homes and the state of Michigan routinely turned out in the 1940s. I was in the middle of what was being called the "rock revolution," but I was in my 30s and that, according to political activist Abbie Hoffman, made me too old to trust. (On the other hand, Gerri Aquino, who helped me run the Sunshine Festival, was quoted in the *Advertiser* as saying, "K-POI FM manager Tom Moffatt is very understanding even though he's over 30 and a good businessman.") My musical tastes were well tuned and the kids loved me, and in a way I was ahead of my time with the eagle tattoo on my left arm. But at the same time, I didn't smoke grass and I never took LSD—and I wore long-sleeved aloha shirts to hide the tattoo, because of the animosity between the local population and the sailors on Hotel Street, a strip I visited for its good jazz and blues clubs.

At the same time, this was the late '60's, and however "hip" a growing part of the young population might have been, Hawaii was pretty conservative. Nobody used four-letter words on the radio. Even "damn" was extreme.

Anyway, once the FM format was up and running successfully, Jesse came to me again and said we needed to do a promotion to introduce FM Sunshine properly. He said he'd talked to the National Guard, and they were okay about letting us use the big field inside Diamond Head for a New Year's Day party. We called it the Sunshine Festival, and its focus was totally on arts and crafts and Hawaiian music and dance.

I should now introduce Mel the Moneyman properly, although the word "proper" may not be exactly right for him. He was a minority partner of Arena Associates—Ron, TR and I each had a 30-percent interest and Mel had the remaining 10—but he was no less than a major influence, as well as a classic character. He was born in Brooklyn and, after service in the Army and earning a degree in speech therapy at the University of Hawaii, he got involved with a family counseling service near the UH campus and volunteered as a subject for some LSD experiments. (It was legal then.) After that he became an instructor at a school of Scientology in the Royal Hawaiian Arcade, which is where he met TR.

When TR was made program director of KFRC, he hired Mel as his promotion director, and together they hatched a charity event called the Magic Mountain Music Festival, so called because it was held on Mt. Tamalpais in Marin County, across San Francisco's Golden Gate Bridge. This was in the spring of 1967, in the months before the "Summer of Love."

Most people think the first pop music festival was held in Monterey, California, part of what made that summer so special, but Mel's and TR's preceded it by several weeks. Police estimated attendance at the Magic Mountain Music Festival over the two days at 60,000, with a lineup of nearly two dozen bands. Many of them were from the Bay Area (Country Joe & the Fish, Steve Miller, the Grateful Dead, Jefferson Airplane, the Sons of Champlin); others were from L.A. (the Doors, the Byrds, Modern Folk Quartet, Captain Beefheart); and there was a handful of singer-songwriters as well—Tim Buckley, Tim Hardin, P.F. Sloan and Smokey Robinson.

Then came Monterey Pop, a three-day blowout in the town of the same name, known up to then as the site of a jazz festival and some of northern California's most magnificent scenery. This was the first time big record companies paid any attention, signing two relatively unknown acts, the Jimi Hendrix Experience (this is where and when he set fire to his guitar to such great effect) and Janis Joplin and her band, Big Brother and the Holding Company. Our own Mel the Moneyman was the operations manager of the festival and, in answer to his urgent request for flowers, I bought and air-shipped every orchid I could find on the Big Island.

Right after Monterey, Mel was offered another job, as operations manager of another "gathering of the tribes" in Orange County, California. (For those too young to remember, in the 1960s the so-called "hippies" were frequently identified with Native Americans—it had something to do with the founding of communes and extended lifestyle families. We had a few of those in Hawaii, especially on the outer islands.) Newspapers in Los Angeles said attendance at the outdoor mega-concert topped 100,000, and that's when Ron called me in Hawaii and suggested we do the same thing—but better—and introduce the pop festival concept to the culturally deprived East Coast.

Ron said he wanted to do it in December, but he didn't want cold weather. He said he remembered an old Connie Francis song, "Where the Boys Are," which took its name from a movie about all the college kids who spent their spring break in Florida.

That's where we're going, Ron said. Miami. 🎤

The young and hip gathered inside Diamond Head at our annual Sunshine Festivals, which featured Hawaii's music, dance, arts and crafts.

CHAPTER 9

Miami Pop

We were feeling pretty cocky at the time. A feeling we'd too soon regret.

As Arena Associates, we opened a couple of nightclubs for the kids. One was where the Hyatt Regency Waikiki is now, and we couldn't get a long lease, so we took it for the summer and called it Fat City. Mel the Moneyman pretty much ran it, and because he was born in New York, he brought in Hawaii's first egg creams. We had these young bands from around town playing in there: the Spirits, Mopptops, Undertakers, Val Richards V, Telstars and, *á la* go-go, the Fat City Dancers. There was a line around the block every night. A lot of the same bands played in our weekend nightclub on Kapiolani Boulevard facing the Ala Wai Canal, the Funny Farm. Steve Nicolet was the host, and it was a big success, too.

Our shows at the HIC continued. Pat O'Day, a disc jockey friend in Seattle, started a company called Concerts West with Tom Hulett and Terry Bassett. Pat called and said, "You want to do Three Dog Night?" We booked them, and by the time they arrived, "Joy to the World" was the number-one song not only in Hawaii, but everywhere. Chicago was coming back from Japan and they wanted to appear here, too. So we put the two together. I don't think Chicago was too happy about it, but because of the strength of their record, Three Dog Night was the closing act. We did two shows in one night—a double sell-out.

The rock festival we staged in Miami featured some of the biggest bands of the day. Opposite: We partnered with Concerts West to present the legendary Jimi Hendrix at the Waikiki Shell.

There were always lines around the block at Fat City, our Waikiki club for kids offering New York egg creams, go-go dancers and music by hot local bands like the Mopptops, the Undertakers and, above, the Spirits. The logo was drawn by the *Honolulu Advertiser's* wonderful cartoonist, Harry Lyons.

We also presented Aretha Franklin, a joint promotion between K-POI and K-POI FM. This was after her big hit, "Respect." It looked, when she came in on Monday, like we might have two sold-out shows on Friday and Saturday in the Arena. She won't fly any more, and I think it's because of the airline I brought her in on: $99 round trip. You got all the champagne you could drink because you didn't want to remember the experience. Believe it or not, it was called Pink Cloud Airlines—I used it several times myself. Anyway, I remember going to the airport to meet the plane, and Aretha and her band

and crew pretty much filled all the seats. There was this guy shouting and cursing, raising hell because one of his bags was lost, and I asked who he was. He turned out to be Aretha's brother—"the Reverend Franklin."

Aretha was staying at the Colony Surf, and the night she arrived she had a few drinks and went out in a small boat at 1 o'clock in the morning, and it tipped over. She hurt her leg. Her manager said not to worry about it. Then the day of the concert, just before the show was to start, the manager told me that the doctor had set what turned out to be a broken leg, and Aretha was in such pain she couldn't go on. The Arena was about sold out. I've never seen so many black people in one place in Hawaii at one time.

This black guy, a former UH football player, Bob Cole, was working for me, and I looked at the crowd and said to Bob, "I'm not going to go out there and tell them there's not going to be a show—you are." We said their tickets would be honored for Sunday night. Some couldn't come back and they were pissed off; they wanted their money back; and there wasn't enough cash at the box office to handle it. It wasn't close to a riot scene, but the momentum stopped and sales fell down for Saturday. When she came out in a wheelchair she did a hell of a show, but what should've been a big weekend was marginal.

We partnered with Tom Hulett and Concerts West in presenting Jimi Hendrix at the Shell for two nights. This was when he stacked his Marshall amps on each side of him and used them as monitors. He was using so much power that when the lights came up toward the end of the show, that affected the amps, and he wasn't getting the sound he wanted. We couldn't hear what he was hearing (or not hearing), but at the end of a song he came off the stage and told Tom and me, "Man, I can't continue, there's something wrong with the sound system."

The lights were on the same power line and were pulling his sound away. And we didn't know that. He'd

Aretha Franklin, the "Queen of Soul," put on a hell of a show at the HIC Arena—from a wheelchair.

already been performing for more than an hour, so we asked him to go back out and do one more song and say goodnight or something, and everybody would be happy. He said he couldn't do that to his fans, and went out and said he wasn't going to continue and everyone was invited to come back on Sunday. This was Friday, and this was mainly a military audience and a lot of them couldn't come back. The box office was closed by then and people started lighting fires around it. Tom said, and I agreed, "Let's get the hell out of here."

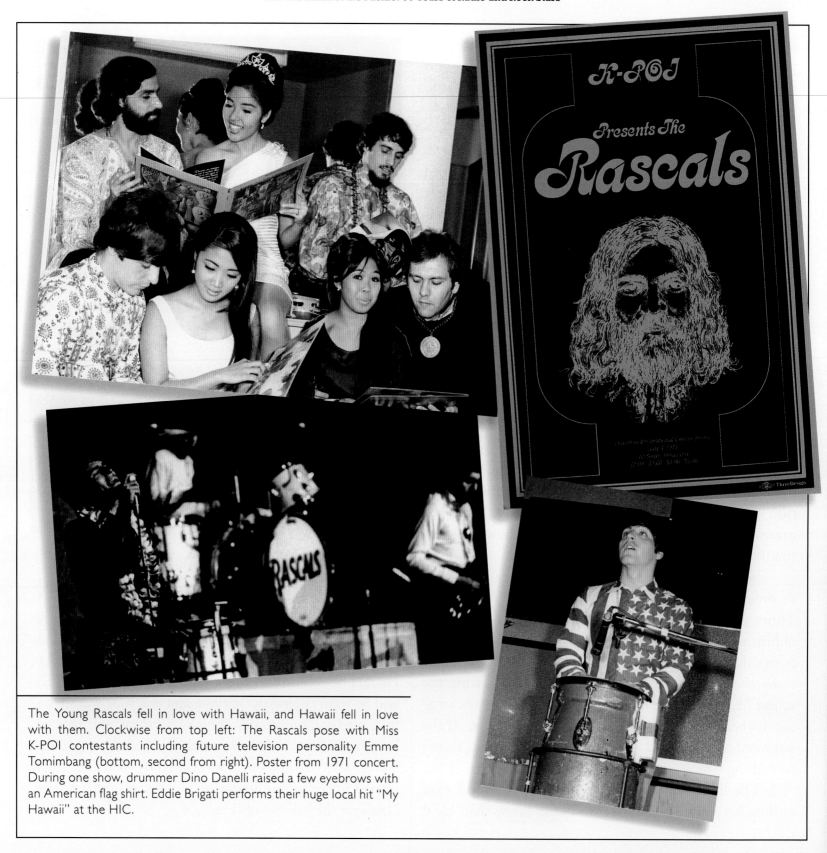

The Young Rascals fell in love with Hawaii, and Hawaii fell in love with them. Clockwise from top left: The Rascals pose with Miss K-POI contestants including future television personality Emme Tomimbang (bottom, second from right). Poster from 1971 concert. During one show, drummer Dino Danelli raised a few eyebrows with an American flag shirt. Eddie Brigati performs their huge local hit "My Hawaii" at the HIC.

The "British invasion" brought every big English group but the Beatles to Hawaii, including the Kinks (top left), the Animals (top right) and Herman's Hermits (above).

Big stars of a hit TV show, the Monkees featured an English lead singer, Davy Jones.

Those were our only real crises. Most of the concerts went off without a hitch. The so-called British invasion reached Hawaii with Peter & Gordon in 1964, but it wasn't until 1966 and 1967 that it rolled in like a tidal wave, when we presented shows by the Kinks, Herman's Hermits, Them, the Yardbirds, the Animals, the Hollies, the Who and the Rolling Stones, five skinny kids who carried in their own amplifiers and were thrilled to see that we provided free Cokes. The Byrds appeared with the Young Rascals (who by now had fallen in love with the Islands and were regular visitors), and the Grateful Dead came in for two nights at the Civic for $12,000, and even paid their own way.

Fat City, indeed.

Arena Associates was exploding. Three of its partners were programming the most popular radio stations in three markets—Honolulu, San Francisco and Los Angeles. We were staging successful concerts. With Ron and TR sending us the acts, Mel and I kept busy promoting the shows in Hawaii. It was a hell of a relationship between the four of us. We had complete trust in each other and remain close friends to this day.

Expansion seemed to be the name of the game, so we decided to get into film. Peter Gardiner had created a 15-minute-long documentary of TR's Magic Mountain Music Festival, and when John Rath, a retired Air Force colonel who was KFRC's new general manager, arrived, TR showed him the film. He was horror-stricken: "My God, there are people with long hair in these pictures!" By now, Peter was doing some filming for Jacobs with a cameraman named Allen Daviau, and together they approached TR with an idea about starting a promotion film business to create what would become some of the industry's first "music videos." TR quit KFRC "to avoid," as he put it, "the wrath of Rath," and organized Charlatan Productions.

At the same time, and under the Arena Associates umbrella, we also launched The Entertainment Company, a joint venture with Drake-Chenault (Drake being Jacobs's old nemesis in Fresno whose new company was now programming KHJ, KFRC and several other stations nationwide), to promote concerts in the Drake-Chenault radio markets.

All of this was going on at the same time. The clubs in Waikiki, concerts all over Hawaii, the new film company and on top of all this, we had our individual radio careers. It seemed we could do no wrong. We were growing like Topsy and having fun.

Then, between Christmas and the end of 1968—it was December 30, actually, my birthday—on a racetrack in Hallendale, Florida, not too far from Miami, we learned a little about humility.

As soon as we had calculated the budget for what we called the Miami Pop Festival, Drake-Chenault backed out of The Entertainment Company, deciding, I guess, that we were out of our cotton-pickin' minds. We might have been successful, but we didn't have a huge bank account. We needed an angel, and fast. This is when we met Tom Driscoll, whose family controlled the strawberry business in California, which was worth a lot more than you might think. He was a rocker at heart, and wanted to get into the business—and he did so by writing a check for $285,000 to pay for the festival's production, talent and marketing. I'm not making light of Driscoll's commitment. It went deeper than some of us might have

Hailing from the Pacific Northwest, Paul Revere & the Raiders weren't really British, but they made as big an impact on Island music lovers.

thought at the time, and, in the years following, he became a valued partner—not just because of his cash flow.

Advertisements were already running from coast to coast, offering, not so humbly, "A Thousand Wonders and a Three Day Collage of Beautiful Music." We promised "strolling entertainers and musicians at a meditation grove" and, so help me, "sporadic runnings, jumpings and crawlings of the 1968 invitational walking catfish derby in the paddock." It's hard to believe today that we'd say such things. Did you ever wear flowers in your hair? I didn't.

As all this was being masterminded in L.A., and Jesse Sartain was handling the last-minute stuff for the first K-POI FM Sunshine Crater Festival, I went to Europe to meet Sweetie, where she was dancing with a promotional group from Hawaii. Then we flew back to the States a week before the festival in Miami began, stopping in New

Echoes of Shea Stadium

by Sid Bernstein

Strawberry magnate Tom Driscoll (left) was our angel at Miami Pop.

I first met Tom Moffatt on August 26, 1966, when I arrived with the Rascals for their debut concert in Hawaii. Accompanying me on that trip was my lovely wife, Gerri, and our first-born, Adam, who was just a baby then. I was managing the Rascals, and this was the first of many shows and wonderful visits to Hawaii. Tom introduced me to the sugary malasadas at Leonard's Bakery in Honolulu; when he visited us later on the East Coast, I returned the favor by introducing him to a real New York egg-cream soda.

Starting with that very first concert, Tom and I became great friends; today I think of him as a brother.

Just days before that first trip to the Islands, I had presented the Beatles at Shea Stadium—a landmark event that many people consider one of the greatest and wildest shows ever. But even with all that hysteria ringing in my ears, I was unprepared for the mass excitement that greeted us when we landed in Hawaii with the Rascals a few days later—thanks to Tom, Bob "the Beard" Lowrie and the other POI Boys. The Rascals played that first Hawaii show at the K-POI Teen Fair in the HIC Exhibition Hall, and it was truly unforgettable.

The Rascals' thunderous reception in Hawaii rivaled that of the Beatles at Shea Stadium.

York. There, my dear friend Judy Tannen told me that Bobby Darin wanted to be added to the Miami lineup. I knew Bobby. I was a big fan. He was a big star when I introduced him at the Civic Auditorium, but it was mostly rock and roll, "Splish Splash" and all that. Then he came out with this big-band album that had "Beyond the Sea" and "Mack the Knife." I sent him a telegram congratulating him. But I had to tell Judy no. I said, we can't do it; the show's full. I felt bad about that. I was the president of the company and all, but we just couldn't fit him in.

We had booked more than 30 acts. From the early days, we had Chuck Berry and from Nashville, Flatt & Scruggs. Three Dog Night signed up to play all three days. James Cotton, John Mayall and Paul Butterfield came in with the blues. In addition, we had Booker T. & the M.G.'s, Ian & Sylvia, Buffy Sainte Marie, Country Joe & the Fish, the Grateful Dead, Iron Butterfly, Jose Feliciano (whose cover of the Doors hit "Light My Fire" was a current smash), Fleetwood Mac, Procol Harum, Marvin Gaye (who also had a big record at the time, "I Heard It through the Grapevine"), Steppenwolf and the Turtles.

Three Dog Night, which played all three days at Miami Pop, later performed in the HIC Arena (above).

Jacobs and Driscoll and TR and Mel the Moneyman were already in Miami when I arrived. We also had the "dean" of rock lighting, Chip Monck, who had worked in Bill Graham's Fillmore Auditorium and at Monterey. He came up with a plan to use two stages for non-stop entertainment, one in front of the 14,500-seat grandstand to be called the "Flower Stage," the other built out of foam in an open field, shaped like the Waikiki Shell and called the "Flying Stage."

When I arrived, I noticed that we weren't getting sales in Florida and other southern states. I thought I knew what the problem was. We had both blacks and whites on the show, and the South wasn't ready for that. Segregation had been illegal for several years, but it was clear to me that the South hadn't yet fully accepted the letter of the law. Bottom line: we were in trouble again, and this time, Driscoll couldn't help. So it was tense, even after the music began.

Ron and I decided to go have a bite to eat after the first show. There was this bar-restaurant across the street from the racetrack. Our lawyer was with us, and after we ate, they wouldn't accept his credit card. Jacobs got furious and said it was because he and the lawyer looked Jewish and the restaurant didn't want us bringing in all these Jewish people. We had this bag full of money in the back of the car to start the next day's ticket sales, so Jacobs got the bag and whopped it down on the counter and started pulling out money. I really thought we were going to get mugged on our way back when we left.

Sweetie went home and I stayed in Miami. It was very successful musically, and the *New York Times* called it "a monument to pop, an excellent model for future events of this kind." One night we had someone check the cars in the parking lot, and if we didn't have much regional support, we noticed that there were license plates from every state in the country.

But I knew we had lost money. Big time. It was the end of the year, and I was expected back in Honolulu for the first day of 1969, when the Sunshine Festival in Diamond Head Crater would kick off a day of music and arts and crafts. My plane to L.A. was late, so I missed my connecting flight and spent my New Year's Eve with friends there. Next day when I got on the plane, I knew one of the stewards and he started bringing me drinks, so when I got to Honolulu I wasn't in any shape to go to Diamond Head. I said the hell with it and went home. I didn't even go to Sad Sam's annual New Year's Day party, the first one I'd missed in years.

Weeks later, we learned that we'd taken in more than $350,000, but we'd spent more than $500,000. Michael Lang, a young kid who loved our festival, said he thought we should try again, maybe go to New York. Driscoll, Rounds, Jacobs and I passed, but Michael took Mel the Moneyman and Chip Monck with him. Again, Mel was named director of operations, and he selected the final site: acreage belonging to a dairy farmer, Max Yasgur, in Bethel, New York.

They called it Woodstock. 🎤

Aloha to the Rolling Stones
by Mel "the Moneyman" Lawrence

Back in the 1960s, the great Tom Moffatt and I were partners, producing scores of shows under the Arena Productions banner. We were the top promoters in the Islands. We did everyone, from the Beach Boys to the Kinks to the Rascals to the Monkees to the Rolling Stones. I was "Mel the Moneyman," coming on the scene after Ron Jacobs and Tom Rounds left to be program directors at KHJ (Los Angeles) and KFRC (San Francisco), respectively. Tom was the emcee and promotion maven, and I was the nuts-and-bolts line production guy. Tom taught me everything I know about promotion, and we had a million laughs and adventures.

"Moneyman!" Tom would always address me like that, in a friendly bark. He had so many great axioms that I still use today. For example, when I'd suggest some far-out group for a show, Tom would remind me, "Know your market, Moneyman!" In promoting these shows, we spent countless hours creating radio spots. Back in those days, that involved splicing together audiotape, and I can still see Uncle Tom with tape draped around his neck, looking for that "perfect" nuance.

Miami Pop was a great steppingstone for Mel the Moneyman.

Tom was a great friend, too. He and Sweetie would have me over at their house a lot (especially if I'd had a break-up with a wife or girlfriend). Sometimes I'd be staying in the upstairs rooms with Tommy Sands, Arthur Thurston from Australia, Morgan Montague from San Francisco, Uncle Frank Day from Los Angeles or a Tahitian dancer who was a friend of Sweetie's. Tom and I had a ritual of sorts: having a martini at Elliott's Chuckwagon (across the street from the HIC) after a sold-out show. Come to think of it, practically every one was sold out! And speaking of drinking: we'd also gather after Blaisdell Arena fight nights at Sad Sam's on Hotel Street with Sad Sam Ichinose, Tom's adopted godfather, offering his famous toast to the battered warriors. Then we'd drive home up Nuuanu Avenue, arguing over who could drink the other one under the table. Of course, Uncle Tom was always the designated driver.

One of my favorite stories is when we first brought the Rolling Stones to Hawaii, in 1966. It was the last stop on their tour, and the local kids went wild over it. I thought the show was going to be a piece of cake, because I had gone to high school with Jerry Brandt, the band's agent at the William Morris Agency. Well, there were a few twists and turns: when the Stones found out that the show was sold out, they lobbied for more money, which we couldn't really afford. There was some talk about canceling the show if we couldn't reach an agreement. When Jerry came to me with the problem, I got Ron Jacobs on the phone. Ron was then running the most powerful radio station in the country, KHJ, and he reminded Jerry that listeners might hear a lot less of the Stones on KHJ if they cancelled the show. So things ended up just fine. The Stones got their fee per their contract, and the kids got their show. They only played for 27 minutes, but it was still a great performance and everyone left the Arena happy.

Now, here's where things got really crazy. After the show, the Stones returned to the Kahala Hilton and found out that there was a domestic airline strike, so they couldn't get back to the West Coast. Tom asked me to entertain the group during their extended stay. Little did I know that I'd be securing large quantities of Maui Wowee, taking the boys shopping and sailing, and getting besieged by girls who wanted to meet the band.

Now, this sounds like fun, but it soon got pretty exhausting. After three days, Tom suggested that if they really wanted to get out of Hawaii, they should get on a flight to Japan, where they could then fly back to the West Coast, as foreign carriers were not involved in the strike. Tom said it jokingly, but the next day, the band boarded a flight to Japan. I think they ended up spending their entire fee by the time they left. I took them to the airport and happily bid "Aloha" to the Rolling Stones.

Mick Jagger at the HIC Arena, 1966: Stones stranded by strike.

CHAPTER 10

The Rock Explosion

Tom Driscoll seemed relatively unaffected by Miami. I guess, for him, it was like losing a strawberry crop because of the weather—next year he could be on top again. It wasn't like that for us. We were devastated. We'd lost our nest egg. With earlier profits, we'd bought some property on Kauai as an investment, a couple of homes above Pearl City, a nice piece of land in Kona, a healthy amount of IBM stock, and we lost all of that. We pretty much lost everything.

But Driscoll had had such a good time that he was now up for anything, and we started still another company, called Watermark, the purpose of which was to put on more shows, especially pop festivals. I remember going to Monterey, where his family business was based, and flying around in a small plane with him looking for another festival site. It didn't pan out, though. Except for my K-POI FM Sunshine Festivals in Diamond Head Crater, we put festivals on the shelf.

There were another couple of things that hurt around that time. On the way to a meeting with the Minneapolis company that owned K-POI, Sweetie and I went on vacation for about 10 days to the Virgin Islands, Puerto Rico,

Elton John made his first appearance at the HIC (Blaisdell) Arena with Kiki Dee in '71 and returned on October 18, 1972, before a sell-out crowd. Opposite: Fronted by Jagger in a jumpsuit, the Rolling Stones made their second Hawaii appearance at the Arena in 1973.

Guitar great Eric Clapton rocked the Arena with Hawaii's own
Yvonne Elliman as one of his back-up singers.

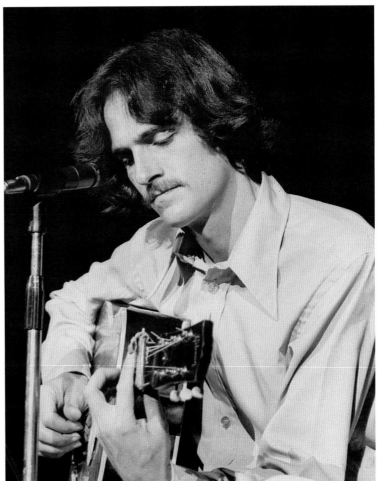

The dynamic duo of Carole King and James Taylor shared the Arena stage in 1971 when Carole debuted her brand-new album, *Tapestry*.

Haiti and Jamaica. While I was on this trip, Colonel Parker was organizing a tour for Elvis, who had gone to Vegas and was a smash in one of the big showrooms. Now he was going back on the road for the first time in more than 10 years, and we were offered the first date in Los Angeles. Aside from the huge guarantee the Colonel was asking for, it didn't look that profitable, and we had to pass. Jerry Weintraub, along with Tom Hulett, got Elvis, and not long after that they were promoting a lot of

Elvis' shows. I was sorry we hadn't been able to promote Elvis again.

A greater hurt was to come. Charlatan had been doing very well: in a short time Peter Gardiner and Tom Rounds, along with Allen Daviau, had produced over 40 of what would today be called music videos. They *were* the first music videos, long before MTV. Only they were called "mini flicks" by the *Hollywood Reporter* because they were on film. Copies were sent to over 150 TV stations across the country. Charlatan shot Aretha Franklin singing the Rascals' song "Groovin'," and for Jimi Hendrix we

Led Zeppelin at the Civic Auditorium in '71: some didn't believe a band this big would play the Civic.

La Cienega Boulevard in Los Angeles. Pretty soon we created *American Top 40* with Casey Kasem, a weekly countdown show based on *Billboard* magazine's Hot 100, which went on to become the world's best distributed and most popular of such shows. The others wanted me to join them in L.A., since I was the president of Arena Associates, but I didn't want to leave Hawaii. I'd fly in for meetings, hang around for a while and come home again to focus my energy on the concerts.

In Hawaii, each year's promotions got bigger and more numerous. From 1964, when the Beatles started the British invasion, one new music scene after another developed, from London to Detroit to San Francisco to Los Angeles, each producing dozens of new acts, as older scenes in New York and Nashville were rejuvenated. The music business was exploding. Top 40 radio, as defined by Bill Drake and Ron Jacobs in southern California, had swept across the country, and there were network television shows like *Shindig* and *Hullaballoo* promoting the same music. Warehouses were turned into concert halls in dozens of cities, and small clubs opened everywhere. All of this came together

filmed "Purple Haze" in Rudolph Valentino's old home in Hollywood. We got the Who in a warehouse somewhere, the Cowsills from a helicopter in Rhode Island and Eric Burdon on the Golden Gate Bridge in San Francisco. Others we shot included Steppenwolf, the Rascals, Paul Revere & the Raiders, Connie Francis and Rick Nelson. I think our budget was $2,000 or $3,000 for each. Peter and Allen also created the special effects for the Peter Fonda-Susan Strasberg-Bruce Dern movie *The Trip*, which was written by Jack Nicholson.

But in 1968, Peter died. That was a really big blow. It also led to the dissolution of Charlatan Productions. (Allen Daviau would later go on to become the cinematographer for many top Hollywood films, including *E.T.*, *Bugsy*, *The Color Purple* and *Van Helsing*.)

By now, Jacobs had produced a groundbreaking 48-hour-long history of rock and roll that was broadcast on KHJ and other RKO stations and was then syndicated around the world. We coaxed him into leaving KHJ to produce other shows for Watermark. The offices and a small studio were upstairs over a dry cleaner's shop on

The Civic meets the wrecking ball: during its 40-year run, the historic facility hosted circuses, wrestling matches and entertainers from Meadowlark Lemon to Liberace.

The Day the Civic Died

by Ron Jacobs

It was 1974 and I was vacationing back home, on leave from the southern California rock-and-roll radio station wars. Uncle Tom Moffatt had just departed K-POI to start his solo impresario career. He wanted to raid the condemned Civic Auditorium (opposite, bottom) for its anthropological treasures. The plan was to do this just before the wrecking crew arrived to demolish the arena.

A phone call from Uncle Tom to his buddy K.K. Chang, puller of strings, and it was all set. "Meet me at the Civic tomorrow morning, Ronny," said Uncle Tom, and the mission was on.

I pulled into the parking lot just in time to see a mournful Velasco, slippers slapping, walking towards the front of the building. He was about to open its doors for the last time.

Velasco, the custodian, had been there forever. He was at the Civic when, as a wide-eyed 11-year-old, I sold programs at the wrestling matches. He didn't remember me, of course, but in those days my fellow program hawkers and I were terrified of him. He scared us more than the wrestlers did, acting like he owned the building, which of course he didn't. We were sure Velasco lived in the Civic, though we didn't know exactly where.

Bobby Krewson, beach boy to the stars, drove up in his station wagon with Uncle Tom riding shotgun. They looked like crazed expeditionaries approaching Pharaoh's tomb.

A funereal Velasco reluctantly unlocked the main front doors. Uncle Tom, Bobby and I pushed our way in like teenyboppers at a Fabian concert.

Velasco padded about in the dark, finally turning on some work lights. The main floor, with its basketball markings, was torn up, a tossed wooden salad. In the gloom I could see Ronnie Kekuda triggering the McKinley Tigers' fast break. I could hear Meadowlark Lemon and the Harlem Globetrotters whistling and dribbling. I could feel the masonite Roller Derby track tremble as John "Porky" Parker rumbled by in hot pursuit of Freddie Noa, the Flyin' Hawaiian.

"I got the Lippy Espinda clock! Dibs on the clock! Bring the tools, Bobby."

Uncle Tom was claiming the Civic's huge neon clock, which advertised the town's most famous service station. Before I could even make a move, Moffatt and Krewson were removing the seats from Section 7. And 8. And 9. I shuddered and headed for the box office. I couldn't compete with those scavengers!

The Civic box office. I thought of Gentleman Al Karasick and his pinochle-playing cronies, their cigar smoke heavy in the air. Someone had already ransacked the file cabinets. Picking through a mound of papers, I struck a vein of cancelled checks. Payday for Curtis "The Bull" Iaukea! A championship purse for Lucky Simunovich! Through the open door, I could hear Krewson crowbarring his way into something.

Chuck Berry was chanting, "Up in the morning and off to school." Bo Diddly was letting fly on "The Jupiter Thunderbird," his square guitar. Uncle Tom was yelling, "Lemme the hammer, Bobby."

Feeling like a cat burglar, I pulled open the cashier's drawer. Empty except for a cigar box crammed with every rubber stamp ever used at the Civic Auditorium. Stamps saying *General Admission* and *C.O.D.* and *Servicemen Only* and *Pro Tennis* and *Complimentary*. I smugly carried my treasure back into the arena, where Krewson had backed his wagon through the rear exit. He and Moffatt were loading in a pair of ancient red-enameled boxing stools. I could see Dado Marino feinting, Bobo Olson pummeling. It was a sad moment. What to say to the grieving Velasco?

Then I spotted two team benches from the Roller Derby and, with a straight face, convinced Uncle Tom of their great historic value. He and Krewson shifted their hoard around in the wagon, making room for the battered red artifacts. When would they discover that under each bench was a 20-year collection of spent chewing gum, stuck there by berserk Roller Derby skaters? A gross, gummy, pockmarked landscape. A chewy, gooey typography of tumult.

I bade a final farewell to the anguished Velasco, as he bravely awaited the wrecking ball. Then I quickly said goodbye to Uncle Tom and Bobby.

Hopefully I would be back on the mainland before Uncle Tom checked out the bottom of his benches.

The Doobie Brothers

America

to create a network of promoters that stretched from coast to coast, and across the Atlantic and Pacific as well, as hundreds of bands went on the road.

Arena Associates might have gotten out of the festival business, but otherwise we were in the middle of all this. From Miami onwards for us, each year got bigger and better, as Hawaii became an increasingly popular concert venue, with bands stopping on their way to or from Japan and Australia or making it the place where they ended a tour, giving them the opportunity for a holiday on the beach.

By now, the Young Rascals had become regular visitors to the Islands, and we brought Jimi Hendrix back to play the HIC. Next year came Vanilla Fudge, Jimi again, Creedence Clearwater Revival, Donovan and Crosby, Stills & Nash. Jimi returned still another time in 1970, along with Dionne Warwicke, Led Zeppelin, and Santana twice, playing first with Country Joe & the Fish and the next time with Elvin Bishop. (No, I did

Creedence Clearwater Revival

not tell Country Joe how I reacted to "Fixin' to Die Rag" the first time I heard it on my FM station.) In 1971, James Taylor appeared twice, the first time with Carole King. Elton John played his first of many Hawaii shows. So did Neil Diamond, Guess Who and Grand Funk Railroad.

A year after that, we booked the HIC for the Beach Boys, the Carpenters, Rare Earth with Climax and, for more return visits, Santana and Elton John. Canned Heat and Deep Purple with Buddy Miles went into the Civic. The Doobie Brothers appeared in 1973 with Tower of Power, the Spinners with Dr. John, Ray Charles and, making her first hometown appearance since becoming a big star on the mainland, Radford High School's Bette Midler. We put her in the HIC Concert Hall. Barry Manilow was her pianist, and when her mother came to the show, she cut out all her profanity. I saw her a year later in Vegas *with* the profanity, and I didn't think she needed that. She was much, much better in Honolulu.

The following year was the best and busiest yet. My friend Lou Adler (who

Tower of Power

The Rolling Stones

had come to Hawaii with Jan & Dean and then with the Mamas & the Papas) talked me into bringing Cheech Marin and Tommy Chong to Honolulu for one of the first shows of 1974. I wasn't sure how their hip kind of humor would go over. So I asked Lou if they'd do a couple of bits for me to run on the radio to promote the show. In one, they played a man and a wife in Waikiki, and the guy says, "Martha, what're we gonna do now; we been in Hawaii four days and if I see another luau I'm gonna puke!" Then they said, "Well, there's a show at the Shell—Cheech & Chong!" They even mispronounced their own names. It was classic. They were incredible. They were as far off the wall in what they were doing as Bob & Ray were in what they did back when I was starting out in radio. With one big difference. With Cheech & Chong, half the audience was as stoned as they were.

They did so well in the Shell, I brought them back again at the end of the year and put them in the Concert Hall, and in between we had the Eagles and Linda Ronstadt, the Moody Blues, Joe Cocker, Steely Dan with Jesse Colin Young, Cat Stevens (the same night we had War; both sold

Grand Funk Railroad

out), and
Bonnie Raitt with Jackson Browne. Back again were Elton John and the Doobies, this time with Mountain.

For some of the acts, we rented the Otani mansion on Diamond Head Road. This was a private home near the Diamond Head Lighthouse that I put Sonny and Cher and the Monkees in, and then Jimi Hendrix and the Rascals. It had plenty of rooms, it had privacy, and the view—if you looked hard enough you could see all the way to Maui. Jefferson Airplane got busted for grass in that house. Led Zeppelin liked it so much that one time when they were coming back from somewhere, they wanted to stay there again and offered themselves at a bargain rate. The Blaisdell wasn't available, so we put them in the Civic Auditorium.

Nobody had done this before, renting a private mansion for a band, and some people thought I was being extravagant. It wasn't true. Ten hotel rooms for a band and road crew cost me between $400 and $500, and I got the Otani place for $100 a day. The only problem was sorting out the

Cheech & Chong at the Waikiki Shell: their hip and hilarious radio spots helped sell lots of tickets to two shows in the same year.

The funny thing was, the show didn't sell out. Maybe it was too soon for them to come back to Hawaii, or maybe people thought it was a bogus group, because they didn't believe a band that big would play the Civic. They were the hottest group in the world, and we paid them peanuts and still lost money.

Many of our acts stayed in hotels. When Herman's Hermits were passing through Honolulu, they were one of the hottest English groups going, and when they arrived at the Kahala Hilton, the reservations were screwed up and they didn't have rooms. Their manager, Harvey Lisberg, called me, said he had 15 kids with him and they were tired. They'd done an Asian tour and Australia, and this was a rest stop on the way back to the mainland.

It was Sunday and I was on the air, so I asked my news director to call every hotel on Oahu if he had to, but everything was overbooked. As he made his calls, I remembered the first time Peter Noone (Herman's real name) and his band came to the Islands, in 1965, when Elvis was filming *Paradise, Hawaiian Style* at the Polynesian Cultural Center. Peter had been an actor on England's most popular daytime soap opera, *Coronation Street*, so he was a seasoned performer and

phone bills when they came in afterwards, though of course the talent agencies always paid them. (We paid the agencies and the agencies, after deductions, paid the acts.)

Tom Hulett and I were like roadies for Led Zeppelin when they came back to play the Civic. We were a little embarrassed about putting them in such a small place. We made sure the sound was set up, and we went to this little superette around the corner—it's still there—and bought three or four cases of Coca Cola, because there was no air conditioning at the Civic and it was hot.

So the band came in and asked, "Where's the coke?" I proudly led them to the dressing room and showed them the chilled-down Coke—which of course was not what they were looking for.

more sophisticated than "Henry the VIII" and some of his other hits might indicate. When he said the biggest thing that could happen in his lifetime would be to meet Elvis, I knew exactly what to do. The Colonel always liked to have visiting stars come to the set, so when I called, he said, "Yes, sir! Bring him on over. We'll be filming at the Polynesian Cultural Center." When we got there, he had a letter ready welcoming Herman's Hermits to Hawaii on behalf of Elvis and the Colonel, typed on the Colonel's stationery.

In this way, Peter and I became friends. So when my news guy failed to find hotel rooms, again I knew what to do. Sweetie was touring with Emma Veary—where else? In Scotland, not far from Peter's hometown—and I had my big house sitting empty, so I told Harvey that as soon as I got off the air they could follow me home. They stayed there for two days. They couldn't walk around the neighborhood, because if word got out, it'd be a disaster. They stayed in the house and listened to records from my collection. I think they enjoyed being out of a hotel room for the first time in weeks.

Another time when I was on the air, the newsman said the Beatles' manager, Brian Epstein, was calling. This was about 6:30 in the morning. He wanted to know how I thought the group would do in Hawaii. I said I thought they'd do fantastic. Then Brian died, and it never came to

Local girl Bette Midler made her only hometown appearance in the HIC Concert Hall in 1973, with Barry Manilow backing her on piano.

Sitar master Ravi Shankar brought his special brand of world music to the HIC Concert Hall in 1968. Thirty-seven years later, I presented his daughter, Norah Jones, next door in the Arena.

Drummer Buddy Miles (opposite) joined Carlos Santana at a Sunshine Festival. (That's me wearing the muttonchops.) Following pages: The Sunshine Festivals were huge draws inside Diamond Head Crater.

be. But I did get to meet three of the Beatles, briefly.

The first were John and George, who came to the Islands with their wives on holiday. I think they thought Hawaii was out in the middle of nowhere and they could come and have a nice, quiet vacation. I sent one of our jocks, Steve Nicolet, to the Royal Hawaiian Hotel, where they and their entourage had rooms. There, because of Steve's long hair, hotel security assumed he was with the Beatles and waved him through, and he covered the whole thing for us.

A local PR company was handling their visit, and they suggested John and George be taken to Kailua Beach. Word got out, and there was practically a riot. Pan American's PR guy, Bill Bachran, who was a friend, told me they were leaving for Tahiti and said he'd get me onto the tarmac at the airport; bring a tape recorder. When Bill and I got to the plane, the two of them were just standing there. I guess their wives had already boarded. I said, "How do you like Hawaii?" John got a sort of smile on his face and George gave me a nasty look and said, "How would you feel if everywhere you went, somebody stuck one of those in your face?" That was all I got. Later, the Associated Press in Papeete reported that when the two couples arrived, nobody knew who they were and didn't care, and they had no car to get from the airport. So they finally got what they wanted, in spades. I think that's one of the reasons they didn't play Hawaii—because they got hassled. I think that if they'd been taken to a beach more isolated than Kailua, they'd have found the Hawaii they were looking for.

With the Colonel looking on, I interview Elvis as he arrives in Honolulu for *Aloha from Hawaii*, the HIC Arena concert broadcast around the world by satellite (right), which reached the biggest TV audience in history.

Ringo came later with Brian Epstein. I got a call from my friend Morgan Montague in San Francisco, who told me that Ringo was aboard a flight to Australia and in the care of another buddy, Art Thurston, the plane's chief steward. The plane had to stop in Hawaii to refuel, and on the way Art was going to prime Ringo on who I was and the importance of his not talking to anyone else.

So there were thousands of people waiting at the airport when the plane came in, and other radio stations were each saying they were going to have the only interview. But the only one out there, inside Customs, with a microphone, was me. The plane was on the ground for about 45 minutes, and I got a pretty good interview—which of course was aired shortly thereafter on K-POI.

At the time, Arena Associates and K-POI promotions were one and the same. Everything I did would be on K-POI. The station would promote the shows, and when we ran an ad, K-POI's name was on it and on the tickets and on the stage and so on. It was good for everybody. But when K-POI was sold a second time, after 15 years, I left. I felt like I was getting a divorce.

We'd done some significant things in that "marriage." Not only had we introduced a new programming format to Hawaii—rock and roll, 24 hours a day—we'd built a cast of characters that people are still talking about more than two generations later. I was the first person to hire a female disc jockey, Roberta Wong. She did the news, too, which made her the first female newscaster in the Islands.

I helped Hermits singer Peter Noone fulfill a lifelong dream by introducing him to Elvis Presley, who was in the Islands filming *Paradise, Hawaiian Style*.

At Sears, my long-time trusted assistant Liz Hudson presents leis to singer Danny Couch as he promotes a new album release.

There were women's shows and women doing shopping shows, but it was unheard of to put a woman into news or rock and roll. K-POI gave me that freedom. We also introduced K-POI FM Sunshine radio, and I did Hawaii's first AM-FM simulcast. That's quite common now, but then it was unheard of.

But things were changing that were beyond my control. One of the reasons the station was so powerful was because we had this terrific ground system, where underground lines went out from the tower like a spider's legs, and as construction around our building cut the lines, and building after building went up, we lost power. Then, when the station was sold, and I didn't think the new owners and I could work together, I took off my POI Boy hat and asked Liz Hudson if she'd like to leave with me.

She'd had been working at the HIC box office, and I'd offered her a job a few months after I was made general manager. And now, with Liz's help, in 1974 I became a full-time promoter. Liz was born in the UK and had worked for promoter Harry Miller in New Zealand and Australia before coming to Hawaii. She stayed with me until she died. I still have a picture of her on my desk, hugging the diminutive piano great Erroll Garner—which reminds me of a funny story. Often musicians put "riders" in their contracts, meaning something has to be provided for them when they perform—special food, drinks, whatever. Erroll's rider was simple: three phonebooks, so he could reach the piano keys! Liz made sure he had those phone books.

I have been fortunate to have two outstanding assistants since I became a fulltime promoter, Liz and, now, Hawaii-born Barbara Hallberg Saito, who after 25 years is my right hand—or maybe both! 🎤

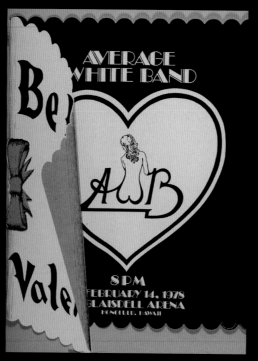

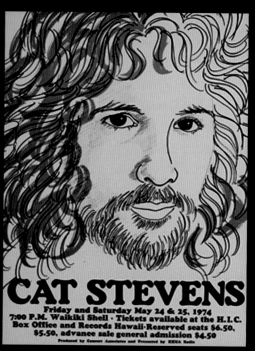

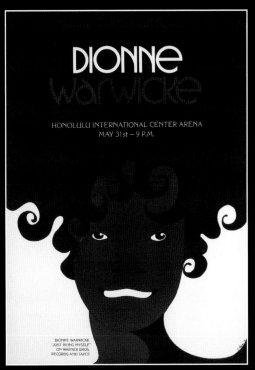

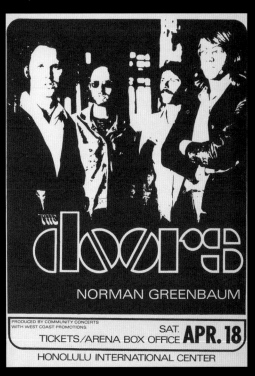

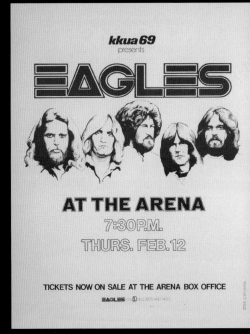

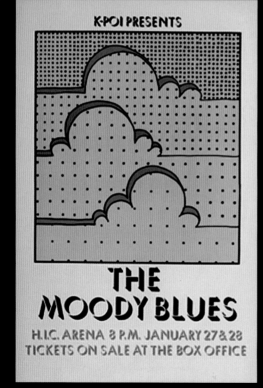

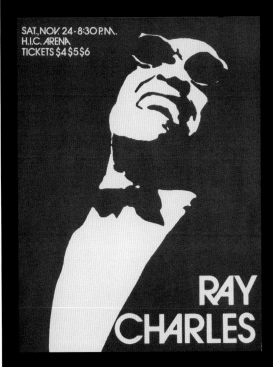

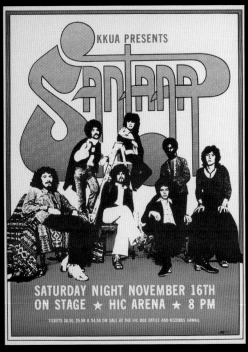

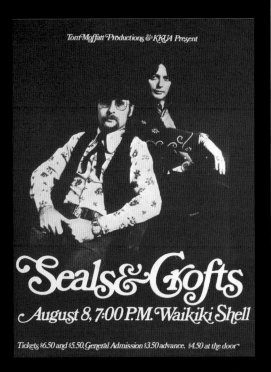

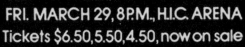

CHAPTER 11

The Hawaiian Renaissance

By the time I left K-POI, a homegrown revolution was brewing. I didn't know it at the time—nobody did—but soon much of Hawaii's culture would do something it hadn't done in such numbers since the Islands were annexed by the United States and Queen Kapiolani was put under house arrest.

It got up and danced.

Amazingly, I found myself in the middle of it.

This was a period that would extend into the 1980s and beyond, when the Hawaiian population rediscovered its "roots and rights" in a way somewhat reminiscent of what happened 15 years earlier on the mainland when African Americans did the same thing. The music, here as there, was a big part of it.

In fact, it wasn't a single river of musical change, but two. One was characterized by a revival of the traditional, where Gabby Pahinui and Aunty Genoa Keawe and the Sons of Hawaii and the Kahauanu Lake Trio and others of their generation found themselves in demand in both nightclubs and recording studios. The Merrie Monarch Festival in Hilo stopped being a little-publicized Big Island tourist event and became the focus of a statewide flowering of the ancient hula; even the men started dancing again.

At the same time, what came to be called "contemporary Hawaiian music" emerged, and before long names like Olomana, C&K (Cecilio Rodriguez and Henry Kapono Kaaihui), Sunday Manoa (which split into the Brothers

The first album I produced, *Honolulu City Lights*, is still top ranked in the Islands. Opposite: Gabby "Pops" Pahinui, performing here at a Diamond Head Crater Festival, led the Hawaiian music renaissance.

Cazimero and the Peter Moon Band), Kalapana, Country Comfort and Keola & Kapono Beamer were finding success as well. The music they played was a blend: some of the lyrics were Hawaiian, more were English; some took the form of "protest" songs; some used traditional instrumentation, most did not. Where earlier performers

It was a packed house when Cecilio & Kapono played the Waikiki Shell in the summer of '74 (right), with a little-known group called Kalapana as the opening act. The next time we booked them together, it was in Aloha Stadium (far right) before more than 20,000 people—an amazing turnout for a couple of local groups.

took Alfred Apaka and Bill Lincoln and Johnny Almeida and other older artists as role models, this new generation had grown up listening to the Beatles and Bob Dylan.

When I came to the Islands, it was pretty much "*hapa-haole*" music, not traditional Hawaiian. "Waikiki," "Lovely Hula Hands," "Beyond the Reef," "Little Grass Shack," "Keep Your Eyes on the Hands." That was pretty much the music. Tony Todaro, who wrote that last song, was publishing a book on Hawaiian entertainers, and he would not recognize the young groups. His book was pretty much devoted to artists who performed traditional and hapa-haole songs, and to some outstanding dancers. There's a full-page picture of Sweetie in there. I told him a whole new thing was happening, but he didn't recognize that.

Now the young people finally had their own music. Dick Jensen, under the name of Lance Curtis, had recorded a rock version of "Leahi." The Royal Drifters recorded rock songs about Hawaii, "S'why Hard" and "Da Kine." I came out with that campy rock version of "Beyond the Reef." All this was happening starting in 1957, 1958, and was featured in the Show of Stars. And in the 1970s we got the writers and musicians who grew up with hapa-haole music and rock and roll, and all that came together.

C&K had been singing at the Rainbow Villa right around the corner from K-POI, but with my crazy schedule I'd never seen them perform there. Bill Thompson, their manager, called and said they were getting ready to record an album for Columbia records and were rehearsing for it and performing in Vail, Colorado. They wanted to do a concert in Hawaii. Bill said, "Why don't you come over and see them?" So I flew to Vail, and I knew the players who were going to be on the album; they were, like, James Taylor's rhythm section. I liked what I heard, and we did a show in the spring at the Shell. C&K weren't that well known then, but they got a respectable crowd, about 4,000 people.

Country Comfort: the challenges of managing the hard-partying boys from Waimanalo soon got me out of the management business.

When the album was to be released, I booked them back into the Shell. Some guy on the mainland booked a bunch of acts, including Black Oak Arkansas and War, into Hawaii Raceway Park the same weekend. It wasn't a bad lineup. The guy called me a month ahead and said he thought I should reschedule my concert. I said C&K were getting real hot and I had had the Shell booked way before he put his show together. He said if I went ahead with my concert, I might find it difficult to get acts from the mainland in the future. I was pissed about the threat. I'd just left K-POI, and I went all out to make it a successful concert. I sold 10,000 tickets and the capacity was 8,400. I hired extra ushers to squeeze people in on the lawn. By the way, the opening act that night was the relatively unknown (at that point) Kalapana.

The Keola & Kapono Beamer Show in our Ocean Showroom was a blend of music, comedy and innovative showmanship.

The other promoter's show turned into an ugly event. Some of the acts said they weren't going to perform unless they got their money up front. Some local guys got rough and forced them to go onstage. A fight broke out. Before it was over, one of the roadies for Black Oak Arkansas got a brain concussion. And we had a big success.

Bill Thompson was the brains behind C&K. He believed in them and got the contract at Columbia, a very big deal then for artists from Hawaii. Back when "Hawaii Calls" was at its peak, Hawaiian artists and their songs were released under that name (on Capitol), but mostly it was the other way around—established mainland artists recording songs from the Islands. This had been going on since the 1930s when Bing Crosby had a big hit with "Sweet Leilani," continuing through the soundtrack albums of the movies made in Hawaii by Elvis Presley.

Bill also coined the name C&K. It was a difficult partnership at the beginning, because the guys weren't getting along. Henry's pure Hawaiian and Cecilio is a Latino who came to Hawaii from the West Coast after being a guitarist for Little Anthony—that was his background. They tried careers separately, but there was nothing like these guys together. The blend of voices, the charisma, everything. It was like magic.

I booked them with Kalapana again, this time into Aloha Stadium, for the day after Christmas, 1976, and everybody said I was nuts. I had a new partner then, Irv Pinensky. He was a big record distributor for MGM and Warner Brothers in San Francisco who had sold his business and come to Honolulu for the slower pace. He continued to work with the mainland record companies, but now on a much smaller scale. We became friends, and after I left K-POI he said, "Let's start a company together." That was when I started Tom Moffatt Productions, and our record company was called Trim, after our sons, Troy and Kim.

At one Blaisdell Arena concert, we paired Keola & Kapono with the brilliant comedian Rap Reiplinger—here as one of the characters from his smash album *Poi Dog*—who later became another victim of the drug culture.

booked the C&K and Kalapana show. I told him I knew it was right, I could feel it. Irv said, "If you feel it, go for it." Bill Thompson was out of the picture by then, and a fellow named Ed Guy was managing both acts. He said each wanted $50,000, which was unheard of at the time. And each had to have the same billing. So C&K were on the cover on one side of the programs and Kalapana was pictured on the other side. They also changed positions top and bottom on the posters, and on the radio spots we had to do the same thing. I think we flipped a coin to decide which group would go on first, so Kalapana opened the show. And they played to a crowd of 20,000. The *Star-Bulletin* said twice that, but it was actually just over 20,000, still an amazing turnout for two local acts at the Stadium.

Country Comfort was a band I decided not only to record but also to manage. Actually, Irv had started recording the group, but the project had just lain there for a while when we formed our partnership. I first heard them when I was just leaving K-POI and saw them at The Sty, a nightclub out in Niu Valley. They were doing great business in an out-of-the-way place, and the reaction they got was good. So with Irv's blessing, I brought in Cyrus Faryar to help me produce the album. Cyrus had been a member of the Modern Folk Quartet (one of the acts at the Magic Mountain Music Festival) and at the time was

(Irv also was the distributor in the Islands for ABC, and he got a line on Ray Charles, so we booked him into the HIC. The show was a loser. Somehow I'd miscalculated, and the audience for this giant wasn't there yet. I was just devastated when tickets didn't sell. I remember Irv saying, "Don't worry about it, we'll make it up in the next one." It was the same thing I'd heard from Ralph and Earl when one of our early shows didn't do so well.)

So I was sharing Irv's office in Kakaako when I

Keola Beamer and I produced a Hawaiian revue at the Maui Surf on Kaanapali Beach, starring Keola and the talented Audrey Meyers.

the hotel's general manager. It was midnight, and I knew it was trouble. He told me the band had gotten into a fight on stage, and one guy had hit another over the head with a guitar stand and cut his head open. People were walking out. That's when I decided I wasn't going to manage any more. That was the end of my management career.

By then I'd already recorded them, and the album became a best-seller because of "Waimanalo Blues." This was a song written by Liko Martin, one of the most talented young Hawaiian composers, and it was originally called "Nanakuli Blues," for the town on the Leeward side of Oahu. It was changed to Waimanolo because that's the town where Country Comfort was based.

As much as any other act at the time, I thought Country Comfort captured the mood of the time. "Waimanalo Blues" talked about "the beaches they sell / to build their hotels / my father and I once knew." Another of Liko's songs, "We Are the Children," was more optimistic: "We are the children / we are the dawn of light / together we are changing / to an endless night." The album sold 25,000 copies—huge for locally produced product. I also produced their second album with Country Comfort's Chuck Lee, and it sold very well. But not long after it was released, for a variety of reasons the band broke up.

I also recorded *Shells* by the Surfers with Irv. That's an album I'm really proud of; I think it's one of the nicest Hawaiian albums ever made. Irv and I also managed the Aliis, formerly Don Ho's backup group, and we had the showroom at the Outrigger Hotel where they performed. We were doing okay financially. I don't remember why Irv and I decided to part, but it was friendly. We were together about four years.

So, we'd split, but I was still working out of Irv's office when I got a call from Kapono Beamer, who asked if I'd like to produce an album for him and Keola. Irv was very generous when our partnership ended, and I had a good amount of money and intended to spend some of it on cre-

living in Hilo.

As their manager, I tried to expose Country Comfort to new audiences. I put them on with the Eagles at the Shell, which wasn't a wonderful start. They got through the sound check okay, but then one of the guys in the band started drinking. Come show time, after two or three tunes, the rest of the band walked off the stage, pissed off because the other guy was out of control. I didn't have a problem with the Eagles; they didn't take offense. It was just embarrassing.

Another time I got a call from the Kauai Resort from

ating a new record company of my own. I called it Paradise Records and also started a music publishing company to go with it, naming it Niniko Music after my home.

I met with Keola and Kapono and gave each of them a little money. I told them to go out of town and write some music. Couple of weeks later, Keola called and said, "I think I got a song." He said he wrote it about when he had to leave the Islands for some appearances on the mainland and realized how much he hated doing that. He was living up at the top of Alewa Heights—that's high up—and he asked me to come up and give a listen.

It was just before sunset when I took a seat facing the window that looked down over Honolulu, and the sky turned from orange and red to black. Keola played "Honolulu City Lights" just as the lights came on below. Keola set me up, but I knew the song was a hit. "Each time Honolulu city lights / Stir up memories in me... / Each time Honolulu city lights / Will bring me back again." I still get chills when I hear those words.

Teddy Randazzo happened to be staying at my house. He agreed to do the arrangements. We recorded the album, and the rest, as they say, is history. *Honolulu City Lights* became an immediate hit and continues to be a Hawaiian favorite, so much so that when *HONOLULU* magazine polled a music-industry panel to create a list of the 50 top Hawaii albums of all time, it was number one.

The Beamer brothers came with a first-class pedigree. Their family traced its musical roots to the 15th century, and their grandmother Helen Desha Beamer was one of the most prolific composers in Hawaii in her time, as well as teaching the hula openly in defiance of local bans. An uncle, Mahi Beamer, had recorded for Capitol Records, another uncle, Keola, had performed in the Hawaiian show at the Lexington Hotel in New York and their mother, Auntie Nona Beamer, taught dance, chant and Hawaiian language at the Kamehameha Schools. The Beamer style of hula was one of the four main branches that went back to

The beat goes on: in the summer of 2004 Kalapana reunited on the Waikiki Shell stage for a 30th-anniversary concert.

when the goddess Hiiaka danced on a Big Island beach.

Keola was the older brother and was thought to have the better voice, along with more sex appeal. Both were exponents of slack-key guitar, but Kapono was a more dedicated picker, and he played a haunting nose flute, a bamboo tube that was played by blowing into it with the nose. About half of their repertoire was Hawaiian, songs learned at their mother's knee. The other half was sung in English. Some of it was so romantic you wanted to die, some of it humorous, like "Mr. San Cho Lee," a takeoff on the Islands' different ethnic groups. They had the right mix of voices. Everything worked.

Producer Kimo Wilder McVay got them a 90-minute television broadcast from the Royal Hawaiian Hotel that was shown without commercial interruption, a Hawaii first. We thought it was important to have them working in Waikiki, so the three of us formed a partnership to open a club. A room was vacant at the Reef Hotel. It was right on the water, so we named it the Ocean Showroom. A hot new comic named Andy Bumatai opened the show and a former Miss Hawaii, Kanoe Kaumeheiwa, danced.

That sustained interest in the album and got us into the tourist market.

I saw something Diana Ross did, and we tried it with the Beamers. You saw them walking down the beach towards you on a big screen, the curtains opened and they walked out, as if walking right out of the picture. Nobody'd done anything like that before in Hawaii. We did some innovative things. They had these fat suits they wore in a takeoff on some of the heavier *hula halau* members. I did a lot of shows with them, with Andy and then with Rap Reiplinger, another local comedian.

After I put out the Beamers' album, and then one by Marlene Sai, a guy approached me from something called Kalei Productions to do a show in San Francisco with the Beamers, Marlene and Andy Bumatai. The Mark Hopkins Hotel, one of that city's most prestigious, was owned by Charlie Pietsch, who built the Kahala Hilton and the Kahala Beach condominiums next door. I knew Charlie, and I talked with John Spierling, who was one of his partners, and the show was booked into the Mark Hopkins. Everyone in the hotel and the sold-out audience loved the show. Then, after the Mark Hopkins, the show was taken to Oakland and Orange County.

My contract for the other shows was with Kalei Productions, whose owner was always so religious you had to pray before the shows. He finally stiffed me. I had to sue him, and when I got a judgment, he disappeared. I always thought about the Sterling Mossman joke: "The missionaries came to Hawaii to do good, and they did well. Very well. They asked the Hawaiians to bow their heads in prayer, and when the Hawaiians looked up, their land was gone."

Sadly, the Beamer partnership didn't last. Keola and Kapono weren't getting along, and when they went on tour on the mainland, we started bringing other acts into the Ocean Showroom. Some came from the mainland. Tower of Power was successful. We even tried the Brothers

Entertainers who played big roles in the Hawaiian renaissance included comic Frank Delima (above, at center) as well as, opposite, the Peter Moon Band and, later on, the Hawaiian Style Band.

Cazimero, another popular local duo, but by then there were things happening that changed Waikiki at night. Suddenly there was a lot of traffic and people couldn't get to the hotel or find parking. I remember one night with the Cazimeros: every table was reserved, but traffic was backed up and we ended up with a 50-percent house.

It wasn't just the traffic. The package tours had something to do with it, too. They would sell "An Evening at the Outrigger" or something, and then the packager would want a kickback. So the cover charge had to go up, and the local people were priced out of Waikiki. That's when I decided to get out of the nightclub business.

There was something else, too. I asked a friend what was causing the big drop in club attendance, and he said it was because the cops were enforcing the DUI laws and a lot of residents were now staying home so as not to run the risk.

It was really, really sad that things fell off. There was a time when you could go from the old Queen's Surf in Kapiolani Park all the way to the Hilton Hawaiian Village

put it into the Maui Surf Hotel in Kaanapali. Keola put the whole thing together and recorded the music. We even recorded the orchestra tuning up, so that people thought there was a house band backstage somewhere. It really sounded live.

We were able to keep the cost of the tickets down; the food was good; we had one show a night, six nights a week. It worked, and the people liked it. We didn't have a big cast, just Keola and Audrey Meyers, who'd had her own revue in Waikiki, along with a comic singer, Lui Williams, and some dancers. I'd go over once a month and watch a couple of shows, and it never ceased to amaze me how good they were. I think if developer Chris Hemmeter hadn't bought the hotel and closed it for remodeling, the show would still be running.

As it was, it lasted two years. We tried another venue and it didn't work. The first room was perfect for the show—the stage wasn't real big, but it was a stage and you knew you were seeing a show. The ceiling was high. The other room had a temporary stage, the ceiling was lower and it just didn't work.

Some people compared the Hawaiian music renaissance to what happened on the mainland with the folk music boom, the British invasion, the San Francisco sound and all the rest. Unfortunately, there were tragic parallels, too. Just as the deaths of Jimi Hendrix, Janis Joplin, Jim Morrison and Elvis Presley (and too many others) were drug related, in Hawaii we lost Billy Kaui of Country Comfort, Robert Beaumont of Olomana, Mackey Feary of Kalapana and Rap Reiplinger to the same damned thing.

But the Hawaiian renaissance came about because of a return to the roots, a surge in respect paid to Hawaii's past. For the first time in too long, a lot of young people got interested in their culture. And that didn't go away. Life in the Islands went along—sometimes *kapakahi*, cockeyed, but Don McLean got it wrong in his song "American Pie": the music didn't die. 🎤

(originally Mr. Kaiser's hotel), and every hotel had a show. There was a show at the Moana Hotel in the Banyan Court, another at the Royal. The Marketplace was full of places. The Surfers were at the Canton Puka, the Invitations were at the Korean Village, Tavana and the Martin Denny Group were at Don the Beachcomber. At the Shell Bar at the Hawaiian Village Hotel you had Arthur Lyman and Rene Paulo. Then, one by one, the lights went out.

I did give it one more try, but not in Waikiki. Keola and Kapono had split up, and when Keola told me he had written a Hawaiian revue, he and I formed a company and

CHAPTER 12

Tommy and the Rat Pack

The first time I crossed Frank Sinatra's path was during the 1960 presidential election, when I was working with Ralph and Earl. He came to Hawaii to do a fundraiser for John F. Kennedy at the Waikiki Shell. Ralph and Earl were heavy into the Democratic Party, so Ralph was asked to coordinate the show, and he asked me to be the emcee.

Now, Sinatra was a good friend of Frank Valenti, one of the all-time greats in Island broadcasting and also one of my idols when he was the man with the fastest mouth in radio. His ability to ad lib was phenomenal. He did a sports show; he recreated baseball. I was in awe of Valenti. For a while I dated his niece, who lived with him and his wife. She was attractive and a very nice girl—and I also hoped I might run into Valenti sometime, picking her up.

At the Shell fundraising event, I introduced Frank Valenti, who then introduced Peter Lawford, who introduced Sinatra. There was a comedian named Paul Desmond—same name as the alto sax player with Dave Brubeck. He was supposed to do 15 minutes. There were some important people in the audience, including Abe Lastfogel, one of the most powerful men in Hollywood and the head of the William Morris Agency. And

Desmond was connecting, he was making them laugh, and all of a sudden he'd been on for 25 minutes. And Sinatra went ballistic. I never heard of that comedian again.

Another time, I interviewed Sinatra on the phone for some charity. Tommy Sands was a good friend by then, and he was married to Sinatra's daughter, Nancy. They came to Hawaii for their honeymoon. I was on the air when they left on the *Lurline*, and I played Elvis' "Hawaiian Wedding Song" for them as the ship rounded Diamond Head. They told me later that they were listening and it was a special moment for them.

When Tommy and Nancy broke up, Frank soured on Tommy. Where once he'd gotten Tommy a part in a major movie he was starring in, *Only the Brave*, now he was…well, unfriendly. When I was doing the interview with Sinatra, I said something about "Tommy and Nancy," and he corrected me and said, "Nancy and Tommy." He pretty much blackballed him. Tommy came and stayed with Sweetie and me for a while after the breakup, and the

Tommy Sands had come a long way since headlining at the 10th Show of Stars. Opposite: I promoted the 1989 Sammy, Liza & Frank concert on the marquee of the Hawaii Theatre.

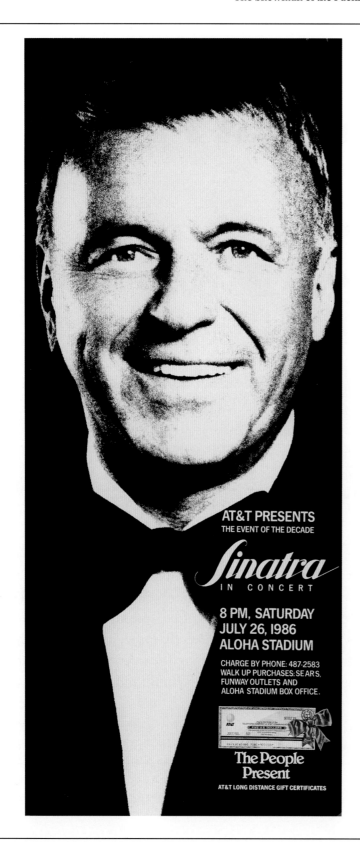

AT&T PRESENTS
THE EVENT OF THE DECADE

Sinatra
IN CONCERT

8 PM, SATURDAY
JULY 26, 1986
ALOHA STADIUM

CHARGE BY PHONE: 487-2583
WALK UP PURCHASES: SEARS,
FUNWAY OUTLETS AND
ALOHA STADIUM BOX OFFICE.

The People
Present

AT&T LONG DISTANCE GIFT CERTIFICATES

rumor was that his former father-in-law had put the word out that he wasn't to get work.

Long before his first appearance in Hawaii, Tommy had a lot of fans here, and I played his records often on the radio. In the spring of 1957 the Farrington High School paper, *The Governor*, ran a student survey that named Tommy the favorite male vocalist, with 1,685 votes. Elvis received 1,001.

Tommy and I had remained friends since he appeared on the Show of Stars. I remember one time, shortly before he married Nancy, his manager invited me to visit him on the set at Disney Studios where he was doing *Babes in Toyland*. Walt Disney came on the set just to meet Tommy, and I met Walt Disney. Tommy was that important.

Honolulu Advertiser columnist Eddie Sherman, a friend of mine since my earliest days in Hawaii radio, took an interest in Tommy, and we started looking for a room where Tommy could perform. We went to Roy Kelley, who owned the Reef Hotel, and he had this empty conference room. We thought this was an ideal location, but Roy didn't. It later became the Polynesian Palace and Don Ho's home base. There was another room at the Outrigger Hotel, which was owned by Roy with tour company honcho Bob MacGregor, and Roy's son Doc ran it. Mike Hickey was the manager for Doc Kelley and the spearhead who put the thing together. We named it the Main Showroom of the Outrigger Hotel and started auditioning, and we put a show together around Tommy. Sweetie and Rose Marie Alvaro danced, and we got some

Despite my initial misgivings about presenting Sinatra at Aloha Stadium, the show was everything we'd hoped it would be.

musicians, including Jack Thompson, later better known as Tihati. The room opened on June 21, 1968.

Tommy was very successful there. Don Ho was across the street at Duke's, and both shows were doing well. I leased a Jaguar XKE for him. He got a good part in *Hawaii Five-O*, and there was a TV producer in Hollywood who believed enough in Tommy that he wanted to do a special. The producer got a crew to come in and do *Tommy Sands in Hawaii*. The producer was Dale Sheets, who managed Mel Torme up until the time Mel died. Dale brought in his two daughters to dance on the show. (One of them married Island radio and TV personality Michael W. Perry, and they have a big family now.)

Tommy had recorded this song that he wanted to release as a single, "Seasons in the Sun," written by Jacques Brel and Rod McKuen. Had it gotten record company support, it would've been a hit. Terry Jacks, a singer in Australia, covered it a couple of years later and it went to number one in *Billboard* in 1974. It was still a great year for Tommy. We had taken a meeting room at the Outrigger Hotel on the beach in Waikiki and turned it into a major showroom. The room is still a mainstay in Waikiki and has been a home for years to the singing group Society of Seven. Tommy remarried and has a lovely daughter, Jessica, who inherited her dad's talent and is a successful entertainer.

There's a funny footnote to Tommy's tenure in Hawaii. When the show closed I inherited his Jaguar, because my name was on the banknote. I already had a car, so I gave it to Sweetie. So here's Sweetie, a dancer for Danny Kaleikini at the Kahala Hilton, arriving for work in this pricey Jaguar XKE, when the hotel manager, Bob Burns, was probably driving a company car.

The next time I got involved with Frank Sinatra was in 1986, when AT&T wanted me to present him in concert at Aloha Stadium. There was no question that Frank was the number-one vocalist in the world, but

It was billed as the Ultimate Event—three of the biggest stars in the world "in the round" at the Blaisdell Arena. What could go wrong?

I wasn't sure he was right for the Stadium. I thought he needed a more intimate venue. It wasn't a sell-out, but it looked good. We dressed the house a little, so when Sinatra came out on stage it looked okay. AT&T didn't want to "paper" the house—give tickets away to fill the empty seats—so I worked with Earl McDaniel, the general manager of KSSK, the sponsoring station, to devise a way to make it a real bargain for the public, and they bought it. Earl was a great GM and salesman. A sign he had in his office really impressed me: "A TERRIBLE THING HAPPENS IF YOU DON'T PROMOTE...NOTHING." For everyone involved, Earl wanted to make sure it was a successful promotion. We really promoted this event, and it was.

But Sinatra was so anxious about getting to the Stadium that instead of waiting for his scheduled limousine, he caught a cab there by himself. When he arrived, there was no one to greet him and he started a tirade. Sinatra had good people around him, including Nelson Riddle and his orchestra, and the performance was everything you'd have hoped. When he finished his last number, he was like a little kid. Hawaii's elite was there in full force, including Imelda Marcos. This was right after she and her husband defected from the Philippines. Sinatra had one of his buddies peek around the side to check the audience reaction. He was so excited that they reacted the way they did. But I remember that temper tantrum.

Not long after that, the Hyatt Waikoloa Resort on the Big Island

I first met Tommy Sands at a Show of Stars at the old Civic Auditorium.

wanted to do something big for New Year's Eve. I flew to Maui to meet Sinatra's guy, Elliott Weisman, who was vacationing there, and he suggested Liza Minelli, who he also represented. So we did a handshake deal, and just after Christmas Elliott called to say he wanted me to meet her at the airport, fly over to Kona on the chartered plane with her, make sure she got checked into the hotel. Leslie Bricuse, the guy who co-wrote *Stop the World, I Want to Get Off,* and his wife were traveling with Liza and her husband. I got them checked in and everybody was happy, including me, returning home, the only passenger in the chartered plane on one of those special, cloudless nights with all the islands in view. Elliott came in for the show, and I was there, of course. Liza's was the second big show in the room, and everything went the way it was supposed to.

Two days after the show, she was leaving and I went to the Honolulu airport to make sure everything was okay. She got to the Kona airport and was furious because one of her bags couldn't make the plane. It was a different chartered plane from the one that took her to the Big Island, and there wasn't room. I made some calls to Hawaiian Airlines, and by the time she landed in Honolulu, the missing bag was there, in plenty of time to make her connecting flight to the mainland. That didn't matter. I don't think she ever forgave me for that.

Two years later we got Frank, Liza and Sammy Davis Jr. for two nights on their way back from Japan. I figured we shouldn't have a problem with a $60 ticket, and we did it in the round at the Blaisdell Arena. Every seat was great; you were looking right down on them, three of the biggest stars in the world. How could anything go wrong? So I was feeling pretty good when Sweetie and I went to the party that Sinatra was having at the Kahala Hilton for just the people traveling with the show. (Elliott invited us, the only outsiders there.)

So we got to the Kahala, and the word was that Sinatra wasn't coming because his wife didn't want to attend and he had a terrible cold and his voice wasn't in good shape. Sinatra did end up coming, though, with his friend Jilly Rizzo. Mrs. Sinatra sent a message that Frank was to have a cup of tea. What got me is that all three of them, Frank and Liza and Sammy, were chain-smoking. The staff at the Kahala were in awe and were afraid to enter the room. Finally, Sweetie had to get up and empty ashtrays. I saw Sinatra nod and I saw Jilly nod, and pretty soon there was a bottle of Jack Daniels in front of Sinatra and the party continued way past midnight.

Next day, I showed up at the Arena and heard that Sinatra's voice was so bad he might not make it. I went backstage and saw Frank Jr. "How's your dad?" "Well, he's really sick, but my dad feels that a cancelled show is bad for the business, so I think he'll make it." He showed up. Liza, then Sammy, and after the intermission, Frank. And they all did something together at the end.

The conductor for Sammy Davis was Morty Stevens, the guy who wrote the theme song for *Hawaii Five-O*. And Frank Jr. conducted for his dad. I told Sweetie, who was in the dressing room, "Come on out and watch." She said, "No, he's singing flat," and my best friend, a record producer, agreed. I said, "Yeah, but when you're watching, he's got such charisma you don't notice it that much." She came out, and he was amazing, especially after he toasted the audience with a well-filled glass of Jack Daniels. I still have the Jack Daniels bottles from both shows, at the Stadium and at the Blaisdell, with a little of the bourbon left in them. I put backstage passes on the bottles.

Tom's First Jewish Deli
by Eddie Sherman

We were having lunch at Canter's, the legendary delicatessen on Fairfax Avenue in Los Angeles. Moffatt claimed he'd never been in a real Jewish deli. I ordered one of my favorites, a whole smoked whitefish, which is small. Moffatt said he'd have the same. He'd never eaten one before.

When the delicacy was served, Moffatt asked how to eat it. So I held the whole whitefish between my fingers like a cigar and put the head of the fish in my mouth. I handed Moffatt some matches and asked him to give me a light. He looked at me like I was nuts.

"Schmuck!" I said. "This is smoked whitefish. You smoke it!"

So there I sat, puffing on the whitefish head while Moffat lit one match after another, and the waitresses and other customers are looking at these two crazies and laughing their heads off.

We were lucky not to get thrown out of Canter's deli when Eddie tried to teach me to smoke a whitefish!

The Blaisdell show was pretty much of a bust, financially. The audience wasn't ready for $60. Even the professional people who had money to burn said it was too expensive. They'd go to Vegas and pay a bundle to see Sinatra, but they wouldn't drive to the Blaisdell for a fraction of the price.

Frank and Liza. The greatest pipes in the world. And hard to be with. Even when Liza came back with Frank and Sammy, she was cold.

Still, Honolulu will never see the likes of that show again. Too bad so many people stayed at home. 🎤

CHAPTER 13

Flying Fists and Feet

I was always fascinated by boxing. I never saw a live fight as a kid, but the Hock family had a friend who was a referee at a Joe Louis fight, so I always listened to Joe Louis' bouts on the radio. Twenty years later, hanging out with Ralph Yempuku and Sam Ichinose at the Civic exposed me to the Hawaii fight scene, and I could see how many people supported it.

Initially, it wasn't the local contests I presented; it was the championship bouts beamed in to Hawaii from the mainland. In those days, if you wanted to see, say, Muhammad Ali take on one of his brave and always-defeated challengers, you had to go to the city where the fights were held or watch it at a closed-circuit location.

In Hawaii, everything came in by satellite, but you couldn't buy it on pay TV. I was lucky to get into this at just at the right time and to meet a very creative and bright projectionist named Keoki Akana, who devised an octagonal screen that could be suspended in the middle of the Blaisdell Arena. So if you were watching it, it was like you were actually there. It became very successful, and I was able to sell every seat in the Blaisdell for the Marvin Hagler-Sugar Ray Leonard fight. And prior to that I had a near sell-out for Hagler vs. Tommy Hearns.

I presented those satellite fights in the Arena, in the Concert Hall, in hotel ballrooms, on Oahu and on the outer islands, too. One time, at the ballroom of the Hawaiian Village, we kept losing the signal and the

By scheduling Hulk Hogan and Ric Flair on both sides of the International Date Line, we did two Saturday-night events in as many days. Opposite: Boxing champion Brian Viloria, who hails from Waipahu, is a world-class athlete and a terrific person, too.

audience got out of control. Somebody threw a bottle at the screen. Next thing I knew, the riot squad was there in full regalia: the tear gas bombs, the police batons, the whole nine yards. There was a National Football League

me anything to refund all those tickets. I think whatever other costs I had were covered, too. You had to have insurance. Don King and Bob Arum, the mainland promoters, insisted on it. They wanted their investment protected, too. But then came something I couldn't take out a policy against: pay-per-view. When fight fans could stay at home with their friends and pay less than I was charging to watch the same bout on their TV sets, that ended my presentations. It also put me back in the ring with what my old mentors Ralph Yempuku and Sad Sam Ichinose taught me. I still promoted some closed-circuit fights in hotels, rather than in the Arena, but from then on I mostly promoted live fights with local favorites.

Kickboxing became very successful for me. It started when I got a call from a guy vacationing on Maui named Dennis Alexio. He said he was known as "the Terminator." I'd never heard of him. He said he was the heavyweight kickboxing champion of the world, and he wanted to fight in Hawaii. I had UB-40 coming in three days, and they were going to play Maui, so I told Dennis to call me when I got to my Maui hotel.

Then I called my son, Troy, who was into martial arts, and he said, "Oh, yeah, Dad, he's big." So I got interested and went to Maui; we met, and I made a deal with him. I said I'd pay his training costs and once we took the expenses off the top, we'd split everything 50-50.

Dennis gave me this footage where he was kicking this guy called Robocop in the face four times—bam-bam-bam-bam! Dennis got him to come to the island for a rematch, and I used the film in the promotion to sell

convention going on in town, and a lot of football players were there that night—including, I learned later, O.J. Simpson. It looked like it was going to be completely nuts. It was scary going up to the ballroom with the riot squad in a freight elevator, not knowing what to expect. The HPD officer in charge looked at me and said, "Someone is going to have to go out and talk to this crowd." So I went out there and said the magic word: "Refund."

I was covered; I had insurance. It really didn't cost

Kickboxing card sets Blaisdell attendance mark

The Honolulu Advertiser   Tuesday, July 14, 1992   D3

By Stephen Tsai
Advertiser Staff Writer

More people attended the kickboxing fight between Dennis "The Terminator" Alexio and Dennis "Mad Dog" Downey last Saturday night than any other single-day event in Blaisdell Arena history.

John Fuhrmann, events and service manager for Blaisdell Center, said the crowd of 8,907 was the largest for a Blaisdell event since the arena opened in 1965.

"I'm glad I've broken the record," Alexio said. "I hope they put in more seats for the next fight so I can break it again."

Tom Moffatt, who promoted the event, said expanded seating allowed the kickboxing card to surpass his World Wrestling Federation promotion in attendance.

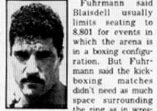

Alexio

Fuhrmann said Blaisdell usually limits seating to 8,801 for events in which the arena is in a boxing configuration. But Fuhrmann said the kickboxing matches didn't need as much space surrounding the ring as in wrestling or boxing, allowing Moffatt to add more than 100 seats for Saturday's event.

Local boxing records show that the largest crowd for a Blaisdell boxing card is 8,516 for a Domi Manalang fight on July 16, 1968.

The kickboxing card also proved to be profitable. A spokeswoman for Moffatt said Saturday's event is expected to gross in "excess of $160,000." That would be the second-largest gross for a sporting event in Blaisdell history.

The second World Junior Lightweight title fight between Ben Villaflor and Kuniaki Shibata reportedly grossed $184,710 on Oct. 17, 1973.

Alexio would not disclose how much he earned for the fight, although he said his purse is larger on the Mainland because he fights in

> "I'm glad I've broken the record. I hope they put in more seats for the next fight so I can break it again."
>
> — **Dennis Alexio**

larger arenas. One bout in Las Vegas drew more than 16,000 last year.

"I don't fight out here because of the money," he said. "I fight here because of the love I have for Hawaii. I want to be a role model to the youngsters."

Alexio said he plans to fight in Tahiti next month and hopes to return to Hawaii for a bout in September.

Downey, whose WWF-like hyperbole probably stimulated ticket sales, won't return. He announced his retirement after the

---

tickets. It worked. And Dennis destroyed him again.

This was my first live fight, though, and we had forgotten something very important. With less than a minute remaining in the first round, we realized the ring stools were still in the Arena's storage room. My two buddies, Bobby Krewson and Morgan Montague, had seats at ringside to "assist" our ring girls, and they quickly sacrificed their chairs so the fighters could sit down when the bell rang and they returned to their corners.

There was another guy called Dennis "Mad Dog" Downey, who'd gone to prison for doing something violent, I don't know what, and when he got out, we brought him to Hawaii. He was a great talker and we got videotape of him shooting off his mouth, and we sold the show out. Dennis kicked the stuffing out of him. Dennis seemed invincible.

I thought, what are we going to do next? That's when I remembered the *Rocky* movies. I went to Alexio and said, "Let's get a fighter from Russia!" So we made a deal for one of the Soviet Union's elite soldiers to come in, and he was supposed to be a killer. We used the same hype as in *Rocky* and sold every seat in the Arena.

Dennis trained hard, and he could kick. Like a mule.

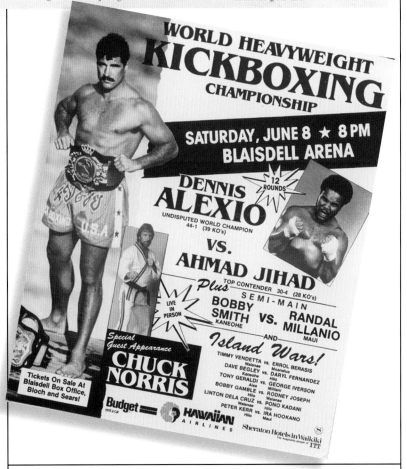

We broke the Arena ticket sales record when kickboxers Dennis Alexio and Mad Dog Downey met in 1992.

Dennis had a manager then, an ex-fighter named Bob Wall. Bob was the bad guy opposite Bruce Lee in *Enter the Dragon*; that was his claim to fame. Bob loved Dennis, and he'd help whenever he could. He was into commercial development by then, and I don't think he ever took any commission. He helped get the Russian fighter and his entourage in, because we had a visa problem and we'd already sold the fight out. Bob pulled whatever strings

Even with all his movie and wrestling exposure, the Rock told me that coming home to wrestle in Hawaii was the biggest thing that ever happened to him.

needed pulling and got them through immigration.

We played Russian music when he came into the ring and gave him a cape to make him look bigger, more villainous. And Dennis beat the crap out of him. The word was, he got exiled to Siberia when he went home.

I'd visited Tahiti a number of times by now, and I knew of the anti-French sentiment there. So I made a deal and got this French fighter from Monaco. I figured the Tahitians would all come out to see a French guy get kicked around. So we got there and the press was going crazy, and the poor guy knew there was no chance against Dennis. He even looked frail, though he had a good record, but you could see that he idolized Dennis. And Dennis did what he always did and the Tahitians went crazy.

Dennis never lost a bout. People said he used set-ups, but he did not. Some said the fights were fixed, that the action was mapped out ahead of time, as it is in professional wrestling, but that wasn't so. He fought tough guys and he was a magnificent specimen. I thought he was very dedicated. He was in his late 30s, and for the first time in his life he was consistently making big bucks. In 1992 when he fought Mad Dog Downey, he broke the Blaisdell Arena record for number of tickets sold. A year or so later Mad Dog came back for a rematch, and when he learned that tickets were going slowly, he said he'd bite the head off a mouse for publicity. I thought he was kidding, but the next day at a press conference at the Blaisdell, he pulled this live mouse out of his pocket and bit its head off. The Humane Society and others went crazy.

I really believed Dennis could beat anybody; he was that good, and I don't think he was afraid of anybody. There was a movie guy into martial arts, Don "the Dragon" Wilson, who had beaten Dennis when they both were young. I told Dennis this guy might be available for a $50,000 guarantee, and I said we could take it to Aloha Stadium. Dennis didn't want to hear about it. There were a couple of other big fighters who wanted big money, too, but Dennis wasn't interested. He wasn't afraid of them. He just didn't want to give anyone that kind of money. He didn't want to spend anything on anything. *He* wanted the money. He wanted to change our deal and I brought my share down 10 percent, but in the end he decided he could do it better himself.

When I was a disc jockey at KHVH, there was a parking lot attendant at the Hawaiian Village named Harry Fujiwara, who went on to become a wrestler called Fuji and joined the likes of Handsome Johnny Barend, Curtis "the Bull" Iaukea, Lord Tallyho Blears and Gentleman Ed Francis during the 50th State wrestling heyday at the Civic Auditorium. After that, he went to the mainland and became a star with the World Wrestling Federation, eventually becoming a manager. When the WWF wanted to come to Hawaii, the guy who used to park my car said, "Call Tom Moffatt."

So I started promoting wrestling, and we did okay, until Hulk Hogan came in and, all of a sudden, BOOM! We sold out! He was a superman, a superhero. He was on his way to Japan, and I told the WWF that if they came back, I thought we could do Aloha Stadium. I suggested doing Guam on the way, so they could appear in Guam on a Saturday night, then get on a plane and cross the International Date Line and get here Saturday afternoon, so we could do two Saturday nights in a row. We sold out the Field House in Guam and pulled a crowd of 25,000 the Aloha Stadium, a record in Hawaii for a wrestling event. Hogan defeated his opponent, Ric Flair, in both venues.

Anything after that was anti-climactic. We brought in the Undertaker, the Ultimate Warrior and other WWF stars, but none had the Hulk's pulling power. Then, after a slow spell, someone else came along who gave the business a new spin.

Dwayne Johnson had grown up in Hawaii, and he'd grown up around wrestling. His dad, an African American, wrestled for Gentleman Ed Francis, and his mother was the granddaughter of the Samoan WWF star Peter Maivia. Later he became known as the Rock.

By now the WWF had become WWE, for World Wrestling Entertainment, after losing a court battle with the World Wildlife Foundation, the conservation outfit that claimed prior ownership of the initials. So, when the newly renamed WWE called me about the Rock coming in, I knew it was a slam-dunk. He was local, he'd never wrestled in Hawaii, he was an actor with a new movie career and he was coming off a major motion picture, *The Scorpion King*. I'd already done 25,000 with Hulk Hogan in the Stadium, and I knew that I could do at least that with the Rock. I said it'd sell out in one day, and the WWE was really surprised when it sold out in four hours.

I wanted to make it special, so we called a press conference and I got one of the Samoan chiefs to come. They did a traditional Samoan ceremony, sitting on the floor on tapa mats in the Blaisdell Galeria. The local media came out in force. Everybody was there. I introduced him, and he was so serious about it. The chief honored me by asking me to sit with him and the Rock, who was really into it. He was only half Samoan, but he was very proud of it, in the same way many part-Hawaiians call themselves

Hawaiian—and you better not call them anything else!

The Rock told me afterward that of all the things he'd done in wrestling, the movie, everything, wrestling in Hawaii was the biggest thing that ever happened to him.

I don't promote much boxing or wrestling nowadays. I still promote a couple of WWE programs a year in the Blaisdell Arena, but I stopped the satellite feeds of world championship boxing into the Arena when sports bars came on the scene. The bars could charge less than I could, because of my high technical set-up costs. I still promote fights, but I do it on a smaller scale, in the bars with the bar owners. I presented the Evander Holyfield-Mike Tyson fight at the Sheraton Waikiki when Tyson took a bite of Holyfield's ear. But most fights I present at sports bars. I make less money, but my expenses are much lower and all I have to do is promote.

One exception is another local boy, Brian Viloria (right). I've presented him three times and expect I'll do some more. I got a call from ESPN, the cable sports network, for the first time in 2001, and they wanted to broadcast a live fight in Hawaii. I thought the Blaisdell Arena was the place for it, but ESPN wanted—insisted on having— palm trees and the Ala Wai Canal in the show, and that meant taking the event to the Hawaii Convention Center, which I thought was all wrong. But that's where we did it, and ESPN used the canal and the palm trees outside the building in the opening shot, and that was the last we saw of them. The other two times, I took Brian into the Sheraton Waikiki ballroom and the Blaisdell Arena. Brian is one of my favorite people, a great athlete and a wonderful person, and I hope to someday present him in a world title fight in the Arena. 🎤

BOXING
BLAISDELL ARENA • MAY 17, 2002
PRESS

CHAPTER 14

Hollywood and Las Vegas

Rock and roll and Hollywood have used each other well. Once the excitement surrounding rock made it clear this "new" music was here to stay—to quote Chuck Berry—television and movie studios made it clear that they wanted a piece of the action. And the rockers said back to them: here I am, come and get me…and I want a little piece, too.

At the same time, TV and movie stars decided they wanted to be recording stars. Ricky Nelson, Johnny Crawford, Shelley Fabares, Connie Stevens, Annette Funicello and Fabian were in the early wave, and after them, just about everybody started jumping the fence. Nowadays there's almost no distinction, with rappers taking leading parts in movies and the likes of Bruce Willis and Keanu Reeves forming rock bands and performing in clubs.

I wasn't the only disc jockey to have a romance with the large and small silver screens. Alan Freed and Dick Clark produced, and appeared in, some of the earliest rock-and-roll movies. So did I, but in an extremely limited way. I was just a young guy doing an afternoon dance show on TV when I was invited to read for a part in *Hawaii*, the Hollywood movie based on an early section of James Michener's big novel of the same name. The casting director told me to come to the Ilikai Hotel and to report to a room where she was holding auditions. I think she was forced to audition me because of my popular TV show. I

Bruce Willis played a mean blues harmonica when he and his band performed in Honolulu. Opposite: I landed a bit part as a war correspondent (far right) in the John Wayne-Kirk Douglas movie *In Harm's Way*. At left is *Star-Bulletin* editor Riley Allen.

could feel her resentment, and it unnerved me. So I did my reading and thanked her and opened a door to leave and walked into a broom closet. Needless to say, I didn't get the part.

One other time, when I was in Hilo, I was told I had a part in a new John Wayne-Kirk Douglas movie, *In Harm's Way*. Otto Preminger was the director. They called me the night before and told me to be on the set on Sand Island at 8 the next morning. I rushed back to Honolulu on the first flight, and of course, nothing happened until close to noon. Bob Krauss and Eddie Sherman of the *Advertiser* and I played war correspondents, along with Bill Ewing, the editor of the *Star-Bulletin*. After that, I happily satisfied myself with a supporting role behind the camera, and always with my friend Glen Larson.

Glen was the leader of the Four Preps, who starred in one of the early Show of Stars performances, and over the years he became one of my closest friends. The Preps had played Hawaii two or three times when he called me to say he wanted to come to the Islands for a second honeymoon and asked me to set them up with a nice home. So I did, not realizing it was *the* Glen Larson I'd been seeing on TV credits. Even when his group was touring, he was writing scripts, and now he was producing them, too. The first script he got a credit on was the Robert Wagner series *To Catch a Thief*.

He called me one day to say he was coming to Hawaii to shoot an episode of *McCloud*, the show with Dennis Weaver. That was another one of his early series and one of the most successful. Glen used me to introduce a singer in the show. The singer was Don Ho, whose name was changed to Al Moana. We all chuckled about that.

After *McCloud*'s last season, Glen wanted to do a pilot with Dennis about a guy who'd come back from Korea and stayed in Hawaii for a few days. His character stayed at the Halekulani Hotel and loved it. He then went back east and became a famous lawyer who represented the underworld. A doctor tells him, "Either you get out of this business or it'll kill you." A hotel is for sale in Hawaii, and he buys it (they used the old, low-rise Halekulani for the set). Bernadette Peters played a hooker; Sheldon Leonard was the gangster. (Leonard was a producer at Desilu by this time, but he had been a tough guy in the Humphrey Bogart movies in the 1940s.) And Dennis' character was just a guy trying to succeed with a small hotel, competing against the big ones. Glen called it *The Islander*. I got Dick Jensen involved—by then he'd dropped the Lance Curtis stage name. He played a singer, and he was good. Dick's daughter, Summer, was born about that time, and I was named her godfather. It was a hell of a show pilot and should've made it, but there was a change in the network's executive lineup and it wasn't one of the new guy's projects. It was broadcast as a made-for-TV movie, but it didn't become a series.

ROB MAILHOUSE • BRET DOMROSE • KEANU REEVES

DOGSTAR

LIVE IN CONCERT

FRI • DEC 4
8:30PM
WORLD CAFE

TICKETS AVAILABLE NOW AT: WORLD CAFE
BLAISDELL BOX OFFICE, TOWER RECORDS KAHALA & PEARL KAI
TOWER VIDEO KEEAUMOKU

Keanu Reeves played with his band, Dogstar, just before the release of *The Matrix*.

Glen called me another time. He gave me a script and I just loved it; I couldn't put it down. I read it while waiting for a flight to Kona where I had a show, and I was so caught up in the plot I missed my flight. The script was for the pilot for *Magnum P.I.* The title character was played by an actor I'd never heard of. Glen said Tom Selleck was a model turned actor and some other studios were after him, so he wanted to bring him to Hawaii and show him a good time.

I was doing a promotion at the brand-new Prince Kuhio Hotel at the time, and I arranged for a dinner party for Tom at the hotel. The next day we had a barbecue at Glen's apartment next to the Kahala Hilton. Glen set up a helicopter ride for him and pretty much sold him on coming to Hawaii to do the show. Glen put all the pieces together, and the show went on to introduce the Islands to millions of people around the world.

After *Magnum P.I.* had its run, then came *One West Waikiki*, with Cheryl Ladd and a talented new actor, Richard Burgi. Glen made me associate producer. If there was any problem locally during production, I'd get involved. I also cleared the music for the show. I went to the City coroner's office and got the assistant coroner to act as a consultant—Cheryl Ladd played a forensic scientist. Later, the *CSI* series became the hottest shows going with a format similar to Glen's show, but *One West Waikiki* ran for only a season and a half. Once again there was a change in the network leadership, and the show didn't get the sup-

port it deserved.

In 1978 Glen filmed an episode of *The Hardy Boys* in Hawaii. At the same time, I had David Gates & Bread playing at the Blaisdell Arena, and Glen got David involved. When they moved the location to L.A. to finish it, Glen decided he wanted to put David Gates on at the Santa Monica Civic Auditorium as if we were in Hawaii, with a marquee outside that read "Blaisdell Arena with David Gates & Bread." Glen wanted me to come and introduce David Gates on stage, so he sent me a ticket and set up a dressing room in a trailer for me. David's manager, my good friend Bill Leopold, put my name and a star on the door. All that for walking out on stage and saying, "Ladies and gentlemen, welcome to the Blaisdell Arena! Let's give a big Aloha welcome to David Gates and Bread!"

Glen also created one of the biggest cult shows of all time, *Battlestar Gallactica*, as well as *Knight Rider* with David Hasselhoff. *Quincy* was a very innovative show of Glen's. *The Fall Guy* was his, with the Million Dollar Man, Lee Majors, as the star. Sometimes he had several projects going at once.

20th Century Fox built Glen his own building; they thought that much of him. And the biggest kick I got was to borrow his car and go out somewhere and then drive back onto the Fox lot. The guard at the gate would wave me through, and I'd wander off onto the old sets. Wow! This is Hollywood! You got a car with the right sticker on it, you can go

I'm still not sure why Jay Leno wasn't a bigger draw at the Waikiki Shell. After all, he'd just been named Johnny Carson's successor.

anywhere.

My friendship with Glen dates back to 1958, and whenever he's in town it's dinner and late nights over drinks and memories; and when I go to L.A., I stay with him.

Glen was the King of Hollywood for me. He never, ever "went Hollywood" on me, though. When I do an oldies show, he'll be there if he can. Once he put the Four Preps back together for one of my shows. One of the original Preps was sick, and he was replaced with a special friend, Dave Somerville, the former lead singer of the Diamonds. They came off great.

I've promoted some TV-related productions, and usually they're hits. *Star Trek*, the TV series, had run its long and successful course; the *Star Trek* movies were still coming out, and the fans had raised the show to cult status. There were *Star Trek* clubs and fan magazines and conventions where memorabilia was sold and the stars were paid to show up and pose for pictures and sign autographs. So I guess it was no surprise when Gene Roddenberry, the man who created *Star Trek*, went on the road. He had some filmed outtakes from the show that made everybody laugh, showing how Mr. Spock and Captain Kirk and the others blew their lines or cursed. He talked about what it was like to know those guys. I was never that big a *Star Trek* fan, but I booked him into the Shell and the Trekkies, as they call themselves, made it a big success.

Another behind-the-scenes

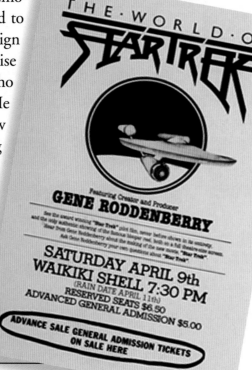

Star Trek creator Gene Roddenberry shared behind-the-scenes stories of his long-running TV show, still a cult favorite among Trekkies.

show came to town with a different approach. This was some years later, when *Everybody Loves Raymond* was such a hot show that its star, Ray Romano, a onetime stand-up comedian, was being paid 1.4 million dollars for each episode. Just after the series finale in 2005, I brought in the show's producer, Phil Rosenthal, who had created the series, along with Ray and eight of the show's writers. They played for two successful nights at the Blaisdell Concert Hall, and what they did, basically, was tell how they created a show from a real situation. For example, one of the writers had taped a football game over his wedding tape. That was the premise for one of the shows—what happened when his wife brought the tape out to spark a romantic evening at home, and a football game came up instead. The audience loved seeing how these comedy situations were put together and got a big kick out of seeing the results on an overhead screen.

A comedy act that failed was Jay Leno, and to this day I don't know why. He'd been guest-hosting the *Tonight Show* and had just been named Johnny's replacement, and when I booked him into the Shell, I figured it was a slam-dunk. But tickets weren't selling at all, and I told Jay's agent that the show was going to flop. I figured if I gave him a chance to get out of it, he'd take it rather than embarrass his client. I was wrong, and Jay came and played to a quarter of a house. Why would a guy in that position want to have a flop? It wasn't that he wanted the trip to Hawaii, because he just flew in, did the show and flew out. He might not have been told by the agent, who just wanted his percentage.

I've also had the pleasure of presenting two of Hollywood's biggest on-screen stars, Bruce Willis and Keanu Reeves. They're both musicians, and when they brought their bands to Hawaii, I promoted them as rock performers, not movie stars.

Keanu Reeves was passing through Hawaii with his band, on his way back to L.A. from Japan. I think everybody knows that his name, Keanu, is Hawaiian. His mom was Hawaiian; his parents split when he was young and he was raised in Texas. But he still had family in the Islands. I remembered when I was the general manager at K-POI and the staff went on strike—the union guy leading the strike was named Hank Reeves. So I asked Keanu if he was a relative. Keanu said if he was from Kuliouou, he likely was. All the people named Reeves in that part of Oahu were.

Keanu was a delightful guy and serious about his music. I booked him and his band, Dogstar, into the World Cafe on Nimitz Highway, a club that seated 1,400, and I promoted him as I would any other act. He played bass, and someone else did the vocals. This was just before *The Matrix* came out. If he'd brought his band to Hawaii *after* that movie was released, I probably could've put him into the Arena!

A few years later, Bruce Willis' agent called me from L.A. and said Bruce was making a movie in the Islands. He'd been in town for three months and wanted me to set up a night for him and his band somewhere. The movie was called *Tears of the Sun*, and Bruce was playing the usual tough guy with the curled smile, this time a Navy SEAL who led a group of refugees out of Nigeria, which was in the hands of a ruthless military dictator. The film was shot on Oahu.

I booked Bruce into the same club on Nimitz. It was mainly because he liked to get up on a stage and perform, to play rock music in a club. So he flew in his rock-and-roll buddies from the mainland, guys he'd played with and

Ray Romano and the writers of *Everybody Loves Raymond* kept their Blaisdell Concert Hall audiences in stitches.

who called themselves the Accelerators. They did some standards, and Bruce played a good blues harmonica. I met him just before the show—nice guy. Whatever I wanted him to do was okay with him. I'm sure Bruce didn't make a cent, after deducting the cost of flying his band in and

A David Gates & Bread concert in Honolulu prompted my unusual walk-on appearance in *The Hardy Boys*.

putting them up in a good hotel, but it was obvious he had a ball.

I tend to think of Las Vegas as a kind of extension of Hollywood. They sure have a lot in common. Glamour. Spectacle. Talent. And money. My connections to Vegas were mostly social, and one of the most important of these was Wayne Newton. The singer who later became the biggest name in Vegas was very young when he started playing in a club near the Honolulu airport, the Dunes (before the place became notorious for its lunches served by naked waiters). Sweetie and I got to know him then, along with his brother Jerry and his manager, Tommy Amato. Tommy conducted the orchestra, Jerry played guitar and Wayne sang.

Anyway, next time they returned, they moved into the Monarch Room at the Royal Hawaiian Hotel, and suddenly Wayne was the hottest act in Waikiki. By now, Jerry was dating Sweetie's friend Rose Marie Alvaro, who was dancing in Japan with Sweetie during the latter part of Wayne's engagement at the Royal.

One Friday night I was supposed to have dinner with them at the hotel. So I got a call from Sweetie just as I was leaving the house. She said she was coming home from Japan the next day, and the house was a real mess. I called Tommy and said I couldn't come down; I had to get the house ready. After Tommy, Jerry and Wayne finished the

show, guess what? They drove up to the house and helped me get everything in shape. I had Wayne Newton helping me clean house!

Wayne later dated Masako, a Japanese singer who was in the Hilo Hattie Show at the Hawaiian Village. She'd come out in a kimono and bow. Very Japanese. The music was traditional Japanese, too. Then the kimono came off and the music changed; now it was rock and roll. I was at K-POI at the time, and when Don Ho came out with the classic Kui Lee song, "I'll Remember You," I thought it'd be a good idea to record Masako doing the same song. Aside from performing nightly at Duke's, Don was the afternoon drive deejay on KHVH radio opposite me at that time, and I didn't want to have to promote my competition.

Well, Wayne and Masako broke up, and one day he and his new girlfriend, Elaine Okamura, a Pan Am stewardess whose parents owned Okamura's Store on Kapahulu Avenue, came by the house to visit. So what did I do? I forgot about him and Masako, and I put her record on, "I'll Remember You." It did not go over well. The new girlfriend, who later married Wayne, knew all about the old one.

I stayed in touch with Wayne, Jerry and Tommy after they went to Vegas, and I visited them on my next trip to the mainland. After the show one night, I said I had to go back to Hawaii the next day. They asked me to go with them to L.A. the next morning and sent a limousine to take me to the airport. Then I got into a Lear jet for the trip. Wayne had made it big.

I was invited to a party for Wayne at Chasen's, the old-line Hollywood restaurant where the guests fairly shouted respectability and establishment. It was to celebrate Wayne's 21st anniversary in show business. Why celebrate the 21st? Why not? I got the invitation via a telegram from Jack Benny, who was to host it, but at the last minute he couldn't make it. Danny Thomas was the

Early in his career, Vegas legend Wayne Newton played a Honolulu nightclub later famous for its naked waiters.

Tommy and Jerry, and it was kind of sad. They were such a tight-knit group. I don't know what happened. Tommy died suddenly a couple of years ago. I'm still friends with Wayne. I saw him again two days before 9/11, when he was playing the Sheraton Waikiki ballroom. I knew his voice wasn't as strong as before, and I wanted to see how he carried the show. He was such a master performer. He had a group of girls doing vocals, and they just covered him—made the notes he couldn't hit. And he was such a charismatic personality on stage that when you watched him, it didn't register that he wasn't singing like he used to. He has always been a great entertainer first. Good people.

There were two other notable trips to Vegas. One was when Ron Jacobs and Tom Rounds wanted to see Sinatra, and I called Elliott Weisman in Florida and he got us a good table. That's when I realized that Concert Sinatra was one thing, but Saloon Sinatra was a lot better. It was a big room, but it was still a saloon setting, with people sitting in front of him drinking.

Another time, I was there for Eddie Sherman's birthday. Eddie had tickets to see Elvis at the Hilton International Hotel, and he invited me to come along. He was married to Peggy Ryan then, and the three of us got there at the last minute and went in through the normal channels since I didn't see anybody I knew. This was before Eddie worked with the Colonel to make the Kui Lee Cancer Fund the beneficiary of Elvis' Blaisdell Arena satellite TV show, so what happened next came as a complete surprise. During a break in the music, Elvis recognized Ann-Margret, who was in the audience; they'd done *Viva Las Vegas* together. Then he said he had a special friend from Hawaii in the audience, and while I was looking around to see who was from Hawaii, he introduced *me*. I didn't see anyone from Elvis's entourage, so I don't know how he knew. It was a big thrill, one I'll always remember. 🎤

emcee, and George Burns told a couple of jokes. Others there included Keenan Wynn, Jackie Kahane, Forrest Duke (the Vegas newspaper columnist), Louis Belson (Pearl Bailey's husband as well as a hell of a drummer), Jane Powell, Mr. and Mrs. Kirk Kerkorian (owners of the Flamingo and, later, MGM Grand), Rona Barrett (the Hollywood gossip columnist), Michael Landon, Lucy Arnaz, Bobby Darin, Abe Lastfogel, Ed Ames, Edward G. Robinson, Johnny Ray, Dale Robertson and Lucille Ball. Sweetie and I couldn't believe it.

Later, Wayne went out on his own and separated from

NORFOLK ISLAND
JANUARY 1987

158

CHAPTER 15

Tahiti and Points West

When I first stopped in Guam, it was 1959 and I was on my way to Japan, just before K-POI went on the air. It was a U.S. military institution and you couldn't even leave the airport. I sometimes wondered what it would be like to promote a concert there, but it was almost 20 years before it actually happened. I got a call from the head of McDonald's in Hawaii, who also ran the franchise for Guam. The biggest-grossing McDonald's in the world was in Tamuning, Guam, and he asked me if I could set up a concert to celebrate the opening of the second store, which would be in the capital, Agana.

I went there looking for a concert site, and I found an old baseball field that looked like something out of Abner Doubleday's time, back when he invented the game. I walked into the park, and a couple of kids were coming out and one of them was singing a Kalapana song. I thought that was a good omen.

One of the biggest challenges in this business is to take a site that has never been used as a concert venue and turn it into one. Paseo Stadium in Guam qualified. Sweetie was doing promotions for Hawaiian Airlines at the time, so I got Hawaiian to fly her and some other dancers and musicians to Guam to open the show. It was a sell-out, and from the stage all you could see was a sea of faces—and, off in the distance, a black cloud coming fast. The Hawaiian group had just started, done only a couple

The opening of the University of Guam's Field House gave us a bigger venue to stage crowd-pleasers like Gloria Estefan, the Stars of the Bolshoi Ballet and the Harlem Globetrotters (above). Opposite: Jimmy Buffet and I visited Norfolk Island to track down some very distant relatives.

Bobby Brown played the University of Guam in the summer of 1990.

stations were off the air, so we couldn't announce it.

This was in 1977, when Guam was pretty much unexplored territory. At that time, the only way to get there was on Air Micronesia, stopping at every island on the way, which amounted to something like a 12-hour journey. You stopped at Majuro, you stopped at Kwajalein, Pohnpei, Kosrae, Chuuk. I loved it, because each island had its own personality. On some of them there was no ground control, and if the pilot was uncertain about the winds, he'd make a pass over the field to check the windsock.

I took Cecilio & Kapono to Guam for the first time, and word got out that we were going to pause at the airport at Majuro. Not many outsiders went there, and hardly any entertainers. The planes were primarily freighters, with only 18 to 20 seats. When we got to Majuro, we found they'd let school out so the kids could come to the airport and see C&K. I said it'd be nice if C&K could do a couple of numbers for the kids, but we didn't have time. The airline staff said, "We'll make time." So they held the plane while C&K did a mini-concert.

I've taken quite a few acts to Guam. I took Gloria Estefan there in 1988, and the Stars of the Bolshoi Ballet in '97—that's a story I'll tell later. By now we were using the new University of Guam Field House, which seats about 3,000. That's also where I presented Hulk Hogan and the Harlem Globetrotters. The Stylistics played a Guam hotel. I put C&K in the Guam Greyhound Track. I also took Mike Love and his Endless Summer Band to Guam, and they performed at Jeff's Pirates Cove, not far from where the last surviving Japanese soldier from World War Two was found. Acts liked to play Guam for the

of numbers, when the sky opened up. It rained. And it rained. And rained. In Hawaii, we sometimes call rain a blessing. This was not a blessing—it seemed like a curse. The concert couldn't go on. This was something that'd never happened to me before.

That wasn't the end of it. That night, a snake crawled into a transformer and blew the whole island out. There was no power. McDonald's was to open a few days later and they had a generator, so we borrowed it and were able to get the show on the next night. But we only had half an audience because the people didn't know it was happening; the rest of the island was still dark and even the radio same reason I did: we knew the people were starved for entertainment, and people hungry for more than TV and movies make great live audiences.

Another time my partner in Guam, "Banana" Dan Bradley, called me and said a radio station there wanted to do a promotion where the winners would fly from Guam to Fukuoka, Japan, to see Paul McCartney. The station was willing to buy the tickets, but they'd been told that the show was sold out. They said if I could score the tickets, I'd get a free flight to Japan and get to see McCartney, whom I'd never seen in concert. So I called my friend Al Arashida in Japan, who was promoting the concert, and he said, "What do you need?" I said, "Six tickets—for four winners of a contest and two for Dan and me."

When the six of us arrived in Fukuoka, a sumo tournament had the town fully booked, so our hotel was a half-hour away by train. At any rate, that's what we were told, but we got on a "local," and by the time we got to the arena McCartney was doing his encore. He did three numbers for it, but that was all we caught. The winners were very understanding; they just took it in stride—and that's why I love Guam. Because of the people.

Then we started doing shows in nearby Saipan. One of the first big ones I did there was with Maxi Priest, who was coming in from Japan. A friend told Dan and me to give him all the plane tickets and he'd pre-check us, because we were going on to Guam after the Saipan show. Well, the guy just disappeared. I don't know if he went to a massage parlor and fell in love or what, but there I was with this whole group of Jamaicans. We went to the airport and the ticket agent said, "I can't check you in; you don't have tickets." Banana Dan got her name and

told her, "The concert is a promotion for this airline, and when the show doesn't go on tonight and 3,000 people are disappointed—including the head of the airline on Guam—I'm going to give him your name, because you're the reason the show isn't going to happen." She let us on the plane.

When I first decided to take Kalapana to open the new McDonald's on Guam, I walked down the beach to the Continental Hotel, which was owned by Continental Airlines. It was all bungalows, and I thought it was perfect for our accommodations. Better still, the manager was James Komeya, part of the student delegation that went to the Big Island back when we were classmates at UH.

Over the years, our paths kept crossing, as Jimmy went from that hotel to the Continental on Palau, and then became general manager of a small, upscale resort built by Larry Hillblom on a tiny island that he also owned off the coast of Guam. Larry was the "H" in DHL, the world's largest courier service, a company he organized in Hawaii. A part owner of Continental Airlines, he was now living in Saipan, where he also owned a bank. We're talking major money here. His Cocos Island Hotel was very private—you could only get there by boat—and when I went there with the "boy band" Menudo, James set me up with all the rooms I needed in exchange for a free show for the hotel's guests, the employees and their families.

Just before Menudo took the stage, I was told that a guy sitting in the front row wanted to meet me. He was sitting next to a beautiful local girl; I figured he was a sailor on leave and she was his date. I was rushed, and I greeted them pretty off-handedly. The "sailor" turned out to be Larry Hillblom—a really laid-back guy. When I

KALAPANA
PALAU MARINA HOTEL
Tuesday, September 24, 1991 ★ 9:00 PM
ADMISSION: $20.00
No Exchange/No Refund

organized a concert at his dude ranch on Saipan, he helped us collect tickets at the door. Anyway, the lack of recognition worked both ways on that trip—Menudo had a ball on the island, because at that time it was probably the only beach in the world they could walk down and not be swarmed by fans.

A final Guam memory, slightly related to my Jimmy Komeya story: I was passing through immigration at the Honolulu airport one time and, without looking up, gave my passport to the officer at the desk. "Oh," he said, "Tom Mafia, eh?" Only one person ever called me that—a friend from my university days, Harry Takane, who was one of the first students to befriend me. Wow! That was a special moment, to see him again after so long. Through the years I had often wondered what had happened to him.

Of all the islands in the Pacific, outside Hawaii, there are none I enjoy more than Tahiti. And I have Jimmy Buffet to thank for a lot of that. The first time I presented him in Hawaii was in 1979 when he opened for the Eagles at Aloha Stadium. A couple of years later, I got a call from a mainland friend suggesting Jimmy for the Waikiki Shell. He said Jimmy wanted to do an acoustic

After wangling great tickets for Paul McCartney's concert in Fukuoka, all we caught was the encore.

show and also go to Tahiti; I said I'd make some inquiries and get back to him. I made a few calls and then told my friend that Jimmy's music might be too lyric-driven—English wasn't spoken widely in Tahiti, so he wasn't all that well known there. And he said, "It's like this: if Jimmy isn't going to Tahiti, he isn't doing the Shell." And I already had tickets on sale for the show.

So I made a trip to Papeete and with help from Gabilou, the Don Ho of Tahiti, got the government to finance the show. Jimmy performed in Honolulu and then we flew to Tahiti, where he and I ran all over the island putting up posters. Nobody was buying tickets. It looked like it was going to be a bust. Luckily, this big research ship came in at the last minute and everyone on it bought tickets, saving us.

Afterward, Jimmy wanted to visit Bora Bora, and a friend of mine who ran the hotel there said he'd comp us rooms. Jimmy wanted to do something in return, so he gave an impromptu concert in the hotel bar, though the sound system was no more than a lonely mike lying on the barstool in front of him.

There was an Australian guy with a Tahitian wife who ran a bar near our hotel. He called it Bloody Mary's, after the character in *South Pacific*. He invited us to dinner. The floor was sand. They had fresh fish laid out. Whatever we wanted, they'd cook. So we had this wonderful meal, and after he closed the place, he said he had a treat for us, and he showed the movie *South Pacific* on an old 16mm projector.

Such magic shouldn't have surprised us. Tahiti was where Paul Gauguin went a 100 years earlier to paint, and it was where many of the first Hawaiians came

I took Keola & Kapono Beamer to Tahiti to perform and to record an album, *Tahiti Holiday*, a musical tribute to the brothers' Tahitian ancestors.

from, sailing in great canoes. Boat Day was still a big deal in Tahiti, even if there was daily plane service between most islands and the big hotels stocked all the latest French wines. It was the end of the 20th century, and Tahiti was still the way the South Pacific was supposed to be, too far away from anywhere else to be spoiled by civilization, the

The Norfolk Island Buffett descendants threw a memorable pot luck, and Jimmy's father (right) and I visited the local graveyard in search of long-lost Buffetts.

way some people insist Hawaii is. (They're wrong, of course. If they'd just get out of Waikiki, they'd see the real beauty of Hawaii.)

The first show I took to Tahiti was Keola & Kapono Beamer. The Tahitians loved their music. Then the weekly plane from Honolulu was cancelled, and there I was with a week to kill in Tahiti—tough break! Gabilou suggested I spend a few days on the island of Huahine, where the only thing I could find to read that wasn't in French was James Michener's *Tales of the South Pacific*. I'd never read it before, and I was struck by a character in a story about Norfolk Island, a sea captain whose last name was Buffet. Jimmy'd always said he was the son of a son of a sailor, and I wondered if this sea captain was one of his ancestors. Jimmy said he was, and several years later, when he decided to visit the island

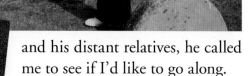

and his distant relatives, he called me to see if I'd like to go along.

He told me he was stopping in New Zealand to hire a private plane to take us to Norfolk and asked me to meet him there. So I was off to Auckland to join Jimmy, along with Sunshine, his assistant and nanny to his young daughter Savanah Jane, his mom and dad, and Doris Buffett—the sister of billionaire businessman Warren Buffett—all drawn by curiosity just as Jimmy was.

According to Michener, Captain Buffet (he spelled it with one "t") arrived on Pitcairn Island sometime after the original Bounty mutineers and then sailed with them to Norfolk Island when Pitcairn was hit with a severe water shortage. Norfolk Island was about as remote as any place could be, equidistant from the east coast of Australia, the northernmost tip of New Zealand and the island of New Caledonia. Michener called it "lonely and lost…the only island in the whole ocean where no man lived before the

Mike Love, performing here with the Beach Boys, also took his End-less Summer Band to Guam, where they played at Jeff's Pirates Cove. Below: In 1988 I produced a live album for Hui Ohana—stars of the '70s Hawaiian music renaissance—recorded at a concert in Papeete.

white man came…a speck under the forefinger of God." All its stone houses, still there when Jimmy and I arrived, were built by convicts sent to the island, the ones too tough for Australia to handle. We landed on an airstrip built by the Americans during World War Two.

It was an amazing few days. Jimmy asked me to introduce him when he gave a little concert in Town Hall. The residents of the small island knew he was famous in America, but they didn't know who he was, just that he was a Buffett (one "t" or two, nobody cared). I was nearby when one of the strings broke on his guitar. He said, "Shit!" and then laughed. "I haven't changed a string in years." He'd always had someone with him to do that.

Before we left, Jimmy's dad and I visited the local graveyard and saw graves marked Buffet and

Fletcher Christian (not the original, of course, but his descendants).

Another special time came a couple of years later in the aftermath of tragedy, when a hurricane hit Tahiti. Gabilou asked if I'd help with a benefit concert, so I got Hawaii's Loyal Garner and New Zealander John Rowles to agree to perform. Jimmy happened to be in town and he volunteered to go, too.

When Jimmy and I went to Tahiti together the first time, he wrote a song with a local musician called "One Particular Harbor." He later recorded the basic tracks when he returned home, and when he was back in Papeete for the hurricane benefit, he recorded the vocal tracks with a Tahitian choir. It became one of his signature songs and one of my all-time favorites. It describes the way I feel about Tahiti and the other remote Pacific islands west of Hawaii: "I don't get there often enough / But God knows I surely try…" 🎤

CHAPTER 16

Classics and Class Acts

Most people who know my name know me as the rock-and-roll guy—the disc jockey who played Bill Haley and Elvis on Island radio before anybody else, who brought the Stones and Michael Jackson to Hawaii. I'm proud of having been in the right place at the right time so I could do that. But I've never forgotten my Midwestern, 1940s musical roots, and little has given me more pleasure than to present people like Sinatra, Tony Bennett, Andy Williams and Count Basie, as well as the younger balladeers, people like Harry Connick, Jr. and Julio Iglesias.

The running joke was, "Julio Who?" I'd seen him in Australia, and most the songs were in another language, so in 1983 when his agent, Dick Alen, called from the William Morris Agency and said Julio Iglesias wanted to play Hawaii, I said, "Julio Who?" I never heard the end of it.

I went to the European manager of the Kahala Hilton—who was well aware of Julio's worldwide popularity—and said I wanted to present him in Hawaii. He knew Julio suited his clientele, so he gave me the rooms. I went back to William Morris and said I'd guarantee them hotel rooms, but I offered no cash guarantee for the show. I thought, who's going to buy tickets for Julio except the upper crust of Honolulu? And they're unpredictable. The agency went along, so my risk factor was way down.

Well, I didn't know it at the time, but Hal "Aku" Lewis was dating a girl from South America. When she heard Julio was coming, she got Aku to start playing his music. No other person in the history of Hawaiian radio has had the power that Aku had. He started talking on the air about this singer from Europe who sang in Spanish, and I sold out one show at the Blaisdell Concert Hall and added a second.

Julio had a rider in his contract: his dressing room had to be stocked Beluga caviar and Cristal champagne—which cost about $200 a bottle. Every concert, this had to be there. Problem was, I couldn't find Beluga caviar anywhere in Hawaii. Here I was, surrounded by an ocean teeming with fish—and no fish eggs. Finally, in despera-

Tony Bennett didn't have a present for my birthday, so he grabbed a napkin, made this sketch and presented it to me. Opposite: Julio Iglesias' champagne and caviar were costing him big-time.

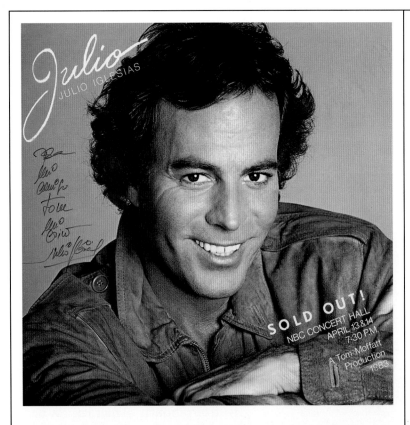

tion, I went back to the Kahala Hilton and said, "What do I do?" The food and beverage manager waved his hand. "Oh, I can get it for you. We have it here." So Julio had his supply in the very place he was staying.

People said Julio could be difficult, but I always got along with him. He called me "TOE-mee," and I remember one time at the Kahala Hilton he was reading a review that said his delivery was questionable. "TOE-mee," he said, like a little boy who'd been scolded by his mother, "how can they write this? I have the greatest vibrato in the world!"

He had a girlfriend with him and another girlfriend in another hotel. That kept him pretty busy. As for the champagne, he'd have a glass and that was it, and maybe he'd never even touch the Beluga! And the next time I brought him in, I looked at the contract and there was no rider for the champagne and caviar. I asked why, and I was told that his accountant figured out how much it

was costing him. For a big act like that, it's cost off the top, and the act gets 85-90% of the net at the gate. That meant Julio was paying for 85 or 90% of the Cristal and caviar himself. According to his accountant, with all the shows he did, that particular expense had climbed to six figures a year.

The second time he came to Hawaii, in 1984, Julio sold out at the Blaisdell Arena on December 29, and two days later I booked him into the ballroom of the Sheraton Waikiki for New Year's Eve. Meanwhile, Jeff Wald, a Hollywood agent and personal manager who'd become a friend, was getting married and wanted to have the reception at my house. I was up to my neck with Julio, so my wife and Jeff worked it out. Julio had rented a place out in Portlock, and after I said goodbye to him, I rushed to my house for the wedding, thinking about Jeff.

He had a reputation for being hard to get along with, too, and it wasn't totally undeserved. Jeff had once punched out a member of Rod Stewart's entourage in the Kahala Hilton lobby. But we went way back, to when he was working as an agent and met an unknown Helen Reddy, whom he later married. (That was an earlier marriage.) After their honeymoon in Australia, I'd gotten a call from Frank Day, who had introduced them, to book a room in Waikiki for this new singer and her husband-manager. So I got them a beachfront room in Waikiki for the unheard-of rate of $30 a night—we've been friends ever since. All the shows we did together we did on a handshake, and everything always turned out well.

One time, I presented Helen Reddy at the Sheraton Waikiki, and after the concert Jeff heard about a young Hawaiian named Eddie Aikau who had disappeared while trying to paddle his surfboard for help when the famous traditional voyaging canoe, the *Hokulea*, was disabled in Hawaiian waters. A fund had been set up in Eddie's name, and Jeff said he had given away most of our earnings to this worthwhile cause. I didn't argue with him.

With these thoughts in my mind, I finally arrived home, where I found the most incredible crowd of people in my ballroom. A lot of Hollywood celebrities stay at the Kahala Hilton during the Christmas-New Year holidays, and they were all there, including producer David Geffen, James MacArthur from *Hawaii Five-O, Westwood One* founder Norman Pattiz, cosmetic mogul Larry Freeman and Jeffrey Katzenberg of Dreamworks. When I meet people like this I'm still in awe.

I've promoted Tony Bennett four times, but one of the most memorable occasions was a New Year's Eve gathering with him and Tony Danza. One of my dearest friends, Judy Tannen, was there—she'd worked with Steve Lawrence and Eydie Gorme for years, and they were vacationing in Hawaii at the time. Judy and I had discovered that we shared the same birthday, so when she was in the Islands, we always got together. We all had dinner after the show, with Sweetie, and it was kind of a birthday party for Judy and me as well. Tony Bennett didn't have a gift, so he took a napkin and sketched me and gave it to me as a birthday present.

Ballet has usually drawn good crowds in Hawaii—from Nureyev and Fonteyn to the Stars of the Bolshoi. When I met her at the airport, I thought the Bolshoi's prima ballerina, Natalia Bessmertnova, (above) was the seamstress.

That's something I still treasure. I never could have imagined such a thing when I was spreading manure back in Michigan!

But that's the way the class acts behave. They aren't in this business exclusively for the buck. I brought in a dance show a couple of times called "Forever Tango." It played forever in San Francisco, but it didn't do well in Hawaii. They were the top tango dancers in the world, and it just didn't happen. I had faith in the act, so I brought them back, thinking word of mouth would make

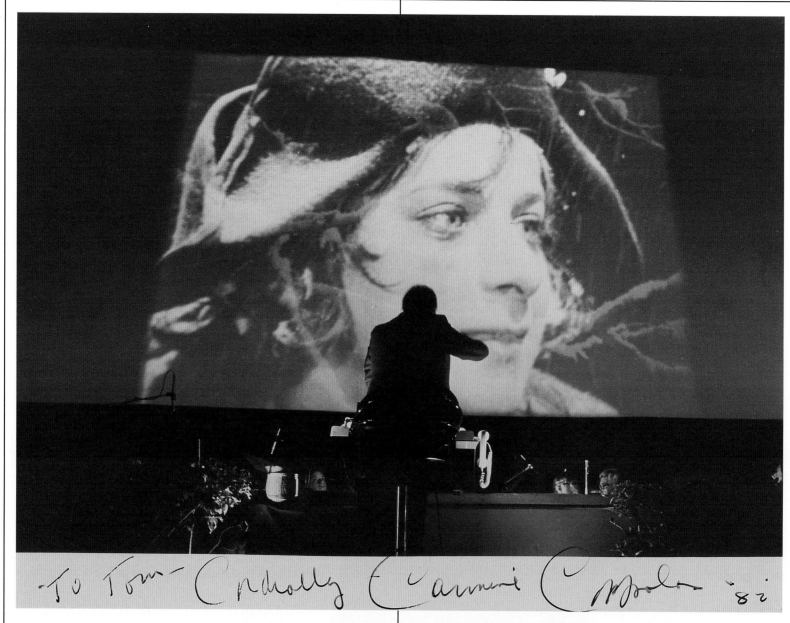

With Carmine Coppola conducting the Honolulu Symphony, the silent film *Napoleon* filled three big screens at the Waikiki Shell.

them more successful the second time. I presented them at the Hawaii Theatre, and it didn't happen again. That time they knew I was losing money, and the show's producer, Luis Bravo, said if I was losing money he didn't want to make any. So I didn't have to pay the rest of the guarantee, reducing my loss considerably.

That doesn't happen very often, though. Tony Bennett is a really nice guy, but when I presented him at

the Blaisdell Concert Hall one New Year's Eve, it seemed people just didn't want a concert situation; they wanted a ballroom where you could sit and drink. When his representatives knew I was losing money with him, they were on the phone to make sure I'd pay. They were on me like hawks. I'm sure Tony wasn't even aware it was happening.

I heard another unfriendly voice at the opening of the posh Hyatt Waikoloa Resort on the Big Island. The hotel wanted a special concert, so I made a deal to get Burt Bacharach and Dionne Warwicke, a five-star act for a brand-new five-star hotel. It was going to be the first show in the ballroom. I was very concerned about the sound, and Burt was really conscious of it, too. So when the concert started, I walked around with Burt's guy, and we were both happy with what we heard.

Then I went and stood in the back of the room, and this young woman was standing next to me, the head of PR for Hyatt Hotels in Hawaii. And there was a guy standing next to her who started complaining about the sound, said it was a cheap system. I said, "Bullshit!" And the woman kind of disappeared; she just melted away. I told the guy it was the best sound system in Hawaii.

It turned out that his family owned the Hyatts worldwide.

My experience with classical shows, meanwhile, has been mixed. Rudolph Nureyev was the first I brought to Hawaii, in 1981. He'd been at the Shell years before with Dame Margot Fonteyn; he was successful then, and he was successful again for me. He was an icon, maybe the single best-known name in ballet worldwide, a cultural superstar—and Hawaii supports superstars.

The next year I brought in *Napoleon,* one of my biggest disappointments. This movie was a spectacular produced the year the talkies hit, so all of a sudden it was an epic that was technologically obsolete and consequently was put on a shelf. (The same thing happened with a lot of silent screen stars, whose voices were weak or so heavily accented they couldn't make the transition to sound.) Well, Francis Ford Coppola found the film in Europe and resurrected it. He was already one of Hollywood's biggest directors, the *Godfather* films having made him one of the industry's golden boys. His father, Carmine Coppola, who'd done the music for the *Godfather* series, arranged and conducted the *Napoleon* music with a live orchestra, and Francis presented it at Radio City Music Hall in New York. It was a smash there, so I brought it to the Shell.

It flopped. It didn't get the Symphony crowd, although I had the Honolulu Symphony Orchestra with Carmine Coppola conducting, on three big screens, just like at Radio City Music Hall. I played it two nights. It was an "artistic triumph," which means you lose money. The classical crowd is tough to sell to in Hawaii. I guess most people thought it was only a four-hour movie in black and white, but it was more than that. It was a symphony by a gifted composer and conductor, created especially for the film. The people who saw it were just blown away.

Not many came out either when I put k.d. Lang on with the Honolulu Symphony. I did remarkably well with the Joffrey Ballet when their theme was Prince and *Purple Rain,* but when I brought them back a year later to perform a classical ballet, it wasn't nearly as successful.

I had a different experience with the same result when I brought in Jose Carreras, who had appeared just about everywhere with Placido Domingo and Pavarotti as one of the Three Tenors. He'd just done a show for National Public Television. I got the Shell and started promoting, and I thought I was doing well. I went to a friend's house on Diamond Head the night of the TV broadcast, and all through the neighborhood, everybody seemed to be watching it. I thought I was home free. Then, suddenly there was a hurricane watch—in July! Jose's show was on a Friday night, and we had bad weather all week and that killed the momentum and stopped ticket sales. What should have been a home run ended up a strikeout.

It's hard to sell culture in Honolulu; it really is.

But I wasn't ready to quit. When Kevin Jacobsen, an old friend and a successful Australian promoter, called and said he had the Stars of the Bolshoi Ballet coming to the Sydney Opera House and that they were available

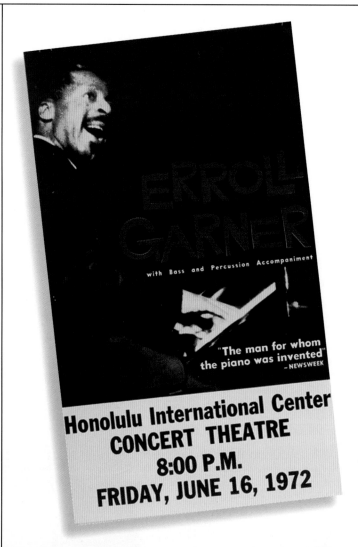

for other dates, I was very interested. He said they were available to perform in Guam and that the Bolshoi's prima ballerina, Natalia Bessmertnova, would be with them. Her husband, Yuri Grigorovich, was the director of the Bolshoi Ballet. That kind of made it for me, that we had the prima ballerina. So I told Kevin that after I'd seen them, I'd say yes or no for Honolulu. I called Banana Dan, who booked a date in the University Field House, and headed for Guam.

I met the company there on the tarmac. I couldn't find the interpreter and was told that nobody spoke English, so I approached a woman I thought was a seamstress and she helped me identify who was coming off the plane. There was a language barrier, but with sign language and a lot of laughter, we got them all together. When the interpreter finally appeared, I asked her who the prima ballerina was. She said it was the woman I'd been talking with.

It wasn't the whole Bolshoi and we didn't have an orchestra, so the music was recorded, but we did well. I was knocked out by them and booked them to appear in Honolulu two weeks later. We did outstanding business.

One of my favorite moments in classical music came with the Shanghai Symphony. They were traveling with a crew from China's national television network, which was making a documentary, and I was asked if I'd give

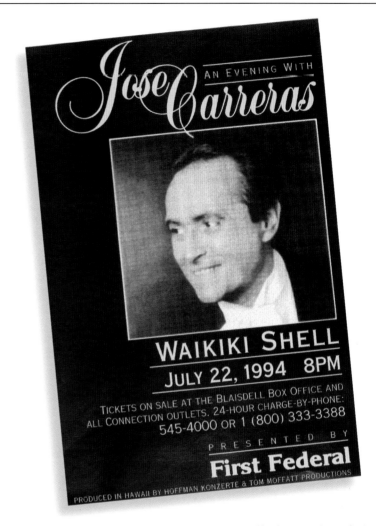

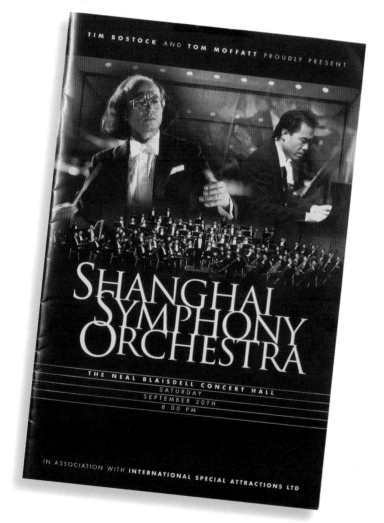

them an interview at the Concert Hall the night of the Symphony's performance. I knew this would be seen by millions of people in China, so I wore a tuxedo. Then I ran into a former director of the Honolulu Symphony, who believes that people should attend classical events dressed in casual Hawaiian wear. Often I go to the concerts dressed even more informally than that, sometimes in jeans and a tee shirt with some rock band's name on it. When he looked askance at my formal attire, I smiled. "I'm just hanging out with the guys in the band," I said. 🎤

CHAPTER 17

Stage Shows and Spectaculars

When I heard about a show called *Elvis – the Concert*, I knew I had to bring it to the Islands. By 2004, when the show was touring the mainland, Elvis had been dead for more than 25 years, but he was even bigger than ever. Graceland, his estate in Memphis, was second only to the White House in number of annual visitors to a home. His records were still selling big numbers. I doubt there was a city anywhere without an Elvis impersonator working the local clubs. And when *Elvis – the Concert*—a re-creation that mixed performance video with live performances by Elvis' original backup musicians and singers—went into Radio City Music Hall in New York, it was a big smash. Elvis had made three movies in the Islands, and some of his most memorable concerts were at Hawaii venues, including the *Aloha from Hawaii* show broadcast around the world by satellite. He vacationed in the Islands, too, until shortly before he died. Elvis had loved Hawaii and Hawaii *loved* Elvis, so I just knew it would be a slam-dunk, and I booked it into the Blaisdell Arena.

The way it worked was they'd reunited Elvis's rhythm section—James Burton on guitar, Glenn D. Hardin on keyboards, Jerry Scheff on bass and Ronnie Tutt on drums—along with two of the backup groups he used, the Sweet Inspirations and the Stamps Quartet, and an orchestra conducted by Joe Guercio. All of them had appeared with Elvis on tour and onstage in Las Vegas. Now they were

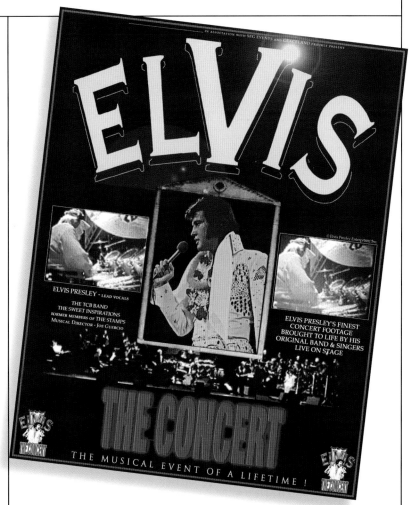

Elvis – the Concert was more like *Elvis – the Flop*, when I presented it at Blaisdell. On the other hand, the *American Idols Live* tour (opposite) was a slam-dunk, thanks to Hawaii's "idols"—Jasmine Trias and Camille Velasco (left and second from left).

Olympic star Kristi Yamaguchi is loaded with leis as she poses backstage at Blaisdell with me and Nohelani Cypriano, after skating to one of Nohelani's hit songs.

I just knew Hawaii would love this—and I was wrong. The technical costs were so high, with all the lighting and the screens and so on, that I could hear Colonel Parker scolding me for spending so much money on production. What was worse was that the public didn't understand the concept. Even the guy doing my radio commercials for the show—a good friend of mine, Dunbar Wakayama, whose production studios were in the same building as my offices—didn't understand. A few days before the concert, he asked me who the Elvis "impersonator" was going to be.

And the people did not come. Bank of Hawaii believed in the show so much it bought a big block of tickets, so most of my expenses were covered. But I still lost money. That's the way it is in my business. Almost every show is a roll of the dice—a comparison the Colonel would approve of. Sometimes you win, sometimes you don't.

A big promotion company on the mainland called and asked if I'd do a show called *Stars on Ice*. I asked who was coming, and they said Kristi Yamaguchi and Scott Hamilton. Kristi was a mainland-born Japanese girl, a former Olympic champion, and the people of Hawaii just loved her. This was a Winter Olympics year—all I had to do was put the sign out. We did that a couple of years running, and I looked like a hero. Everybody made money.

I also presented *Ice Capades* and *Disney on Ice* in the Blaisdell Arena and a version of the old holiday standby, *Nutcracker on Ice*, also in the Arena but on a specially constructed stage. Shows like this require a long set-up time. In the Arena, they start turning the floor into an ice rink on Monday for a Friday show, and it's a 24-hour process. People have to be there around the clock, to keep smoothing and leveling the ice, as well as to provide security for a building that's usually locked up tight at night. One year we filmed the process and gave the film to the local television stations every day, and they put it on the evening news. On the final day, the film showed a rehearsal.

onstage together again, and overhead were two big projection screens, showing film of Elvis in performance. Audiences, especially when sitting in the more distant seats, were accustomed to watching the acts on overhead screens by now. So it didn't seem unusual to watch Elvis on a screen and think he was actually "in the building." It was almost as if he were there singing to a live band. And when Elvis, on film, introduced Joe Guercio, the spotlight went onto Joe Guercio live on stage, taking a bow.

How did I do? *Ice Capades* did okay, but nothing great. When I brought Mickey Mouse with Donald Duck and all his Disney friends on ice, it created a lot of interest, and that's when I learned another big lesson. I went to Oceanic Television for sponsorship, because they had the Disney Channel and I figured we could cross-promote. But even with their help, the costs were very high. So I told myself we'd make money from the concessions. When it was all over, and I got a profit-and-loss statement, I learned about what's called "creative accounting," a term used to explain why even the most successful movies don't make money—on paper. The mainland company had charged off the cost of flying their people to Hawaii against the concession earnings. In this way, I was cut out of the picture. After that, when dealing with the big producers for the first time, I try for a piece of the gross, not the net.

After two successful years of *Stars on Ice*, there was *Nutcracker*, a staple during the Christmas holidays. Looking back, I see the mistakes I made. I'd had *Stars on Ice* the previous summer, and maybe Honolulu just wasn't ready for another ice show so soon. Worse, I put it on a stage, so that instead of looking down at the performance, many people in the audience had to look up. I was also competing with other *Nutcracker* productions (minus the ice), at the Concert Hall and high schools around the Islands. I'll be honest here: I had a condo on Kauai and I lost so much money on *Nutcracker*, I had to sell it to pay for my losses.

I used the Concert Hall for three one-man shows, and they were more successful. The first presented the esteemed actor Hal Holbrook in *Mark Twain Tonight*, in which he did little more than talk, appearing in the wardrobe and makeup that, along with the writer's original words, actually made you think you were spending an evening with the famous author.

My good friend Joe Moore, the long-time Honolulu newscaster, decided to do something similar on Will Rogers, the humorist and cowboy philosopher from the 1930s. To promote the show, I suggested that Joe start ending his newscasts with something Will Rogers said. He was eminently quotable. And in the show itself, Joe was excellent—except when he twirled and threw a lasso over a milk can, a trademark part of Will Rogers's original vaudeville act. It always worked for Joe during rehearsals, but on opening night he missed.

Later, Joe came back with an evening on another of his heroes, John Wayne. His voice was pretty good—if not as perfect as Rich Little's impression—but I have to say he had Wayne's walk down to a T. His voice wasn't bad, but that walk was perfect. Joe and I both did well with both shows.

Sesame Street and four touring Broadway shows followed—*Camelot, Porgy and Bess, Bye Bye Birdie* and *A Chorus Line*. I partnered on these shows with Jerry Lonn. He took care of the technical parts and I did the marketing. There was only one real name, Troy Donahue in *Birdie*, but all the actors were Broadway

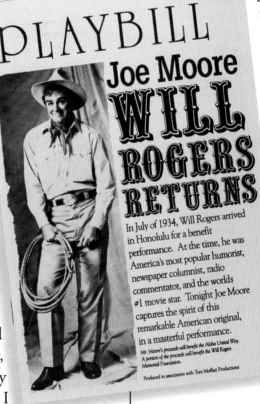

PLAYBILL
Joe Moore
WILL ROGERS RETURNS

In July of 1934, Will Rogers arrived in Honolulu for a benefit performance. At the time, he was America's most popular humorist, newspaper columnist, radio commentator, and the worlds #1 movie star. Tonight Joe Moore captures the spirit of this remarkable American original, in a masterful performance.

Mr. Moore's proceeds will benefit the Aloha United Way. A portion of the proceeds will benefit the Will Rogers Memorial Foundation.

Produced in association with Tom Moffatt Productions

We presented newsman Joe Moore and his one-man *Will Rogers Returns* in Honolulu and at Parker Ranch's Kahilu Theatre on the Big Island.

veterans. The shows had proven themselves on the road, and we did well.

Then came the most successful, no-effort, slam-dunk experience of my entire career—presenting *American Idols Live* in the Blaisdell Arena. It was part of a reunion tour of the performers who'd just starred in the TV competition. And it was even bigger, and easier, than the Rock.

American Idol can be traced back to Major Bowes' *Original Amateur Hour*, a talent contest on radio, and, later, Arthur Godfrey's *Talent Scouts* on TV, and after that, Al Masini's successful *Star Search*. It's an old concept, anyway, of talent competing against talent, almost always amateur vs. amateur. *American Idol* originated in England and, when it was imported to U.S. television, auditions were announced for different parts of the country, including Hawaii. Thousands tried out across the country. The idea was to put the singers on television and let the public vote by dialing toll-free numbers, thereby whittling the finalists down over the course of a season. Toward the end of the season, *American Idol* was doing three prime-time shows a week and all were in the week's Top 10.

In the spring of 2004 two of the finalists were from Hawaii—Jasmine Trias from Oahu and Camille Velasco from Maui. I had no hesitation; I knew the live tour concert would sell out with two local girls involved. Hawaii has always supported its own, just as they turned out for the Rock and before that for Bette

Midler, the Beamers, C&K and Yvonne Elliman.

There was also a change in the technology that made a big difference. In years past, we had sold tickets only at the Blaisdell or Stadium box offices. If you wanted a seat at the event, you had to show up in person and buy a ticket. For some of my shows, at 5:30 in the morning the Blaisdell line ran all the way down Ward Avenue and curled around onto King Street. People wanting good seats for the Stones spent the night outside the box office in sleeping bags! But with the concept of speed dialing in place, it became a whole new ball game. Hawaii had cast hundreds of thousands of votes in supporting our two local finalists, and I knew we'd sell tickets that way, too, so the whole concept of standing in line was gone. Now all you had to do was go online or call a toll-free number.

So I called a good friend who was working with the promotional company handling the *American Idol* tour. He said they couldn't afford to come to Hawaii. I said, "What if I guarantee two shows?" I was that sure of it. And because of that, they came. And I sold out two shows in four hours, and added a third. With all the *Idol* hysteria, we could've sold out another, but the building wasn't available for a fourth night.

The show had three facets. Most important, of course, was the talent. Then there were three judges, who gave their opinions after each performance. Third was the voting. Most of the judges were singers themselves, and they were generally pretty kind. But one was a cynical Englishman who seemed to find fault with everyone.

HAL HOLBROOK in MARK TWAIN TONIGHT!

"Deeper, richer and more uncanny than ever now."
Douglas Watt, N.Y. DAILY NEWS

NEAL BLAISDELL CONCERT HALL
HONOLULU
SANDWICH ISLANDS
FRIDAY EVENING, AUGUST 1, 1986
8 PM

In his one-man show in the Blaisdell Concert Hall, Hal Holbrook made you believe you were really spending an evening with an American literary legend.

This guy pulled out all the stops, telling the singers, "You have no business being here"—that kind of thing. You hated him, but you'd still tune in to see what he was going to say.

Sometimes that worked to the contestant's advantage. When he told one of the girls from Hawaii that she didn't have a chance, half a million people voted for her and she stayed in the competition. The Island girls didn't win, but they and the people of Hawaii sure put on a performance. After the tour, the promotional company said the shows in the Islands were the best. We sold more tickets per capita than any other location, and everybody had fun.

When someone was selected to be on *Idol*, she or he was required to sign up with a production company; they couldn't perform on their own for a contracted period of time. They couldn't even go home and sing at a high school dance. (Which is why Jasmine made her hometown debut in 2005 at her alma mater to help raise funds for a new gym.) They had the performers handcuffed. The three Hawaii shows grossed $883,000, and I'm sure that wasn't reflected in the salaries they received.

I didn't take home very much of the money either, but it was still one of the most successful promotions I've done. And it was a no-brainer. Blaisdell Arena—three nights—boom, boom, boom!

By the way, when I was asked if I wanted to do it again the following year, I said no. There were no local kids involved, and I didn't think I could do half a house.

Far more modest and in some ways more satisfying is a show we've produced for several years now, just before Halloween. Anyone who lives in Hawaii or has visited during the last week of October knows Halloween is celebrated almost out of all proportion to reality, so we thought people would like a really scary haunted house. It's hardly a new concept. Many schools and local organizations have had haunted houses for years. We were ready to spend some money on it, though, and have tried to come up with something that really scares the hell out of people. One year, we had someone positioned just before the exit with a chainsaw. Remember *The Texas Chainsaw Massacre*? Our saw didn't have a blade, but it didn't matter—when that guy cranked it up and came at you out of the dark, you screamed—and maybe wet your pants. In the style of all those Freddie Krueger, slasher and ghost movies, we called our creation Shockhouse.

My staff created it with Rick McCall, who supplies staging and special effects equipment locally, working with little theater groups and drama classes to find people to appear as ghouls in our show. The first year we staged it at Ala Moana Center, then moved it to the Aloha Tower Marketplace, and in 2003 we took it to the Blaisdell Exhibition Hall to accommodate the growing crowds. When we open the doors the weekend before Halloween, the lines are all the way to the Blaisdell parking lot.

ENCORE ATTRACTIONS & MERRINGTON PRODUCTIONS JERRY LONN, MIKE MERRICK, JOHN ADAMS PRESENT

LERNER & LOEWE'S

Camelot

STARRING
JAMES WARWICK

BOOKS & LYRICS BY
ALAN JAY LERNER

MUSIC BY
FREDERICK LOEWE

ORIGINAL PRODUCTION DIRECTED & STAGED BY
MOSS HART

BASED ON THE "ONCE & FUTURE KING" BY
T.H. WHITE

SET DESIGN BY
BRAD KAYE

LIGHTING DESIGN
RICHARD SCHAEFER

SOUND DESIGN BY
WALLY FLORES

CHOREOGRAPHER
DENIZE de LAPPE

MUSICAL SUPERVISOR
WILLIAM R. COX

DIRECTED BY
STONE WIDNEY

PRODUCED BY
ENCORE ATTRACTIONS

BLAISDELL CONCERT HALL
special limited engagement
Wed-Sun, MAY 3 - 7
(Matinees on Saturday and Sunday)
Tickets at Blaisdell Box office and all Connection outlets
24-hour Charge-By-Phone 545-4000

presented by
TOM MOFFATT PRODUCTIONS

National touring shows of hit musicals, featuring Broadway veterans, always seem to do well.

Another promotion that gave me pride was a magic show we did with the Shriners, as a fundraiser for their Children's Hospital. They'd done quasi-amateur magic shows before, but when Tracy Larrua, who'd worked for me and then become a top PR gal in Los Angeles, sent me some material about a professional magician named Franz Harary who wanted to come to Hawaii, I put them together. In the world of magic, Franz was known mainly as the guy who created some of the most imaginative illusions for David Copperfield and some of the other big names in the entertainment field. Franz had his own show by then, and when the Shriners decided to go with him and do their first show with big illusions, I booked a date at the Blaisdell Concert Hall.

To promote the show, Franz said he'd make the Mayor disappear. Mayor Jeremy Harris, a good sport, went along with it. All he had to do was crouch beneath a bench outside the Blaisdell Center—the rest was done with mirrors. The trick went off well, but a spoilsport of a photographer from the one of the daily newspapers sneaked around to where people weren't supposed to go and took a picture of the Mayor under the bench. I'm sure some people thought it was funny.

Nor did I like it when, after the show, one of the Shriners accused us of being in collusion with the stage-hands' union and skimming money from his organization. The Shriners had presented magic shows before on a much smaller scale, where the backstage labor was pretty much done by volunteer Shriners. Well, Franz's show was high tech with an intricate set and rigging, and that meant you had to have seasoned stagehands working, union stagehands, because someone could get seriously hurt if something wasn't properly rigged.

And this guy was saying we stole because the union guys got paid so much. It's true; the union guys do make big bucks. Oftentimes they make more money than I do. But they aren't always guaranteed jobs, so when they're highly skilled and they do get work, they get top money. None of this came out publicly, but it bothered me. It still bothers me, that somebody could be that petty.

But that was just one guy. On the whole, the Shriners were happy—in fact, they were so pleased that the head of the show committee presented me with an Aloha Lodge fez. I was very honored, as they had never made a presentation like this before to a non-Shriner.

When I think of "spectaculars," there's one that stands out above all the rest: the Tube show at the Stadium. Tube was a Japanese supergroup that celebrated its 15th anniversary by staging its first-ever concert in the United States. And it wanted Hawaii's largest concert venue, Aloha Stadium.

This wasn't like any other Stadium show—not even close. This was promoted as more than just a rock concert by Japan's most popular quartet; it was to be a special-effects extravaganza using thousands of gallons of water erupting in fountains and "water pillars." People in the first 20 rows of seats were told to expect to get wet. In addition there were fireworks and balls of flame that emerged from a height of 100 feet. For the finale, a helicopter flew overhead with a spotlight brought in from Universal Studios, just to bathe the audience in brilliant light.

Nor was their stage like any I'd seen before. In comparison, Michael Jackson's was a piece of cake. (He was traveling with Russian cargo planes and a crew adept at setting up and breaking down his light and sound systems and stage in a day or two). Tube started from

My most spectacular "spectacular": the Aloha Stadium extravaganza staged by the Japanese supergroup Tube in the summer of 2000. Opposite: *American Idol* performers who sold out the Blaisdell Arena for three nights in a row include local favorite Jasmine Trias.

scratch and required 10 days to get everything in place, tested and ready to go. Technicians were flown in from the UK, joining a large crew from Japan.

Governor Ben Cayetano proclaimed the date "Tube Day" in Hawaii, and about 15,000 Tube fans came from Japan for the concert. (The Governor's office estimated these fans would add almost $20 million to the state's economy.) The remaining tickets were sold locally, for just $25—a bargain, I thought, even for a band that not many people in Hawaii knew about.

There were some local connections. Tube's newest album, *Blue Reef*, had been recorded in Hawaii Kai, and an English-language song, "Sha La La," was released on my record label, Paradise, a couple of months ahead of the concert as a fund-raiser for the Easter Seals Hawaii education program. (My assistant Barbara, who was very much involved in getting Tube to come to Aloha Stadium, helped write the English lyrics.) But other than that, Tube came and Tube went, roaring through town like a hurricane—but leaving behind only that money the Governor talked about.

I never saw anything like it. When the Stadium cleanup crew came out after the concert, there was nothing to clean up. The Japanese spectators had picked up after themselves completely. And two days later, the Stadium was a football field again. 🎙

CHAPTER 18

The Blaisdell: My Second Home

Ilaugh when I recall the first time Dionne Warwicke appeared at the Honolulu International Center Arena in 1970. Almost timidly, she asked if she could have a hot dog and a Coke, and I went to one of the food booths and got them for her. That was my first experience with "catering." Before that, you had a drinking fountain, a few cans of soda, and that was it. Today, catering for a big show in the Arena can cost as much as $10,000!

How did this happen? I'm not really sure I know, but it might help explain why it costs as much it does to see some of the world's top acts.

Since Honolulu's major entertainment complex—now called the Neal S. Blaisdell Center—opened in 1964 with an arena, concert hall and exhibition hall, I've promoted hundreds of events and spent countless hours there, checking the myriad small details with my staff.

I never get tired of it. The lights dim in the Arena, stragglers hurry to their seats and the audience welcomes the stars I'm presenting: Elton John, Willie Nelson, CSN&Y, Grand Funk Railroad, Led Zeppelin, James Taylor, the Beach Boys, the Byrds, Sonny & Cher, Jimi Hendrix, Carole King, Leon Russell, Steely Dan, Jimmy Buffett, the Carpenters, Tower of Power, Santana, Johnny Cash, the Moody Blues, the Eagles, Three Dog Night, the Doobie Brothers, the Doors, John Denver, Chicago, America, the Stylistics, Steve Martin, Engelbert Humperdinck, Gloria Estefan, Lionel Richie, Cyndi

The Who's Pete Townsend and Roger Daltrey rocked the Blaisdell Arena in the summer of 2004, nearly four decades after the band appeared on the same stage in 1967. Opposite: *NSync hovered above the crowd at a New Year's weekend concert.

Lauper, UB40, Barry Manilow, Rod Stewart, Chubby Checker, the Diamonds, Melissa Etheridge, Yvonne Elliman, Journey, Chuck Berry, the Who, Neil Diamond,

"Captain Fantastic" Elton John made a triumphant return to the Arena for sold-out shows in the fall of 1974.

the Rolling Stones or Sammy, Liza & Frank, to name a few. I still feel the same rush that the audience does.

When I welcome the Harlem Globetrotters to the sound of "Sweet Georgia Brown," the Shanghai Circus acrobats, kickboxers from Russia and Thailand, the flashing blades of the *Ice Capades* skaters and Kristi Yamaguchi, Chinese lion dancers and the choreography of the Lipizzaner Stallions, I know it's a small world after all, just as Walt Disney said, and we are about to see and hear—experience, together—something we'll always remember.

My shows at the Blaisdell Concert Hall have been

less numerous but just as special. That's where I watched Bette Midler clean up her act because her mother was in the audience and where I indulged my long-suppressed love of jazz, bringing in the Count Basie Orchestra, Oscar Peterson, Joe Pass and Erroll Garner. It's where Hal Holbrook and Joe Moore pretended to be people they weren't and where some of the acts from China performed, like the national opera and dance companies, the Shanghai Circus and the Shanghai Symphony. Where audiences saw Broadway shows and the Bolshoi and Joffrey Ballets. Where a bit of class prevails and where once upon a time I wore a tux.

When I started to chronicle my 50-plus years in show business, I tried to put together a complete list of all the acts I've interviewed, promoted and introduced—some of whom I've come to call friends. I was truly, truly amazed.

I remember when I went to Osaka to see Elton John and Billy Joel. A friend was promoting it, so I got tickets to the show. I went backstage and Billy was there. I'd brought leis for both of them, but Elton was going to arrive at the last minute and I didn't get to see him. This was in the late 1990s and he hadn't appeared in Hawaii in a long time, maybe 20 years. There was a girl who worked for my friend the promoter, and I asked her to be sure that Elton got the lei from me. The reason I had *gone* to Japan was to see Elton. I thought if I could see him, I could invite him back to Hawaii, and maybe we could do a concert. I went backstage after the show, but he and his entourage were booked on a bullet train to Tokyo, and by the time I got back there, he was gone. Emme Tomimbang, the Hawaii TV personality, was close to one of the guys who traveled with Elton, and when I got back to Honolulu she told me that she'd talked to her friend, who said Elton was so happy I'd remembered his birthday and brought him a lei. I didn't know it was his birthday! Within a year, he was doing a concert at the Arena, and it was an acoustic concert, just Elton and his piano. To hold an audience for over two hours like that, that's really special. I always wondered if that little misunderstood gesture of mine made it happen.

The first time Elton came to Hawaii, it was because my friend Tom Hulett called and said, "It might not happen right away, but give this guy a shot because he's going to be a giant." I trusted Tom. So we did a concert and did half a house, which meant the money was marginal for both of us. The next time he did a sold-out show, and the time after that, two sold-out shows. The fourth time, we sold out two shows and I wondered about doing a third. I was a bit apprehensive, but I decided to go for it. I was with my son Troy on Kauai and flew back early because I wanted to see what the line was like. I remember getting to the Blaisdell and the line was, like, Woooo! and I knew we had a third sell-out.

After that acoustic concert in 2000, Elton came back to the Blaisdell a year later to perform with his band. He wanted to come back again after that, but he won't stay anywhere in town except the Kahala Mandarin Oriental (formerly the Kahala Hilton). Unfortunately, he was only available that year during the Hawaiian Open, and the hotel was full. He always puts on a great show; he plays all his big hits but is also fresh and surprising. He loves the Islands, and I always know he'll be back. Sir Elton is special.

Another of my favorites only played the Blaisdell once, but I'll remember it forever, because it was one of the few times a local performer filled the place. It's quite a story. Yvonne Elliman grew up in Hawaii. Her mother was Japanese; her father was haole. Just after graduating from

When Sonny and Cher came to town in 1965 to play the HIC Arena, we had a luau for them at the Otani home.

Roosevelt High School she traveled to England and was singing in a coffeehouse in London when Andrew Lloyd Webber walked in. He was there to listen to another singer, who didn't show, so Webber stayed for Yvonne and signed her for the Mary Magdalene role in the original London production of *Jesus Christ Superstar*. She then starred in the Broadway and Hollywood versions of the musical and toured extensively with Eric Clapton. She also sang backup on "I Shot the Sheriff," the song that turned me on to the music of Bob Marley.

The fifth Highwayman? A country supergroup, the Highwaymen consisted of (left to right) Waylon Jennings, Johnny Cash, Willie Nelson and Kris Kristofferson.

On her own, she had a number-one national hit in 1978, "If I Can't Have You," the fourth number-one single from the *Saturday Night Fever* soundtrack. That was the year I showcased her at the Blaisdell, and it was a sell-out and a great show.

I got to know Roger Forrester, Eric Clapton's manager, the first time Eric came to Hawaii, and after that Roger's wife, Annette, and Sweetie became corresponding friends. Annette visited us in Hawaii, and the two of them went to Tahiti together. So we did Eric at the Blaisdell, and when I got home after the show, I got this frantic call from

Roger. He said, "Tom, you've got to do something—they're going to arrest Eric."

Eric and his band were staying at the Hilton Hawaiian Village Hotel, and I heard it was something about his being out on a ledge there. I called Joe Kama, who handled security for me at the show and knows everybody at the police department. Joe rushed to the Hawaiian Village, where hotel security was holding Eric, and got there just as two police officers were arriving to arrest him. One looked at the other and said, "We can't arrest him—he's

Eric Clapton." Seems the officer came on duty after attending the concert. Anyway, Joe helped smooth things over, and there was no arrest.

What was he doing out on the ledge in the first place? Eric and his band had just come from Japan, where he had acquired a samurai sword. He and his musicians and road crew had taken the whole 18th floor of the Hawaiian Village's Rainbow Tower—Eric was on one side of the building, and on the other side was the room of a band member who'd just gotten married. Eric decided to play a trick on him and was crawling along a ledge around the outside of the hotel in a kimono, carrying this sword. When he reached the opposite side, the bride looked out the window and screamed, "Oh, my god, what is it?" Her new husband said, "Don't worry, it's only Eric." But one of the hotel security guys spotted Eric, figured he was a burglar and called the police.

The next night we had a reception, and Eric looked at me sheepishly and said, "You'll have to excuse last night. Every time I have a few drinks, I think I'm a bloody steeplejack."

I haven't been able to get him to stop in Hawaii on his way back from Japan or Australia since. He was married to Patti Boyd at the time and she was traveling with him, and the Customs guys at the Honolulu airport just took her and her luggage apart. They didn't find anything, but she was practically hysterical. So we lost a couple of Clapton shows.

Willie Nelson I know will perform in Hawaii again

We continued to present the Harlem Globetrotters long after the originals retired—old-time players like Hubert "Geese" Ausbie (right), the Trotters' Clown Prince. In 1982 we staged a Blaisdell basketball game reuniting the members of the Fabulous Five—the University of Hawaii's winningest team ever—who had been big fan favorites in the early '70s.

and again, and he likely won't ever have to pass through Customs on his way, because he lives on Maui. Willie is probably the nicest man in the business. He's just genuinely nice. I've watched him with people. The 2003 concert I did with him was special—I'd presented him several times before, but always with somebody else. I did him with Waylon Jennings, I did him with Leon Russell, I did him in the Blaisdell with the Highwaymen: Kris Kristofferson, Waylon Jennings and Johnny Cash. But never Willie by himself. So this time I did, in the Waikiki Shell.

Don Ho was in the audience, and Willie sang "Night Life," Don's theme song. I think he did a little extra for Don; he played a fantastic guitar solo. My sister-in-law

Christina Aguilera, the first pop star ever to play the University's Stan Sheriff Center, required that all the catered cuisine backstage be organic.

Cultural Center, and Willie was in the audience. I didn't know it until Shep Gordon told me. (Anything I do with Willie, it's with Shep as my partner.) I went over and talked to Willie and his wife, asked him if he was home for a while. He said no, he had to get on a plane next day and go to the Super Bowl. I watched the Super Bowl, and he was one of the featured stars. He hadn't even mentioned that. He still has a home on Maui and he does a lot of things quietly, benefits that nobody hears about. Hawaii's kind of his home now. His kids go to school in the Islands—a couple of young sons who are, I understand, good musicians. Maybe I'll be able to present them one day.

Another favorite at the Blaisdell Arena was the Harlem Globetrotters. They came through several times, playing the Civic Auditorium the year Wilt "the Stilt" Chamberlain had his first season with the team. They'd been around for decades, since way before the National Basketball Association began drawing big crowds, doing the same incredible tricks year after year. They'd come out to their theme song, "Sweet Georgia Brown," and do a warm-up that would dazzle the crowd. In the early years, when they'd take on the pros in a demonstration game, the Trotters always won.

Their appearance at the Civic was one of Ralph Yempuku's promo-

wanted to meet Willie, so I introduced her and my brother to him, and they had a nice chat, and when they left he remembered their names. When people came up to Willie, it was like they were the only people who existed. There was never any sign of impatience. I was really impressed with him.

Hawaii has never been a country music kind of place. I once presented Charley Pride in Honolulu and Vince Gill on Maui, but Hawaii just doesn't have a country audience and those shows lost money. But I'll always be able to sell Willie and his family. In January 2004 I was presenting Bonnie Raitt and Robert Cray at the Maui Arts and

The Hurricane Iniki benefit in 1992 also included Jimmy Buffett as a surprise guest.

tions. The POI Boys played a short game with them there and later at the Blaisdell to promote the show. I wasn't promoting them at the time, but I joined Dave Donnelly, Don Robbs and the other POI Boys in a team we called the POI Pounders on the court against the Globetrotters.

Abe Saperstein was the team's owner and general manager. Joe Anzivino, the former sports editor of the *Honolulu Star-Bulletin*, had left Hawaii to join the Globetrotters' company, and when Abe died he became associated with Abe's successor. After that, I'd promote them in Hawaii, at the Blaisdell Arena. I would laugh when asked if I was bringing the original Globetrotters—most of the early greats, like Goose Tatum and Meadowlark Lemon, had long since retired. I was fortunate to bring some of the last of the great superstars, like Curly Neal and Geese Ausbie, when I presented the Globetrotters in Hawaii and Guam. They were amazing.

Of all the Arena shows, one of those I'm proudest of was the 1992 benefit for people affected by Hurricane Iniki, one of the most devastating storms ever to hit the Islands. It caused hundreds of millions of dollars in damage, especially on Kauai, where Graham Nash had a home. I was in my car when Graham called and asked me to do a benefit. He said he had Crosby, Stills & Nash and Bonnie Raitt and Jackson Browne. I added the Pahinui Brothers, sons of the late, great Gabby Pahinui, who performed together. And when I told Jimmy Buffett about the benefit—he was doing a Honolulu concert a few days later—he became a

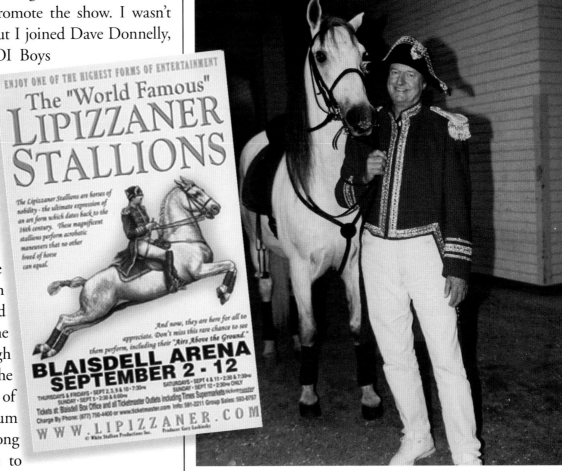

I really got into the spirit of things when Vienna's famed Lipizzaner Stallions rode into town for shows at the Arena.

surprise guest.

As the event came together, I remembered Colonel Parker's advice about how to run a benefit. When Elvis sang at the Bloch Arena to raise money to complete the U.S.S. *Arizona* memorial, everybody paid to get in, including the admirals and the Colonel and Elvis and his father. So I told Graham that that's the way I was going to do it. There would be no complimentary tickets. Everybody pays and every cent of the money goes to the cause.

The Blaisdell had never done this before, but they went along and waived their rent and other charges. I got

Chinese lion dances are always popular events in Blaisdell Arena.

and girlfriends and wives and assorted hangers-on, plus media and whoever else has wangled a backstage pass. And some of the shows have large casts and support teams. It's also more efficient to have the caterer feed the stage crew than to let them go out for their meals, because when they go off-site they seem to lose some of their momentum.

Some acts require special attention, and it's reflected in their contracts. Backstage riders are now sometimes longer than the technical ones. Now on certain days, the acts ask for certain meals. They're on the road, and they don't want chicken five nights in a row. So Thursday may be fish, Saturday steak. Chicago wanted a sushi bar and we set it up, and then they stopped at a restaurant on the way to the Arena and didn't eat a single piece of sushi. Often the show ends, the act leaves, and the appetizer platter's never been touched. Joe Cocker wanted six bottles of the most expensive champagne, and when he ignored it, the crew drank it after they clocked out. (Generally, if the act doesn't eat what's prepared, we invite our crew to join in a late-night snack.) For Christina Aguilera, the first star to do a concert at the University of Hawaii's Stan Sheriff Center, every-thing had to be organic. Others want special wines and cheeses.

We're now also cooking fresh on-site: barbecuing, frying, the whole nine yards. There's never any of the steam-table service that the acts may be getting somewhere else. Steve discovered an artist who can do wonders with a cake; Wesley Oda can duplicate the concert poster on the cake or put on a tropical scene with the message, "Aloha from

the cops, the stagehands, everybody, to donate their time. The only expense we couldn't get around was the State's four-percent tax. And we raised more than half a million dollars.

Speaking of money—back to those big catering bills. How do I explain? I should introduce my caterer, Steve Ozark. I met him in 1975, when he was a lighting guy working for John Rowles and Dick Jensen and others in the hotel show-rooms. When he opened The Meat Bun, a small company specializing in sandwiches, I invited him to bring some for the backstage crew, and after that I asked him to do dinners. Steve watched the caterer who catered for Neil Diamond and thought he could do it better and fresher, and he's been with me ever since.

So why does it cost so much? Well, first you have to know that when I'm catering for, say, the Who, I'm not just feeding four guys. I'm also feeding the Who's road crew

James Taylor has played the Arena a half-dozen times over three decades, including concerts in 1971 (above, in an HIC chair) and 2001 (right).

Waikiki Shell, and even in the Blaisdell Concert Hall—the only facility in the Neal Blaisdell Center that was designed with other than sports performance in mind—the audience sits in front of the stage; they watch the action from straight on. In the Arena there are often seats we can't put people in, because the lights and sound system hanging from the sides and ceiling can block the view. The official capacity of the Blaisdell Arena is 8,800, but for some shows I'm lucky to squeeze in 6,000. When Elton John performed solo we were able to sell most of the seats—just a few were obstructed. But when Frank Sinatra performed in the round, we could have sold every seat in the house.

The arena concept also works for shows like *Ice Capades* and the World Wrestling gang and the Harlem Globetrotters—but they're sports, aren't they?

When it comes to musical acts, Honolulu needs a bigger venue, something that isn't a stadium, because some of the biggest acts really aren't right for stadiums or they themselves don't want to perform in them. That leaves us stuck in the middle. Because of the Arena's limited size—and the University's Stan Sheriff Center is only slightly larger—we can't make a big enough offer to get a lot of the top acts. Stars we've missed because the Blaisdell is too small include Bruce Springsteen, Cher, Madonna and Neil Diamond, to name just a few. I hope that's something the powers-that-be are working on. 🎤

Tom Moffatt!" Some of the acts will take a picture of the cake. That's not in any rider I've seen; it's just something we do for the acts. All of this adds up.

I love the Blaisdell Arena, I really do. It is my second home. But the name tells you a lot about the place. An "arena" was where gladiators fought to the death and Christians were thrown to the lions. Even today, when you say the word, you can faintly smell gym socks and hear locker doors bang shut.

Keep all this in mind the next time you see a show there. It was built primarily with sporting events in mind. The "dressing rooms" were designed as locker rooms for basketball players. (Unfortunately, the main arena floor is too short for hockey, a sport I think Hawaii would love.) So when you put a Sinatra in a locker room and tell him to sing in an "arena," you have to dress it up a bit.

Another thing that makes it difficult is that at the

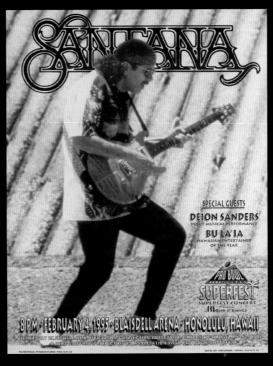

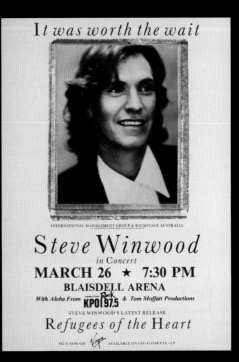

CHAPTER 19

The Stadium Shows

I've already grumbled about the Blaisdell Arena, because it *is* an arena, which was all it was ever intended to be by the architects who designed it—people who, in my darkest moments, I believe never went to a concert in their lives. So what can I say about a stadium?

I can say, "Welcome to Aloha Stadium!" And why not? From the time the Beatles began their first tour of America in 1964 at Shea Stadium in New York, stadiums have been where it's at for the big acts, performers who want the biggest and most of everything. Once presented with this challenge, it remains for the promoter to ask not why, but how?

To be fair, Aloha Stadium *was* designed to accommodate more than sports. With movable grandstands, it was the first of its kind anywhere in the U.S. Using compressed air, the Stadium can be transformed into three configurations, or shapes. The first is a traditional diamond for baseball, which can double as a wide rectangle for soccer. The second is an oval for football. And the third is a triangle for concerts and special events. Actually, the only concert I presented in this configuration was Frank Sinatra's, and

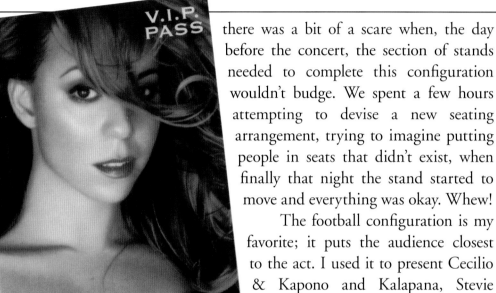

V.I.P. PASS

MARIAH CAREY
ALOHA STADIUM
FEBRUARY 21, 1998
A TOM MOFFATT PRODUCTION

there was a bit of a scare when, the day before the concert, the section of stands needed to complete this configuration wouldn't budge. We spent a few hours attempting to devise a new seating arrangement, trying to imagine putting people in seats that didn't exist, when finally that night the stand started to move and everything was okay. Whew!

The football configuration is my favorite; it puts the audience closest to the act. I used it to present Cecilio & Kapono and Kalapana, Stevie Wonder, Chicago, the Eagles—both with Jimmy Buffett and alone—Billy Joel, Michael Jackson, Janet Jackson and the Rolling Stones.

Once the football season is over the configuration is changed to baseball, and that's the shape I used for the Beach Boys and Heart, Gloria Estefan, Whitney Houston, Mariah Carey and Tube. It all depends on the size of the audience and the arrangement of the performers' sound systems and other equipment.

The number of permanent seats in the Stadium is

Neither a sore throat nor soccer moms could keep Mariah Carey from performing at the Stadium. Opposite: Michael Jackson arrives for what would be Hawaii's biggest concert ever.

around 50,000 total, although many of those can't be used for a concert as they're behind the stage. The maximum I've been able to seat for a concert, including field chairs, was 38,000 for Janet Jackson, an all-time record for a single concert in Hawaii. The size of her brother Michael's stage limited the seating capacity for his show. However, in his two sold-out shows, Michael played to a total audience of over 65,000, a Hawaii record that even the Rolling Stones couldn't match.

The Stadium opened 11 years after the Honolulu International Center, in 1975, and I got my baptism there a little over a year later with Kalapana and C&K. I've already told that story. The second time came about a year later when Don Ho and Big Island rancher Larry Mehau asked me to help organize the talent for a political rally for Governor George Ariyoshi. This was just before the 1976 election, and for a $10 admission, people got a full day of entertainment and a bento lunch. Hundreds of women were busy making the lunches. The food was donated, of course, and everybody worked for free.

I'd never stage-managed a show like that, where dozens of acts had to get on and get off on schedule. (At the Miami Pop Festival, someone else took care of that.) But with the help of Russell Druce, Don's showroom manager, everything went smoothly. The acts pretty much did as they were told, not going over their allotted times (we wanted the show to end at dusk with a giant fireworks display). We were right on schedule when a local comic came

Stevie Wonder agreed to work with me for his performance at Aloha Stadium once we explained there were no black promoters in Hawaii!

on to do his 10-minute act. He was getting a good reaction, and he did what comedians everywhere do when they hear laughter: they stay on. When the show finally ended, we were well into darkness and people were already leaving the Stadium. But those who stayed enjoyed the fireworks. The Governor was re-elected.

Several of my biggest shows seemed cursed, though, and it wasn't the Stadium—it was the situation. It happened with Mariah Carey, Whitney Houston, Stevie Wonder, Chicago and the Rolling Stones.

One of the worst things that ever happened to me in the promotion business involved Mariah. On the dates she wanted, a local soccer tournament was booked at the Stadium. So I went to the head of the soccer association and made arrangements to buy the date out, to pay to have the soccer tournament moved. The guy said fine, no problem, we'll play somewhere else, because soccer wasn't a big draw in Hawaii anyway, and they really didn't need a venue that big.

So we put the tickets on sale and we were sailing along, when some soccer moms got very upset because their kids couldn't play in Aloha Stadium because of Mariah Carey. They started this awful campaign against her, calling radio stations and saying Mariah Carey didn't like Hawaii. A couple of radio guys I knew put one of these women on the air, and she said Mariah Carey had been on *The Tonight Show* and had said Hawaiians were stupid and she really didn't want to come here.

Now, I'd already sold a lot of tickets, so I wasn't in any financial trouble, but it was frustrating because it wasn't true. I checked, and she hadn't done *The Tonight Show* in months. The newspapers called, and I knew if I tried to

A trivia contest was one of many ways we promoted the Rolling Stones when their *Bridges to Babylon* tour rolled into Aloha Stadium in 1998.

My 14-Year-Old Boss

by Shep Gordon

The year was 1974 and I took a bunch of people from my California office to Honolulu for a month. After a few weeks I got bored and called some friends, who told me to hook up with a local promoter named Tom Moffatt. They said he'd help me find something to do.

When I called him, Tom had a concert tour going to the outer islands, so he said I could come along as crew! At the time I was managing Alice Cooper, Groucho Marx, Raquel Welch, Blondie, Anne Murray and Ben Vereen, just to name a few, so I assumed he was joking about the crew part. But, lo and behold, the next day we flew to Maui, where I was introduced to my "boss"—Troy, Tom's 14-year-old son! My job was to sell show merchandise, including the poster. I had my technical director, Joe Gannon along, and he helped sell posters, too. Not that either of us were really needed.

That night, Tom put us up in the Maui Beach Hotel in Kahului, saying that it *used to be* the best hotel on the island. Since there was nothing else to do in Kahului at 11 o'clock at night, Joe and I were watching a movie on TV in our room— you actually had to put quarters in the set to keep it going. We ran out of quarters just before the movie ended; and the hotel office and front desk were closed so we couldn't even get any more change.

After that unexpected introduction to Maui, I decided to move there and continue with my real job—managing talent. I bought a house on the beach in Kihei, and I'm still there 30 years later. I also co-promote concerts with Tom, among them Willie Nelson's and the Rolling Stones'. As for Joe, he moved to Maui, too, with his wife, Beverly, and today they run two of the most successful restaurants on the island—the Haliimaile General Store in Makawao and Joe's Bar & Grill in Kihei. I am forever grateful to Tom for introducing me to that beautiful island. He and I have remained great friends and partners in promotion. It couldn't have worked out better for any of us.

Fifteen years after his first Maui "job" changed his life, Shep Gordon and I joined Gov. Ben Cayetano at a press conference announcing the Rolling Stones Stadium concert.

refute the rumors I'd be adding fuel to the fire. But these women had no basis for what they were saying. Mariah had been *married* on Maui; she *loved* Hawaii!

Then Mariah got a throat problem just before the date. Her manager called me and asked me to meet her at the airport and make sure she got settled at the Kahala Mandarin, since she was traveling alone. She wanted to see a throat doctor, so I called one I knew and asked if he did house calls. He said he was sorry, but he did not. I said, "Well, how'd you like to look down the throat of Mariah Carey?" Needless to say, he rushed right over to the hotel. And Mariah did the show. She talked a lot during the performance. After the press knocked it a bit, saying she'd performed with a throat condition, some people called me for their money back. This, after sitting all the way through a good show without complaint.

The same thing happened when Whitney Houston played the Stadium. She brought her husband, Bobby Brown, along, and they did a few duets—not more than the audience wanted, and he's good. Her hit song from *The Bodyguard*, "I Will Always Love You"—I knew when she was going to sing it, and I took the elevator up to the top of the stadium to listen. It sounded good to me. I hadn't even heard she had a throat problem. But the press mentioned it, and I got some angry letters from people demanding a refund and asking why Bobby Brown sang so many songs. Not one person asked for their money back the night of the show; it was only after the press reports.

In 1998 the Rolling Stones were on the Big Island to perform at a 100th anniversary show for Pepsi-Cola. It's the kind of event even the biggest acts won't turn down, though it's essentially a corporate function, as long as they're paid enough. So they were already in Hawaii as part of their cross-country *Bridges to Babylon* tour, and we wanted to present them at Aloha Stadium. With a venue any smaller, we never would've been able to afford them. The problem was, the date we wanted for the Stadium performance was a week before the NFL Pro Bowl. When the guy who was handling the nationwide Stones tour called the Stadium, he got a flat no. Aloha Stadium management felt the Pro Bowl was too important for Hawaii and that it couldn't be jeopardized by a big concert staged six days earlier. Sometimes 8-to-5-o'clock guys think that way. When I learned that the San Diego Chargers had played on their field on a Sunday, following a concert held a couple of days before, I was incensed. If San Diego could handle the changeover in two days, why couldn't Hawaii do it in six?

So I called news anchor Joe Moore. Over the years he'd occasionally ask on the air, "When's Tom Moffatt going to bring the Stones to Hawaii?" Joe is a good friend, and on the 10 o'clock news that night he announced that

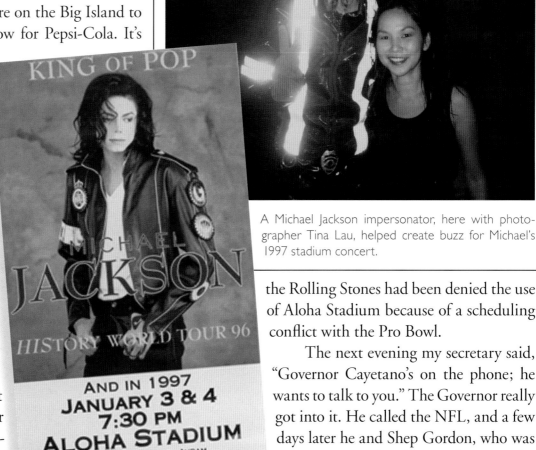

A Michael Jackson impersonator, here with photographer Tina Lau, helped create buzz for Michael's 1997 stadium concert.

the Rolling Stones had been denied the use of Aloha Stadium because of a scheduling conflict with the Pro Bowl.

The next evening my secretary said, "Governor Cayetano's on the phone; he wants to talk to you." The Governor really got into it. He called the NFL, and a few days later he and Shep Gordon, who was co-promoting the show with me, and I held a press conference and announced that the Stones would play the Stadium. The Governor had made some calls and had been told that six days was more than adequate. He also knew the Stones concert would bring a lot of revenue to the state.

The first time I had presented the Stones, at the HIC in 1966, they used the stage we provided. For the *Bridges to Babylon* tour they built their own stage, which included a bridge out over the crowd at floor level. Then they walked the bridge to a smaller stage. But for all the high-tech

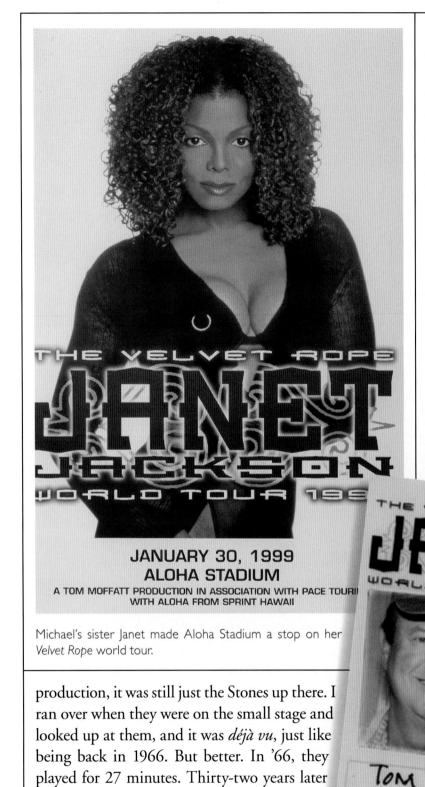

JANUARY 30, 1999
ALOHA STADIUM
A TOM MOFFATT PRODUCTION IN ASSOCIATION WITH PACE TOURI
WITH ALOHA FROM SPRINT HAWAII

Michael's sister Janet made Aloha Stadium a stop on her *Velvet Rope* world tour.

And, by the way, the Stadium didn't have any trouble at all getting ready for the Pro Bowl.

The concert that was probably the hardest to get off the ground was Chicago, in 1979. It was the first time I used the Stadium's football configuration, placing the stage facing the stands behind the south end zone; I named it the Concert Corner of Aloha Stadium, and ticket buyers liked the compact set-up. This way the farthest seat in the Stadium was closer to the stage than the farthest seat in the Blaisdell Arena would be to the stage there. But that was the last thing that went right for days.

On the day of the concert, we were all set up. I had a big crowd, and the band played its first song—and then it started to rain as if someone had unzipped the sky. Suddenly, it was raining everywhere on the island. Even the freeways were flooded, so the show couldn't continue, and it was really difficult for the people in the audience to even get home. That was Saturday night. Sunday was clear, so we tried to get everything dried out so we could do the show on Monday. And then the rains returned and flooded the field again. Jeff Wald, who was managing the group, said, "We're not going to leave you hanging."

He talked to the guys, and they all agreed to stay.

The third time was the charm, and, according to the *Honolulu Advertiser*, the next day the audience was even bigger than it had been the first night. And, man, you should've heard the crowd roar when the band came on and it didn't rain.

Chicago's keyboard player, Bobby Lamm, was quoted in the *Advertiser* as saying, "We haven't blown a concert three times in our 12-year history. And this is our last

TOM MOFFATT
TMP

production, it was still just the Stones up there. I ran over when they were on the small stage and looked up at them, and it was *déjà vu*, just like being back in 1966. But better. In '66, they played for 27 minutes. Thirty-two years later these "old men" played for two hours!

concert of the tour. To blow the last concert would be bad luck. And Hawaii is not the place to blow a concert. And we really like it here." So thanks to Chicago and Jeff, it was a memorable night.

Another Stadium concert that might not have happened was Stevie Wonder's. I was in Japan. My friend Tats Nagashima was doing a concert there with Stevie, and he arranged a meeting for me with Stevie's manager, Ewart Abner. We finalized the deal, I flew back to Honolulu and set everything up, and on the day before the concert I went to the airport to meet Stevie. Right after that, I got a call from Ewart, who said, "We have a little problem. Stevie didn't realize you were white, and he says he only wants to work with black promoters." After meeting me and hearing me talk, he knew I wasn't black, and I guess his manager hadn't thought it would be a problem, what with our multiracial population in Hawaii. I didn't know what we could do at that point. We couldn't get a black promoter involved—there weren't any in Hawaii. As it turned out, Stevie was okay once his manager explained. People still say that was one of the best Stadium concerts.

Hawaii's biggest Stadium concert to date has to be Michael Jackson's in 1997. There'd been a lot of shows in the Stadium by then, but nobody'd had a sell-out. I did this deal on a handshake with Paul Gongaware, who represented Michael's world tour, and I asked him what we should do if we sold out the first morning of sales, because I thought we would. Michael was in Southeast Asia, and by mid-morning, Hawaii time, we knew we had a sell-out. We called Southeast Asia in the wee hours of the morning there and got an okay for a second concert. But they didn't know if Michael would do two shows in two days or would want a break in between. He was sleeping, and they couldn't wake him up to get a final decision. We didn't want to lose the momentum, so we put the tickets on sale at noon, time and date of the concert to be announced. And we sold that one out, too, before the day was over. That was probably

Gloria Estefan and I announce a rare stadium concert for her and the Miami Sound Machine.

a world first, selling out a major concert without a time or date printed on the ticket.

The next week, we got a call that Michael wanted a local act to open his show. After thinking about it, I felt that a surprise act would make this even better. So we decided to leave the act's name out of the promotion and just make the introduction on the day of the show. I felt the element

Britney Spears attended the *NSync concerts at Aloha Stadium, then returned to Hawaii four months later for a free beach concert at the Hilton Hawaiian Village, filmed for a Fox TV special, for which we were the local promoter..

of surprise was important. I wanted sweet-voiced Israel Kamakawiwoole, the hugely popular—and huge—Hawaiian entertainer, but I didn't even want to tell "Bruddah Iz" himself that he was the opening act. The secret would've gotten out.

So I called my old friend Leah Bernstein, who'd worked for me at K-POI and who was now handling Israel for the Mountain Apple Company. She loved the idea and agreed to keep it a secret, telling Iz and the band that they were to play at a private VIP party at the Stadium prior to the concert.

After we explained to Michael's people that an 800-pound Hawaiian was going to open the show for him, and they raised no objection, everything seemed in place. Then a couple of days before the show, Michael changed his mind and said he didn't want an opening act. It's too bad, because it would've been a special moment in Hawaii's musical history.

At the same time, he did ask for a choir for the show.

As a board member of the Honolulu Boy Choir, I thought seriously about suggesting them. But because of the alleged child molestation charges and what people might say, I decided to use a local school group instead. Even with those allegations hanging over his head, by the way, I didn't get a single negative call or letter about bringing Michael to Hawaii.

Another success, but one that went relatively unnoticed, was the Beach Boys' show at the Hula Bowl. Attendance was falling when Larry Little, the basketball coach at UH, was put in charge of the January college football all-star game. Larry asked me if I could help with the entertainment. My old friend Tom Hulett was managing the Beach Boys then, and he put me in touch with a guy who had a stage on wheels. We shipped it over and wheeled it out onto the field after the game and—Bam!—in 10 minutes you had the Beach Boys, included in the cost of the ticket for the game. It was the perfect marriage. The Beach Boys had a wide age-scale appeal, and it worked really well. And it was really special watching the NFL cheerleaders singing along with the Beach Boys.

A promoter should never play favorites and certainly should keep his mouth shut if he has any, but I can't ignore Gloria Estefan. I had worked with her and her band, the Miami Sound Machine, before. I've mentioned her appearance at the Shell, and later she performed at the Blaisdell Arena. She even played the University Field House in Guam for me. Early on, I lost money, but I believed in her, and when she put her name out in front and started billing herself as Gloria Estefan and the Miami Sound Machine, she was easier to sell. Once, I'd even flown to Puerto Rico to see her—this was right after Michael Jackson—and she did the entire show in Spanish. I had no idea what she was saying!

Several years before, I had booked her to come back into the Arena when she got into a really serious bus accident that left her nearly paralyzed. I'd invested some

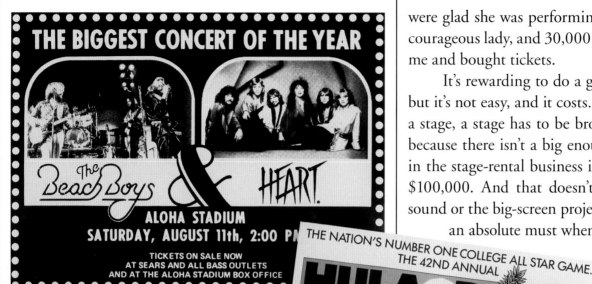

THE BIGGEST CONCERT OF THE YEAR

The Beach Boys & HEART.

ALOHA STADIUM
SATURDAY, AUGUST 11th, 2:00 PM

TICKETS ON SALE NOW
AT SEARS AND ALL BASS OUTLETS
AND AT THE ALOHA STADIUM BOX OFFICE

THE NATION'S NUMBER ONE COLLEGE ALL STAR GAME.
THE 42ND ANNUAL

HULA BOWL

AND The Beach Boys IN CONCERT

Tickets:
Aloha Stadium
Sears Stores
Hula Bowl Office
Military Special Services

JANUARY 16, 1988
KICK-OFF 11:00 A.M.

ALOHA STADIUM

were glad she was performing again. I thought she was a courageous lady, and 30,000 Hawaii residents agreed with me and bought tickets.

It's rewarding to do a good show at Aloha Stadium, but it's not easy, and it costs. If the act isn't traveling with a stage, a stage has to be brought in from the mainland, because there isn't a big enough market for anyone to be in the stage-rental business in Hawaii. The cost for that? $100,000. And that doesn't cover the light towers and sound or the big-screen projection system, the latter being an absolute must when doing any stadium show.

We also have to cover the field with plywood and then a waterproof tarpaulin to protect the field surface. If there's to be seating on the field, chairs have to be rented and secured together in rows. The Stadium provides parking attendants, ticket takers and ushers, but we're still responsible for the stagehands, concert security, cater-ing and cleanup, along with air and ground trans-por-tation.

Now you know why you paid $65 to see Michael Jackson. 🎤

money in promoting her performance, but I let it go. I figured she'd make the show up sometime. Years later, her agent said I was the only promoter with whom she was scheduled to do a show at the time of the accident who didn't ask for something back. She was in such bad shape, I wondered how they could have done that. It's no wonder some promoters have a bad name.

Once she'd recovered and was working again, her agent called me and said she was coming back from Japan and he wanted a big guaran-tee. I thought about it and put in a bid for the Stadium. Her own record distributor came to me and asked if I was putting her in the Waikiki Shell or the Blaisdell Arena. I said the Stadium, and he said, "You're out of your mind! Gloria doesn't play stadi-ums, except maybe in Miami. She plays arenas." But I felt the timing was right and followed my gut instinct. Hawaii fans were very sympathetic about her terrible accident and

CHAPTER 20

Return to Radio

It was 1984, and I'd been off the air for 10 years when I pulled into a gas station in Wahiawa and the station attendant said, "Didn't you use to be Tom Moffatt?"

It was time to get back into radio.

Fortunately, I didn't have to go knocking on doors. About that time Jeff Coelho came to me and asked if I'd like to join the on-air staff at KIKI. Jeff had worked for me at K-POI as a salesman, and now he was KIKI's general manager, running the station for San Francisco-based owners who pretty much gave him free rein. Kamasami Kong—his real name is Bob Zix—was the program director, and I liked both of those guys. I said I'd do it if I could simulcast—broadcast my show on the station's AM and FM stations simultaneously.

At the time, that really didn't mean much, because FM hadn't really grabbed a huge Hawaii audience yet, despite the excitement generated when K-POI introduced Sunshine FM and simulcasts many years earlier. But I was really excited about trying to incorporate television as well, so I could be the first one in the country to do a "triplecast": AM, FM and television. I soon found out that the television part wasn't going to work, but KIKI FM wasn't doing anything much at the time, and Jeff agreed I could broadcast on that. Then he talked me into taking the morning shift, beginning at 5:30! That was an interesting time to start whenever one of my concerts ran late

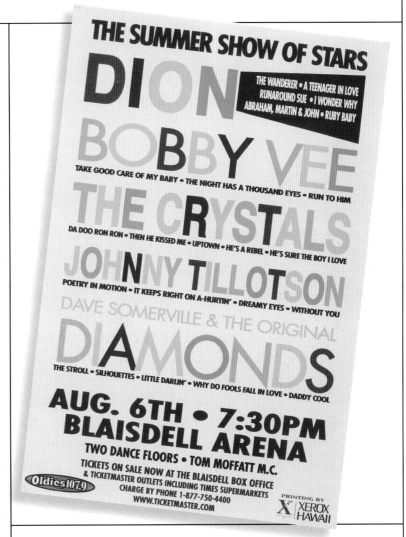

At the Summer Show of Stars and other revival concerts, we bring back many of the acts that first played Honolulu almost a half-century earlier—at our Show of Stars series in the Civic Auditorium. Opposite: Back behind the microphone at Oldies 107.9 FM.

In 1982 Sacred Hearts Academy student Althea Janairo competed in *Brown Bags to Stardom* at the Waikiki Shell. If she looks familiar, maybe it's because she went on to become movie star and *Playboy* model Tia Carrere.

the previous night.

Radio had changed while I was gone. K-POI was still a presence, but the hyphen was removed from the call letters, so now it was just KPOI. It was calling itself "98 Rock," with the tag line "The rock you live on." I always thought that was something servicemen said about Hawaii, and not in a particularly flattering way.

Ron Jacobs had returned to the Islands and for several years was the morning man at KKUA. His show, maybe more than any other at the time, epitomized the sound of the Hawaiian renaissance. On Fridays he interviewed the musicians, and every day he promoted the music of the Beamers, Olomana, Country Comfort, C&K, Gabby Pahinui, the Makaha Sons of Niihau and all the rest. He also introduced the *Homegrown* album concept, where musicians and singers who'd never been recorded professionally would submit songs about Hawaii on demonstration tapes. Ron would then release a long-playing record with a dozen of the best. KIKI answered with *Brown Bags to Stardom*, an album produced with the

help of Frank Day. One of the stars ended up on the cover of *Playboy* with a new name, Tia Carrere, but she didn't win the contest. By the time I was back on the air, Ron had bought his own station, KAHU in Waipahu, and was trying for a niche playing country music.

Another station, KCCN, was riding pretty high at the time as well. This was the "all-Hawaiian" station, whose disc jockeys became almost as famous as the musicians they played. The deejays included Krash Kealoha—his real name was Victor Hoonani Opiopio—and Jacqueline Leilani Rosetti, better known as the "Honolulu Skylark."

The biggest change, in a way, was that Aku was gone. He died in 1984 of lung cancer, at age 66, and was replaced on KSSK by Michael W. Perry and Larry Price. Michael had been at KKUA with Jacobs, and Price had been a football coach at UH and a relief guy for Aku. Then station GM Earl McDaniel wooed Michael away from KKUA (Michael Qseng took his place) and put Perry and Price together. The new partnership worked.

So my morning competition was Michael Qseng and Perry & Price. And I booted it. I did something that lost me my core audience: I became fascinated by a new recording act called Menudo.

At the time, they weren't that well known. Like a lot of other groups that had come before, they were a "manufactured" act, one created by recording companies and managers or sometimes by the musicians themselves. Earlier pre-fab groups included Three Dog Night and some remarkably successful groups aimed at the younger audience: the Partridge Family, the Archies, the Monkees and Dino, Desi & Billy. The angle with Menudo (Spanish for "tripe"; I have no idea why the word was selected) was that the kids were Puerto Rican—the group was created to appeal to the growing Hispanic market. They were recruited when they were 11 to 13, and they stayed until later in their teens or until their voices changed, whichever came first. I was playing their records because kids who

At KIKI, I went overboard with the Puerto Rican boy band Menudo (at left, performing at the Blaisdell Arena) and lost too many of my adult listeners. Above: Ricky Martin was the youngest member, here standing in front of manager Edgardo Dias.

his records.

Anyway, I wanted to bring Menudo to Hawaii and their agent gave me a big figure, although at the time they didn't have any national hits and were just popular in the Puerto Rican neighborhoods in New York. He sent me a video featuring Diana Ross because her son was a Menudo fan, and that got me really interested.

I thought Hawaii would take to them, so I booked them into the Blaisdell Arena and put them up at the Prince Kuhio Hotel. What I didn't know was that Mrs. George Bush, whose husband was then Vice President to

knew about them called me and requested their songs. I got an interview with group member Robbie Rosa in Puerto Rico; I figured he was the only one who'd last. I was wrong. The newest member of the group, who had a squeaky voice and danced like he had two left feet, was Ricky Martin. Eventually, Robbie helped Ricky produce

WE HONOR FIVE
of Hawaii's recording industry veterans at the
Hawaii Academy of Recording Arts'
Lifetime Achievement Awards.

Krash Kealoha
Nora Keahi Santos
Haunani Kahalewai
Noelani Mahoe
Tom Moffatt

In 2002 I felt honored to receive a Lifetime Achievement Award from the Hawaii Academy of Recording Arts at the organization's Hoku Awards ceremony.

Ronald Reagan, was scheduled to make a luncheon speech in the hotel the same day they arrived. You can imagine what the hotel looked like when the kids found out that Menudo was staying there. There were 400 little girls running around, and the Secret Service guys just went nuts.

I did a promotion at Holiday Mart in the Pearl City area. There was this vast parking lot full of kids, and they started pushing. I could see these little girls in front turning blue in the face. They were hyperventilating, and they started fainting. Even Menudo was scared. That's the

one crowd scene I remember, in all my years, where I was really scared that somebody was going to get seriously hurt. Thankfully, no one did.

Then I came up with this idea of doing shows in Hilo and on Maui and chartering a plane, announcing on the radio, "You can fly with Menudo to Hilo and you can fly with Menudo to Maui, and then you can fly home with Menudo." I made a deal with a travel agent, who chartered an Aloha Airlines jet. We advertised it and sold out in one or two days. They started out in the morning and came back at night. These kids who went on the plane were so excited, but they kept their manners. They held back, they didn't bother Menudo on the plane; they respected their privacy. It was only after we landed that things got a little complicated.

Now, there's one thing you have to know. Their music was all on tape. They didn't have a band with them. The kids in the audience didn't care if they were singing to a track, though. The little girls just wanted to see these five little boys. But without the tape, you didn't have a show.

So we did the show in Hilo, and I said we have to make sure these tapes get on the plane. When we arrived at the Maui airport I was relieved to see the container with the tapes coming off the airplane. One thing I didn't notice was that the Hilo cargo tags had not been removed. We got to the building on Maui, and everything's set to go, and where are the tapes? I drove to the Maui airport and couldn't find them and discovered the tapes had been sent back to Hilo. Luckily there was a flight coming back *from* Hilo, stopping in Maui, and we got them on that flight. The show started an hour late. The kids didn't care; the only ones who were mad were the parents who came to pick up their kids and had to wait for them.

It never ceased to amaze me. We sold merchandise at the concerts, and these 12- and 13-year-old girls would pull out $100 bills to buy stuff—we sold a ton of it. I made a deal that Records Hawaii, located at 404 Piikoi

In 1998 Neil Sedaka and the Tokens made a repeat appearance in Honolulu at the Sheraton Waikiki ballroom.

across from Ala Moana Center, would be Menudo Headquarters in Hawaii, and when we announced that the store would offer for sale all the merchandise left over from their concerts, the kids came by the thousands. I had a show on one of the outer islands that day, and as we took off about 8:30, with the opening at Records Hawaii scheduled for 9, I remember flying over Ala Moana and looking down to see this parking lot swarming with kids. All young girls.

Menudo Mania.

The group was so exciting that I took them to Guam, where thousands of kids were waiting at the airport. I also took them to San Francisco for a successful concert in association with my good friend Morgan Montague.

Chubby Checker came back to perform in Honolulu in 2002, this time with Dee Dee Sharp in the Blaisdell Arena.

In the end, I went overboard with the group. To keep the kids tuned in to the station, I played Menudo too much and lost my adult listeners. I had broken my own rule about staying in touch with my audience, and that was the beginning of the end. When new owners came in, they thought I was being paid too much and let me go. That put me off the air for another decade or so.

In the meantime I got a call from KSSK, where Perry & Price were still the morning guys. Earl McDaniel, who had been general manager of the station for about a thousand years, retired, and I was considered, as was Ron Jacobs, as a possible successor. A business consultant to the station interviewed us, and I learned that one of the first things I might have to do if I took the job was fire the morning newsperson, Linda Coble. I got a bad taste in my mouth. Linda was an icon in Island news; there never was, and never will be, anyone to take her place. If they were serious about having me fire her, I wasn't serious about going to work for them.

Still, when the consultant asked me to meet with another consultant, a retired radio guy living on the Big Island, I figured what the hell. I had a concert scheduled there in a week; I'd see what he had to say. This second consultant hadn't been told how much money I was offered, and when I told him it was more than $100,000 a year, his eyes got big as saucers.

Next thing I knew, he was the new general manager.

My next return to the airwaves made more sense. That was in 1997 when, ironically, the program director who had fired me from KIKI, Jay Stone, hired me to take on the morning shift again. This time it was at Oldies 107.9 FM, where he was now the new program director. The match seemed perfect. Wasn't I, by now, a bit of an "oldie" myself?

Radio, of course, had changed again. In 1984, when I'd gone back on the air at KIKI, the technical side of things hadn't altered since I'd left K-POI. Disc jockeys still put records on turntables and used tape decks. Now, in 1997, everything was computerized. There were no records, and CDs were on the hard drive. It was like stepping out of a time machine. It was all foreign. The only thing that hadn't changed was the microphone.

I tried it, but I was uncomfortable; I felt as if it wasn't me on the air. I wanted to take phone calls and do contests. About the third day, the program director came in to run the board for me. I said if someone could do that regularly, I could be Uncle Tom again. I talked to Ron Jacobs about it. He recommended Bart DaSilva, a Hawaiian-born deejay living in San Francisco, who came home at Ron's suggestion and went on the air at Oldies 107.9 and ran my board.

It was rough. I was on the air from 6 to 9, five days a week, and that meant I was in the office running Tom Moffatt Productions until 7 or 8 at night. But I was playing the music I knew. I was also bringing some of those same acts to the Islands to perform. During the three years

I was the morning guy at Oldies 107.9, I became one of the station's biggest advertisers when I had shows, buying commercial time not only for my usual lineup of big-name concerts, but also for oldies shows I put together in the station's name.

I organized the Summer Blast of 1997, the Summer Show of Stars, the Valentine's Hop, the Last Blast of 1998, another Million Dollar Party and a 2 Million Dollar Party. And I put on plenty of shows that featured the stars whose music we were playing: the Rolling Stones, the Shirelles, Bobby Rydell, the Coasters, Teddy Randazzo, the Drifters, Lesley Gore, the Crystals, Neil Sedaka, the Tokens, Dee Dee Sharp, Peter Noone & Herman's Hermits, Brian Hyland, the Champs, Ray Peterson, the Angels, Johnny Tillotson, the Marvelettes, Tommy Sands, the Temptations, Barbara Lewis, Martha & the Vandellas, Freddy Cannon, the Skyliners, Lou Christie, the Beach Boys, Mitch Ryder, Little Anthony, the Platters, Johnny Rivers, the Diamonds, Eric Burdon & the Animals, Jimmy Clanton, the Penguins and the Rascals. And there were Hawaii's own Ronnie Diamond, Lance Curtis (Dick Jensen), Robin Luke, the Royal Drifters and more. Later, I brought in Chubby Checker, Chuck Berry, Little Richard, Jerry Lee Lewis, Gerry & the Pacemakers, Chad & Jeremy and Bobby Vee & Dion.

Despite the success we were enjoying, I was questioned when I played local hits from the 1960s. An interim manager at the station said most people living in Hawaii in the '90s either hadn't lived in Hawaii back then or had been too young to listen to the radio. How did he reach this brilliant conclusion? He probably got the advice from

consultants on the mainland.

My first love is radio, and no matter how much it might have changed, I knew there was one thing that never did, and that was the uncertainty. One day you're praised and well paid, and the next day you're on the street. So when 107.9 changed owners again and a bean counter looked at my salary—which really wasn't all that big—and then factored in the zillions he mistakenly figured I was earning as a concert promoter, I was fired. I think they felt they should've been made partners of my production company.

It wasn't such a bad thing that I left then. The station hadn't spent a dime to promote my show in the newspapers or to say I was back on the air. For a while I had $100 a week to use as prize money for a weekly Treasure Hunt contest I was running, but even that was taken away. Ironically, the same day that happened, the program director of XTREME radio gave me a check for $20,000— they were going to give away tickets to my *NSync shows at the Baisdell Arena to promote their station. Here's the kicker: XTREME's studio was across the hall from mine and was owned by the same company that I was working for, the one that had just cut my prize money.

But time heals most everything. A couple of years later Bart DaSilva and 107.9's new program director, John Matthews, approached me about returning with "Uncle Tom's Rock and Roll Drive In" on Saturday mornings from 8 until noon. They told me I could play the music my listeners wanted, and I agreed to a contract. So every Saturday I return to my first love and really, really have a ball. And from the fantastic response the station is getting, the listeners are too. 🎤

CHAPTER 21

A Promoter Looks Back at 50

I started writing this book by talking about breakfast with my friend Jimmy Buffett. I'm going to finish it with him, too—not with a meal, but with a little plagiarism. A few years ago, Jimmy wrote a delightful autobiography called *A Pirate Looks Back at 50*. His reference was to his age at the time. I call this last chapter "A Promoter Looks Back at 50," but I'm not talking about age, I'm talking about how long I've been in the business.

When I do this, I feel like my Aunt Hazel, who once told me that she remembered seeing some of the first motorcars in New York City and then in her 80s flew to Hawaii in a jumbo jet. In this book, I've reminisced about big-band jazz and 78 rpm recordings, and as I've done so, I've watched radio get so computerized that it's lost some of its charm. At the same time, I've become dependent on mobile phones that allow me to talk to anyone anytime anywhere in the world by satellite.

I don't think I've changed that much over the years. But the years have changed everything else. Most kids today don't know what a 45 rpm record is—forget about a 78. And they don't want to know, or need to. Today, music is reproduced on discs using technology that makes those old 78s sound awful. Technology has improved the quality of entertainment beyond my wildest dreams. I still think Elvis put on one of the best shows I ever saw, in 1957, using only a couple of lights in a boxing ring, but when I put on shows today I'm grateful to have the power-

An early K-POI event. A good promoter can promote just about anything—even dorks! Opposite: It's been my good fortune to call many legends of show business my friends, including (left to right) Jimmy Buffett, Martin Denny and Don Ho.

ful lights and sound equipment that allow me to bring the music to modern-day audiences. Visually, it's better, too; big screens are a standard part of most Blaisdell Arena shows and concerts at Aloha Stadium, and sometimes

Show business has led me into some sticky situations—like stomping grapes at the Taste of Honolulu festival.

complex, it took more than a week to set it up.

As the venues have increased in size, to keep up with the magnitude of the stars, the money has gotten bigger, too. When the Grateful Dead played the Civic Auditorium in 1970, tickets cost $4 at the door, $3 in advance, and now we're asking for $65 for stars like Elton John and all the Stadium acts. (The first time Elton played Hawaii, tickets to his show cost $6.50.) I brought the Rolling Stones to Hawaii in 1966 for $15,000, but in 1997 the costs were staggering. And where once I landed Julio Iglesias by simply guaranteeing rooms at the Kahala Hilton, now an act's guarantee can be well into six figures, plus hotel rooms and a lot more besides.

A word about "guarantees." The word means exactly what it says: you promise to pay the act a certain amount of money—sometimes against a percentage of the box office gross—and that's what you pay regardless of what happens, even if it's more than you take in. Or sometimes the agent will say he needs "x" amount of money to bring an act to Honolulu, and I set the price of the ticket that way. I look at the artist's contract riders to determine production costs and figure out how many seats might be lost to the size of the stage or hanging lights. Most important, I look at how well I think the act will sell in Hawaii. With marginal acts, I look at how well their CDs have been selling; I look at their history. With the Elton Johns and Jimmy Buffetts, it doesn't matter if their last CD was a hit—I know people will go to hear them. The guarantee is then computed, based on the gross potential, with everybody agreeing that expenses will be taken off the top. I'm willing to take risks, but some agents and managers are now asking you to guarantee a virtual sell-out.

While I'm defining words, I want to talk about another: promoter. That's a word I've never really liked, by the way. Say "promoter" to the man on the street and he gets a picture of a fat guy with a cigar, a loud mouth and a bottle of something greasy to sell. I guess it goes

we even get them for the Blaisdell Concert Hall. Even in the most distant seats you can see the performers' facial expressions. The audience gets a better show today.

The special effects are better, too. I remember when dry ice thrown into a bucket of water was used to create what looked like smoke on stage, and we thought that was a big deal. (I also remember how C&K's roadie working the ice for their shows kept getting burned handling the stuff.) Now we have smoke machines and fireworks and fountains and waterfalls on stage. The Tube show was so

Life with Father

by Troy "Satch" Moffatt

Life with my Dad always included lots of love, family, fun and, of course, music. Summed up in one word it would be, "Wow!" There was always excitement and high energy.

One story in particular sticks in my mind: I was just a kid, and Dad got a call from Elliot Roberts in Los Angeles, who was then managing Crosby, Stills & Nash. Elliot needed to rush a contract to David Crosby, who at the time was staying on his boat in Lahaina. So Dad and I took the next plane to Maui and then went down to Lahaina Harbor, trying to track David down. We learned that he had taken his boat out to sea, with Neil Young aboard. Oh, boy—now what? Somehow Dad managed to commandeer a boat in order to chase him down. We raced out of the harbor and, when we caught up with Crosby's yacht, stuck the contract on a pole and held it out for someone on his boat to grab. Then we had to circle around until the contract was signed, take it back with the pole and then send it out on a plane that night to Los Angeles. Obviously, this was before fax machines! But it was all in a day's work for Dad.

There are so many memorable moments of Dad's journey through the music industry, I could write a whole book myself. I especially remember:

- Sitting on Dad's lap as a boy, while he did his radio show at K-POI
- Meeting David Cassidy at K-POI with Dylan Bernstein (son of New York promoter Sid Bernstein—the man who brought the Beatles to Shea Stadium and many concerts to Hawaii)
- Shopping for a bike with Dad and movie/music producer Jerry Weintraub

- Playing in the Kahala Hilton pool on weekends
- Hanging out at Waimanalo Beach Park with Dad and our dog, Czar
- Being on stage with Eric Clapton and watching his great drummer jam up-close
- Having my own section (Troy's Box) at concerts for me and my friends (Dad, you're my hero!)
- Always running for airplanes, and wishing I were at Grandma's house
- Alice Cooper in Australia (now, that was stress—but again, all in a day's work for Dad!)
- Watching Nigel Olsson, Elton John's drummer, pounding his kit
- Getting hugs from Gloria Estefan at the Waikiki Shell
- Going on a cruise with Dad just after 9/11 and meeting Florida Governor Jeb Bush
- Promoting UB40 with Dad in Hilo
- Watching Dad finally relax and unwind at my home

These are just a few of the highlights, and I know there will be many more to come. I feel so blessed having such an amazing Dad—I wish everyone could have one just like him!

Halloween hijinks: Troy and I dressed up as Boy George and friend (top). Above: David Cassidy entertains Sid Bernstein's son, Dylan, and Troy (right) at the K-POI studios.

back to the days when con artists traveled around with a wagonload of snake oil or some other patent medicine, or with a fighter who'd take on anyone: "Knock the bruiser down and win 50 bucks!"

What a promoter really does is figure out what someone or something—a circus, a Broadway musical, a sporting event, whatever—can do in his or her marketplace. (Though I regret there aren't many "her"s.) Know your marketplace; that's the most important thing. Find the venue, price the act, establish a ticket price that you think is fair to everyone, then make an offer to the agent or manager based on gross potential. If the offer is accepted, or negotiated to a point where both sides still think it's fair, then you do the actual promotion—through advertising, stunts, whatever it takes. It's how a new product gets sold or ignored, how a politician gets elected or not, and whether the Waikiki Shell has 1,000 or 8,000 people out front when the show begins.

It helps to believe in what you're selling. I may have come to rock and roll through a door marked "jazz," but music is music is music, as someone once said about a rose.

Backgammon by the Kahala Hilton pool, here with head beach boy Bobby Krewson, was one of my favorite ways to unwind.

And if the music is good, and the promoter truly cares, chances are better that the show will do well, too.

I admit that some of the classic promoters of all time had a bit of the "con" in their pitch. The great circus promoter P.T. Barnum, whose motto sometimes seemed to be "Never give a sucker an even break," started out with a tent full of human oddities and a sign at one end that said, "THIS WAY TO THE EGRESS." People went through the door out of curiosity, not knowing that "egress" is another word for "exit." Colonel Parker was another who got his start in carnivals, where he put a hot-plate under a cage containing a chicken. He plugged in the hot-plate and sold tickets to see what he called a "Dancing Chicken." Later, both Barnum and the Colonel became more respectable.

I've been "guilty" of selling a little more sizzle than steak a few times myself. I've already mentioned that K-POI promotion where the prize was a piece of "the sheet Elvis slept on." And not too long ago I saw how an exaggeration can come back at you. This happened at the funeral of my best friend, Bobby Krewson.

I was a regular at the Kahala Hilton for years, until the hotel closed for renovations in the mid-'90s. I'd go down there every weekend that I could (if I didn't have a show going on), and I'd hang out with Bobby. Talk about a shining star! Bobby was a famous beach boy, one of the first ever to surf the North Shore. He'd also been the head beach boy at the Kahala Hilton since the hotel opened. Everyone who stayed there, including the big stars, loved him. When Bobby was done with his duties, we'd play backgammon, drink some wine and take a swim. And he would entertain me with endless surf stories. So at his funeral, in 2005, I told one of my favorites:

A number of years ago, Bobby was all set to compete tandem at a big surf meet at Makaha Beach. There was just one problem: his partner was stuck in traffic and called to say she'd be late. What was he going to do? The

The first Show of Stars performances (here featuring the Platters) often required little more than a walk-up stage and a microphone. Turn the page to see how showbiz technology has evolved.

waves wouldn't wait! Being a resourceful guy, Bobby asked the crowd for a volunteer. A young lady stepped up—a wee bit larger than his partner—and despite the change in personnel, they won the tandem championship. When I told the story at his funeral, I may have overstated the size of the girl, just to lighten up the crowd. It was a funny story, and I wanted to present it well. Afterward, a slender and very attractive woman walked up to me and said with

a laugh, "I was that big girl." She was such a good sport, and so *not* big, that I started laughing too.

But sizzle's no bad thing; in fact, it's essential. Just look at some of rock and roll's great promoters. The Beatles' manager, Brian Epstein, is one, of course, and Sid

Then and now: In 1968 the Young Rascals played the Arena with a few amps lined up next to the stage, and a ticket cost five bucks.

In 2004 the Who filled the same venue with a high-tech profusion of sound, lighting and special effects—and ticket prices started at $65!

Bernstein, and so is Dick Clark, who may be the greatest of them all. And in the movies there was Mike Todd, the guy who produced the film Jacobs and I tried to promote back when we were at KHVH, *Around the World in Eighty Days*. These guys all had good reputations. They knew how to put the pieces together and then sell the hell out of the show. They were flamboyant and bigger than life.

I'd rather be called an impresario than a promoter, but if you use that word, the guy on the street will think you're wearing fancy underpants. But at the first Chinese event I ever did, the Chinese producer asked to meet "the impresario" and bowed when we were introduced. The word works in many parts of the world and in the classical music world, too, and in opera and ballet. Even on Broadway the word "impresario" carries big-time respect.

But not with rock and roll. So a "promoter" I remain.

A lot of promoting comes down to dealing with money. And the money angle has also changed over the years. Of course, everything costs more nowadays, but a number of factors helped keep ticket prices down in the past. At the Civic, Ruth Eckert ran the box office long before computer ticket charges, and we had the auditorium's handyman, Velasco, come in before a show and turn on the sound, and that was it. Now, stagehand and other labor costs, along with catering, security, cleanup and all the rest, can be enormous. Then add hotel and transportation costs.

A lot of times we find we can't afford to bring an act to Hawaii. Where once musicians carried their own guitars off the plane with them and used the local sound and lights, now they come with *containers* full of equipment, and it's expensive to fly them to the Islands. Up until the 1980s, all planes going to the U.S. from Japan and Australia stopped in Hawaii as a matter of course. Later on, they either returned to Japan and Australia or overflew Hawaii and went directly to the mainland. That meant the acts had to take a second airline to the main-

land after performing here, or fly direct to Los Angeles or San Francisco and then fly back to Hawaii. It cost them (or us) too much to do that.

Even nowadays, though, if an act is on a mainland tour, the lure of the Islands isn't always enough to inspire them take a side trip to Hawaii. Sure, it's a nice place, but in terms of dollars and cents, to move everything and everybody over to Hawaii from Los Angeles on the way to San Francisco—well, they might as well go play Bakersfield or Fresno. It's not as glamorous, but they'll walk away with a lot more money. Again, I give thanks to the Jimmy Buffetts and Elton Johns, who love Hawaii. They don't come back again and again just for the bucks and the applause; it's the *feeling* they get in Hawaii from the local audience.

I have to say there are bigger egos in the business nowadays, too. When I was doing the Show of Stars, big-name mainland acts graciously took second billing to other acts that might have been lesser known on the mainland but were bigger in Hawaii. And remember when the Champs backed Frankie Avalon and the Beach Boys played behind Dee Dee Sharp? Picture me asking a band to do that today! Another ego yardstick is the size of the support staff traveling with the act. In 1966 the Stones came with a traveling party of 12, and now the entourage of a major act will number over 100. Same thing with equipment: for their record-breaking shows, the Rascals used whatever was available at the Blaisdell, but nowadays acts demand several hundred lights and a very expensive sound system.

Another big difference: there are a lot more performers today. And they can come up so fast that I find I'm being offered acts I've never even heard of. If I didn't have young people on my staff to consult with, I'd probably miss a number of good performers.

Some of the biggest changes have happened in radio. In the old days, everybody was a character, but now there's

I'll do anything for a promotion! Here are (left to right) Jimmy Borges, me and Keola Beamer in 1979 as members of a phony punk band we called the Honolulu Dreggs. Honolulu hairstylist Paul Brown did the makeup.

not much time between records to talk and develop an on-air personality or even discuss the music. When I hear music I'm not familiar with on the radio, I want the song and the act identified, and they don't tell me. It sounds as if they're not interested in the music. Music means something to me. On most stations, it sounds as if music is just wallpaper—background noise.

There are some good jocks on the air, but they're handcuffed. They don't pick the songs they play; they follow rigid playlists. Tight playlists aren't new, but they've gotten tighter, and some are dictated by mainland people who own the station and don't have a clue about Hawaii's special tastes. I talk to listeners to find out what they want to hear. Some jocks today hesitate to answer the phone because they may not be able to answer the request.

Technology has revolutionized radio. Where there were records and tapes years ago, now a computer that can hold gigabytes of sound files handles everything. This has eliminated skips and improved sound quality—but,

unfortunately, now the jocks can be pre-recorded too. A station will hire a jock and, instead of paying him or her to do a four-hour shift on the air, they just pay for the 45 minutes it takes to record the intros and "outros" to the songs. Everything else—the music, the commercials, the jingles—is added electronically, instantly. Some disc jockeys work several stations owned by the same company, changing their delivery and names as they move along the dial. When I wanted to release some Norah Jones tickets on the day of her show—to let people know there were still seats available—I could find only one station in Honolulu that was live, so it was difficult to get the word out.

So there are fewer deejays working these days, and the future looks bleak for them. Now there's satellite programming, in which a company programs a variety of

Our Uncle Tom

by Barbara Saito

I remember the day Tom Moffatt interviewed me for a job with his company. I didn't have much of a sense that he was a legend back then; I saw him as a businessman who needed an office person, nothing more. The job involved music, and that was good enough for me.

In the intervening quarter-century, I've learned that the job involves much more than music, and that the man who hired me is much more than just a boss. He is my mentor and my ally, someone who has laid the whole of his expertise on his desk and invited me to learn it all.

At his core he is still that suave disc jockey from the '50s and '60s whose sincerity, integrity and charm made Hawaii a "must-play" stop for the pioneers of rock and roll. He is constantly stopped on the street, in restaurants and at supermarkets to be thanked for the many fond memories he's given his fans. There is a reason he is so well liked: even in the middle of a tough week leading up to a show, he has dropped everything to find someone an elusive song, record it on a cassette and deliver it in person. That's just the way he is.

But beyond the affable personality lies a very savvy marketer. I've often been amazed by his knack for mixing oil and water to further a promotion. In 1982 Stevie Wonder was co-presented at Aloha Stadium by two fiercely competitive (and that's putting it mildly) radio stations. Julio Iglesias, one of the world's top-grossing performers, played two sold-out nights at the Blaisdell Concert Hall, for no guarantee. Michael Jackson, groggy after being awakened from a sound sleep in Southeast Asia, agreed to let Tom sell a second concert at Aloha Stadium even though he wasn't sure what day he would play it—with no contract, without even the proverbial handshake. And no one, in the history of the *Honolulu Advertiser*, had ever gotten them to hold the presses for anything—until Tom needed to change something in an ad.

He has presented the very first show in every major venue in the state of Hawaii. He has rubbed elbows with the likes of Frank Sinatra and Elvis. He'll field a hundred phone calls a day at the office, having gotten in earlier and stayed longer than any of his staff. He's part of a now-rare breed of men who understand that your word can make or break you. And yes,

Barb Saito works the Arena floor before a Blaisdell concert.

folks, he is as good-natured, through both good times and bad, as he seems.

I have watched a dozen promoters attempt to overtake him in this market, and each one has melted into obscurity. The critical key to his success, I believe, is caring about his community. For a half-century Tom Moffatt has not only promoted entertainment in Hawaii, he has promoted Hawaii *to* entertainment—and our state is richer for it. That's why I'm convinced there will never be anyone like our "Uncle Tom."

musical formats—oldies rock, modern rock (hip hop, techno and the like), easy listening, traditional country, modern country, whatever—and records it in 24-hour-long blocks, selling it by subscription to listeners. There are no disc jockeys and no commercials, and you can pick it up at home or in your car. You could drive from New York to Los Angeles and listen to the same "station" all the way.

The recorded music scene in Hawaii has changed big-time, too. When I started Paradise Records, little local acts couldn't afford to make a record, because they had to order a couple of hundred LPs at a time. Now anybody can make a CD at home and press 200 copies just like that, at a fraction of the LP cost. This has given Hawaii the biggest recording scene in the world in terms of number of acts and amount of product—produced for a local audience—but sometimes the quality is lacking in the music and recording techniques.

And, sadly, not as many acts can find work. When I came to the Islands, and for many years afterward, most of the recording stars were working, and Hawaii was a center of live entertainment. Now we've got Na Hoku Hanohano award winners who are unemployed. Waikiki is a live entertainment graveyard. Even the venerable Monarch Room at the Royal Hawaiian Hotel no longer supports a live act. Except for Don Ho, who's still going strong at the Waikiki Beachcomber, and former Beamers dancer Kanoe Kaumeheiwa and a Hawaiian trio at the Halekulani Hotel, and a few solo performers here and there part-time, there's almost no one to listen to.

That's enough bad news—there's more news that's good. When I started in radio, there were only a handful of stations. And even if I do think Hawaii radio was more exciting 30 years ago, today on Oahu alone there are 18 AM stations and 21 FM stations, giving the listener more variety to choose from.

There's more variety in live acts, too, which are also appearing more often on the outer islands. (I'll never for-

Honolulu Advertiser entertainment editor Wayne Harada, here interviewing Jean Terrell of the Supremes, ca. 1970, has been covering Hawaii's showbiz scene since his Farrington High School days.

get when Jimmy Buffett played the Kona Surf Convention Center, a venue that could hold only 1,000 people—just because he wanted to.) We promoted 45 shows in 2004, and more than 60 in 2005.

I couldn't have done all this without a larger staff. That's a big change—and a big plus, too. When I set up my office, it was just Liz Hudson and me. Now my invaluable assistant Barbara Saito is in the catbird seat. She's been with me for 24 years and has a mind for figures that scares agents and managers—but does it so disarmingly that she has them thanking her. George "Cubby" Chun, my oldest friend in Hawaii—who was a disc jockey at KIKI and managed Liz Damon and the Orient Express (he's a jazz-head like me)—runs Paradise Records. The late Frank Day was responsible for much of the success of my recording endeavors and brought a new level of professionalism to the local recording industry. And Rick Smoot is my pair of "young ears." He's in his early 30s, has real insight into the younger market and sounds, does talent scouting for me and helps with production.

And the best is yet to come. I've got some big ideas for new acts I want to bring to Hawaii, new ways to get people interested.

Regrets? As Sinatra sang, I have a few. But they're pretty minor. Jerry Hopkins, an old friend who helped me organize this book, lives in Thailand, and one time when I was there we went to see a company of Chinese acrobats I'd never seen before. Thinking about it afterwards, it occurred to me that in the last 40 years, that was only the eighth time I'd sat all the way through a live performance. (The others were Deep Purple in London, Brian Wilson and Paul Simon in San Diego, Billy Joel and Elton John in Osaka, Frank Sinatra in Las Vegas, Gloria Estefan in Puerto Rico, Fleetwood Mac at the Hollywood Bowl and Julio Iglesias in Australia.) So I guess I'd like to have had some more of that.

But there were some opportunities offered that I think I was wise to walk away from—like when I was approached to get into politics. Ralph Yempuku's friend Dan Inouye dropped by the Civic to say hello to Ralph—this was before Dan went to Washington and became a dean of U.S. senators—and said I should consider running for office. And when I was the general manager of K-POI, I was approached to run for mayor against Frank Fasi. Later one of Honolulu's longest-running mayors, Fasi was then campaigning for the first time. Some politically powerful people talked to one of my dearest friends about it, and I was seriously considering it. Then I thought about how my life would be affected. I had a nice family life; I could go home at night and on the weekends and be with my wife and son. But politicians—five or six nights a week they had to be out somewhere, shaking hands and making promises. I'd seen how some of those guys turned out, and I didn't want to get into that bag. As nicely as I could, I said no way.

I'm sure that's one of the reasons that Sweetie and I are still together. When I'm asked for the secret to such a long and happy married life, I joke and say, "A big house." It's true that we're still in that 19-room mansion up in Nuuanu Valley, purchased when our son Troy was a baby, but the house, and the space it gives us individually, is only a small part of it.

(But what a retreat it's been for both of us. We don't entertain as much as we used to, and it's not every year we fly in a Christmas tree from Maui, but the Civic Auditorium piano that's been played by everyone from Count Basie to Neil Sedaka, and sung to by Caruso and Sam Cooke, is still in the ballroom, and I still enjoy a fire in winter in the fireplace.)

Sweetie and I always kept our careers apart; that was important. We never hung around backstage at each other's shows. She rarely comes to one of my concerts, unless it's to say hello to a friend. She's always been very supportive of what I've done, and I've been the same for her, yet we gave each other the freedom to do our own things.

To me, Sweetie *is* Hawaii. And while it wasn't her being a dancer that attracted me to her—I rarely saw her dance—that's still a special part of who she is. She's retired now, but when she gets up and dances hula for a special friend, or on a special occasion, I get all choked up. When she dances, all of a sudden, wow!

How many hundreds of shows have I done? How many of the biggest and most talented entertainers have I seen in performance? From all over the world?

The best was always at home. 🎤

Sweetie and I, sailing away on the *Queen Elizabeth II*.

Acts from A to Z, 1955-2005

A Chorus Line
Air Supply
Aliis
All 4 One
Al Lucas
America
American Idols Live
Andy Bumatai
Andy Williams
Ani DiFranco
Animals
Anri
Aretha Franklin
Ashanti
Aswad
Average White Band
Barbara Lewis
Barry Manilow
Beach Boys
Berres Hammond
Bette Midler
Betty Everett
Bill Haley's Comets
Billy Joel
Billy Ward & the Dominoes
Blind Faith
Blood Sweat & Tears
Blues Image

Bo Diddley
Bob Marley
Bobbie Gentry
Bobby "Boris" Pickett
Bobby Brown
Bobby Darin
Bobby Day
Bobby Freeman
Bobby Rydell
Bobby Vee
Bobby Vinton
Bobcat Goldthwait
Bolshoi Ballet
Bonnie Raitt
Booker T. & the MGs
Boxtops
Brenda Lee
Brian Hyland
Brian McKnight
Brian Viloria
Brian Wilson
Britney Spears
Brothers Cazimero
Brothers Johnson
Bruce Willis
Bruce & Terry
BT Express
Bu Laia

Buddy Holly
Buddy Miles
Buffy Sainte Marie
Burt Bacharach
Butterfield Blues Band
Bye Bye Birdie
Byrds
Cadillacs
Camelot
Canned Heat
Carl Dobkins, Jr.
Carl Perkins
Carole King
Carpenters
Cascades
Cat Stevens
Cecilio & Kapono
Chaka Khan & Rufus
Champs
Charles Lloyd Quartet
Charley Pride
Cheap Trick
Cheech & Chong
Chicago
Chiffons
Chi-Lites
Christina Aguilera
Christopher Cross

Chubby Checker
Chuck Berry
Chuck Mangione
Climax
Clyde McPhatter
Coasters
Connie Francis
Count Basie & his Band
Country Comfort
Country Joe & the Fish
Creedence Clearwater Revival
Crests
Crosby, Stills & Nash
Crosby, Stills, Nash & Young
Crystal Gayle
Crystals
Curtis Mayfield
Cyndi Lauper
Dan Fogelberg
Danny & the Juniors
Danny Valentino
Dave Brubeck
Dave Koz
Dave Wakeling
David Benoit
David Crosby
David Sanborn
Dee Clark
Dee Dee Sharp
Deep Purple
Deion Sanders
Delfonics
Dennis Alexio

Destiny's Child
Diamonds
Dick & Dee Dee
Dick Clark's Caravan of Stars
Dick D'Agostin & his Swingers
Dick Jensen
Dino, Desi & Billy
Dion & The Belmonts
Dionne Warwicke
Disney on Ice
Dixie Cups
Dodie Stevens
Don & Dewey
Don Ho
Donovan
Doobie Brothers
Doors
Dovells
Dr. John
Drifters
Duane Eddy & the Rebels
Eagles
Earl Klugh
Earth, Wind & Fire
Eddie Cochran
Eddie Hodges
Eddie Holman
Eden's Crush
Elegants
Ella Fitzgerald
Elton John
Elvin Bishop
Elvis - the Concert

Elayne Boosler
Englebert Humperdinck
Eric Clapton
Errol Garner
Everly Brothers
Fabian
Fabulous Five
Famous Amos
Five Satins
Flamingos
Flatt & Scruggs
Fleetwood Mac
Fleetwoods
Flogging Molly
Forever Tango
Four Freshmen
Four Preps
Four Tops
Frank Sinatra
Frankie Avalon
Frankie Ford
Frankie Valli
Franz Harary
Freddie Cannon
Gallagher
Garry Miles
Gene Pitney
George Winston
Gladys Knight & the Pips
Glen Campbell
Gloria Estefan & the Miami Sound
Machine
Grand Ballet of Tahiti

Grand Funk Railroad	Janet Jackson	Johnny Tillotson
Grassroots	Jasmine Trias	Joni Mitchell
Grateful Dead	Jason Mraz	Jose Carreras
Guess Who	Jeanne Black	Jose Feliciano
Gypsy	Jeff Beck	Journey
Hal Blaine	Jerry Lee Lewis	Jr. Walker & the All-Stars
Hal Holbrook/*Mark Twain*	Jerry Wallace	Judds
Hapa	Jesse Colin Young	Judy Harriett
Harlem Globetrotters	Jesus Salud	Julio Iglesias
Harry Connick, Jr.	Jethro Tull	Kalapana
Heart	Jets	Kalin Twins
Heatwave	Jimi Hendrix	KC & the Sunshine Band
Helen Reddy	Jimmy Buffett	k.d. lang
Herman's Hermits	Jimmy Clanton	Kealii Reichel
Hideki Saijo	Jimmy Cliff	Keanu Reeves & Dogstar
Highwaymen	Jimmy Rodgers	Kenny Loggins
Hollies	Jo Mama	Kenny Rankin
Howie Mandell	Joan Rivers	Keola & Kapono Beamer
Hugh Masakela	Jo-Ann Campbell	Kiki Dee
Hulk Hogan	Jodie Sands	Kingsmen
Humble Pie	Jody Miller	Kinks
Ian & Sylvia	Joe Cocker	Kris Kristofferson
Ice Capades	Joe Moore/*Will Rogers/John Wayne*	Kristi Yamaguchi
Infinite McCoys	Joe Pass	Krush
Iron Butterfly	Joe Tex	La Verne Baker
Israel Kamakawiwoole	Joffrey Ballet	Lea Salonga
J. Geils Band	John Denver	Led Zeppelin
Jack Bruce	John Mayall	Lee Ritenour
Jackie DeShannon	Johnny & The Hurricanes	Len Berry
Jackson Browne	Johnny Cash	Lenny Welch
James Cotton Blues Band	Johnny Crawford	Leon Russell
James Taylor	Johnny Mathis	Lesley Gore
Jan & Dean	Johnny Rivers	Leslie West & Mountain

Linda Ronstadt	Monkees	Pointer Sisters
Lionel Richie	Moody Blues	*Porgy and Bess*
Lipizzaner Stallions	Mos Def	Procol Harum
Little Angels of Korea	mrnorth	Rap Reiplinger
Little Anthony and the Imperials	*NSync	Rare Earth
Little Richard	*Napoleon* with Carmine Coppola	Ravi Shankar
Liza Minelli	Natalie Cole	Ray Charles
Loggins & Messina	National Chinese Opera Theatre	Ray Peterson
Lord of the Dance	National Dance Company of China	Ray Romano & Friends
Loretta Swit	NBA All Stars	Red Skelton
Lou Christie	Neil Diamond	Redman
Lucky Dube	Neil Sedaka	Reggae Sunsplash
Makana	Nicolette Larson	Ric Flair
Malo	Night Ranger	Rich Little
Manhattans	Nino Temple & April Stevens	Richard Jeni
Manpower Australia	Noel Harrison	Richie Havens
Marcels	Norah Jones	Righteous Brothers
Marcia Griffiths	*Nutcracker on Ice*	Ritchie Valens
Margaret Cho	Olivia Newton-John	Rivingtons
Mariah Carey	Oscar Peterson	Robert Cray
Marlene Sai	Ozomatli	Robert Palmer
Martha & the Vandellas	Pacific Gas & Electric	Robin Luke
Marvelettes	Pat Boone	Rod McKuen
Marvin Gaye	Paul & Paula	Rod Stewart
Mary Wells	Paul Anka	Roger Williams
Masaaki Hirao	Paul Revere & the Raiders	Rolling Stones
Maxi Priest	Peaches & Herb	Ronnie Diamond
Melissa Etheridge	Penguins	Ronnie Milsap
Melody Makers	Pepper	Roy Orbison
Michael Jackson	Persuaders	Rudolf Nureyev
Michelle Branch	Peter Moon Band	Sam Cooke
Mills Brothers	Peter & Gordon	Sam Kinison
Mitch Ryder & the Detroit Wheels	Platters	Sam Moore

Sammy Davis, Jr.
Sandy Nelson
Santana
Savoy Brown
Scott Hamilton
Screamin' Jay Hawkins
Seals & Crofts
Seawind
Sesame Street
Seeds
Shaggy
Shanghai Circus
Shanghai Symphony
Shangri-Las
Shaun Cassidy
Sheena Easton
Shields
Shirelles
Shirley Valentine
Shockhouse
Sigur Ros
Simon & Garfunkel
Sister Sledge
Skip & Flip
Skyliners
Society of Seven
Sonny & Cher
Sonny Knight
Souther-Hillman-Furay Band
Spinners
Star Trek with Gene Roddenberry
Stars on Ice
Steel Pulse

Steely Dan
Stephen Stills
Steppenwolf
Steve Lawrence & Eydie Gorme
Steve Martin
Stevie Winwood
Stevie Wonder
String Cheese Incident
Stylistics
Surface
Surfaris
Sweet Inspirations
Sweetwater
Sy Klopps Blues Band
Tamayo Otsuki
Teddy Randazzo
Temptations
Them
The Rock
Third World
Three Dog Night
Thurston Harris
Tierra
Tokens
Tommy James & the Shondells
Tommy Roe
Tommy Sands
Tony Bennett
Tony Danza
Tony Orlando
Toto
Tower of Power
Treniers

Tube
Turtles
Twelve Girls Band
UB40
Van Morrison
Vanilla Fudge
Ventures
Vince Gill
War
Waylon Jennings
Wayne Brady
Wayne Newton
Whitney Houston
Who
Willie Nelson
World Wrestling Entertainment
Yanni
Yardbirds
Yazawa
Young Rascals
Yvonne Elliman
Ziggy Marley

Index

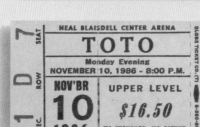